BON APPÉTIT
KEEP IT SIMPLE
EASY TECHNIQUES FOR GREAT HOME COOKING

From the editors of *Bon Appétit*

Condé Nast Books · Clarkson Potter/Publishers

NEW YORK

Stir-fried Sugar Snap Peas and Cherry Tomatoes (page 51)

FOR BON APPÉTIT

Barbara Fairchild, Editor-in-Chief
Victoria von Biel, Executive Editor
Laurie Glenn Buckle, Managing Editor
Kristine Kidd, Food Editor
Marcy MacDonald, Editorial Operations Director
Carri Marks, Editorial Production Director
Lynne Hartung, Editorial Production Manager
Sybil Shimazu Neubauer, Editorial Administrator

Kim Upton, Editor, Bon Appétit Books
Joy Whittemore McCann, Associate Editor
Jordana Ruhland, Editorial Associate
Marcia Hartmann Lewis, Editorial Support
Jeanne Thiel Kelley, Food Research
Susan Champlin, Text
H. Abigail Bok, Copy Editor
Gaylen Ducker Grody, Research
Elizabeth A. Matlin, Index

FOR CONDÉ NAST BOOKS

Lisa Faith Phillips, Vice President and General Manager
Tom Downing, Direct Marketing Director
Deborah Williams, Operations Director
Fianna Reznik, Direct Marketing Associate
Eric Levy, Inventory Assistant

DESIGN BY VERTIGO DESIGN, NYC
Produced in association with Patrick Filley Associates, Inc.

Front Jacket: Roast Pork Tenderloins with
Cranberry-Port Sauce (page 81),
Sautéed Green Beans with Shallots (page 48),
Polenta Triangles with Rosemary and Walnuts (page 65)

Published by Clarkson Potter/Publishers,
New York, New York.
Member of the Crown Publishing Group.
Random House, Inc.

CLARKSON N. POTTER, POTTER,
and colophon are trademarks of Random House, Inc.

Manufactured in Hong Kong

Library of Congress Cataloging-in-Publication Data is
available upon request.

ISBN 1-4000-4636-X

10 9 8 7 6 5 4 3 2 1

FIRST EDITION

Condé Nast Web Address: bonappetit.com
Bon Appétit Books Web Address:
bonappetitbooks.com
Random House Web Address:
randomhouse.com

Contents

Lamb and Zucchini Fusilli with Basil Butter (page 125)

Panna Cotta with Strawberry-Vin Santo Sauce (page 188)

Introduction

For many of us, the kitchen is our haven. It's the place we retreat to when life gets crazy, where we can be renewed by the familiar, comforting acts of chopping vegetables, cracking eggs, sifting flour, browning meat, grating cheese—or, of course, opening the oven door and savoring the aroma of freshly baked cookies.

There's nothing complicated or fussy about any of these activities. They're wonderfully simple, and the end results are entirely satisfying.

That's why we've created a book called *Keep It Simple*. The most delicious dishes start with the simplest of actions, but sometimes we forget that fact—especially in the middle of a busy week. Cooking can seem time-consuming, complex, just too much *work*, and we've got enough work already. Anyone for Chinese takeout? But when we get back to basics, we can rediscover the great pleasures of cooking that led us into the kitchen in the first place—and in the process, discover how amazingly quick and easy it can be to get a homemade meal on the table. Anyone for Stir-fried Chicken with Onion and Hoisin Sauce? (Just see page 93.)

Split Pea Soup with Bacon and Rosemary (page 28)

Steak with Roquefort, Green Onions and Walnuts (page 70)

So to get right back to the basics—and to make this book as simple to use as possible—we've organized the chapters according to a cook's essential ingredients and techniques. These are the dishes you think of first when you want to prepare a meal that you know you and your family will enjoy.

We start with eggs, the most fundamental of ingredients. Then we move into chapters on soups, salads, vegetables, beans and grains, meats, poultry, seafood, pasta and pizza, and breads. Desserts, however simple they may be, deserve *serious* attention, so we've broken that category down into five separate chapters, on cakes, pies and tarts, frozen desserts, custards and soufflés, and cookies.

Throughout each chapter, we present the straightforward recipes and foolproof techniques that should be in every cook's repertoire: the classic cheese omelet, for instance; a perfectly roasted chicken; savory sautéed steak; an all-purpose white cake. Then we build on those timeless dishes with some delicious—and somewhat more challenging—variations. That omelet becomes a sophisticated entrée with the addition of

Yams with Spiced Honey-Molasses Butter (page 56)   Lemon Meringue Pie with Pecan Crust (page 164)

morels, ham and Brie. Fresh wild mushrooms create a delicious stuffing for roast chicken. A simple rib-eye steak takes on an entirely new character when it's accompanied by an elegant yet easy-to-make sauce featuring Roquefort cheese and green onions, then sprinkled with walnuts. And when that plain white cake batter is divided into four cake pans and combined with a citrusy filling, it is re-created as the show-stopping Four-Layer Cake with Lemon Curd.

For those days when you have a little more time or feel like experimenting a bit, there are recipes that will dazzle your guests—and you: dishes like Goat Cheese and Herb Soufflé; Roast Pork Tenderloins with Cranberry-Port Sauce; Chicken and Vegetable Pot Pies with Cream Cheese Crust; Shellfish Cioppino; and a luscious Panna Cotta with Strawberry-Vin Santo Sauce.

At each step of the way, we offer all kinds of helpful information guaranteed to make your time in the kitchen both more efficient and more enjoyable. In every chapter you'll find:

Roasted Vegetables with Garlic-Tarragon Butter (page 52)   New Orleans-Style Shrimp (page 112)

HINTS on purchasing the best ingredients (and how to store them properly so they don't go to waste); **TIPS** that make recipe preparation easier and smarter (at last, the secret of the perfect hard-boiled egg!); **ADVICE** on cooking equipment (which products are must-haves, and which are handy luxuries); and **ANSWERS** to the questions you're most likely to ask (from "What's the best way to keep lettuce fresh?" to "How do I know when a soufflé is done?").

Whether you're an accomplished cook brushing up on your skills, an enthusiastic novice learning your way around the kitchen, or a busy working person who has eaten one too many frozen lasagnas, *Keep It Simple* has what you need. Here are the recipes, the insights, the photographs and the step-by-step instructions that will introduce you—or re-introduce you—to the great satisfaction of freshly prepared foods made with your own two hands. It's that simple.

White Beans with Bacon and Endive (page 66)

Oven-fried Chicken (page 90)

When it comes to keeping things simple in the kitchen, eggs are the cook's best friend—and the best place to begin a book that sets out to do just that. Master a few techniques, from boiling and scrambling to separating eggs and whipping the whites, and you have all the tools you need to create any number of satisfying meals, from breakfast to dinner.

There is just one thing to know about buying eggs: Freshness counts. A fresh egg makes fluffier omelets, whips up lighter and just tastes better. Check the "sell by" date, and once you get the eggs home, store them in the refrigerator in their carton, and use them within a month.

With a supply of eggs on hand, there's always a terrific dish—from a simple omelet to a richly appealing slice of frittata—at the ready.

Eggs

Baked Eggs with Chive Butter (page 15)

Basic creamy scrambled eggs

EGGS, ONE OF THE MOST VERSATILE INGREDIENTS, CAN BE PREPARED ANY NUMBER OF WAYS; ONE OF THE SIMPLEST IS SCRAMBLING. THE KEY TO A CREAMY RESULT IS COOKING THEM OVER LOW HEAT.

10   large eggs

¼   cup whipping cream

2   tablespoons (¼ stick) unsalted butter

4 SERVINGS

Whisk eggs and cream in large bowl to blend. Season with salt and pepper. Melt 2 tablespoons butter in heavy large skillet over low heat. Add eggs and cook, stirring gently with wooden spoon or heat-resistant rubber spatula, until eggs are almost set but still soft, about 4 minutes. If firmer consistency is desired, continue stirring until cooked to desired doneness. Remove from heat. Season with salt and pepper.

Creamy scrambled eggs with asparagus, goat cheese and prosciutto

AFTER MASTERING THE ART OF MAKING BASIC SCRAMBLED EGGS, USE THIS RECIPE AS INSPIRATION FOR OTHER VARIATIONS. TRY ADD-INS SUCH AS GRATED OR CRUMBLED CHEESE, SAUTÉED VEGETABLES OR MEATS.

12   medium asparagus spears, peeled, cut into ½-inch pieces

2   tablespoons (¼ stick) unsalted butter

2   thin slices prosciutto, cut into 2½ x 1½-inch strips

    Basic Creamy Scrambled Eggs (see recipe above), cooked just until soft

½   cup crumbled soft fresh goat cheese

1   tablespoon minced fresh chives

4 SERVINGS

Cook asparagus in large saucepan of boiling salted water until just tender when pierced with sharp knife, about 2 minutes. Drain. Rinse asparagus thoroughly under cold water; drain again. *(Can be prepared 2 hours ahead. Let stand at room temperature.)*

Melt butter in heavy medium skillet over medium heat. Add asparagus and sauté 1 minute. Remove 8 asparagus tips and reserve for garnish. Add prosciutto to asparagus in skillet and stir until heated through, about 15 seconds. Set asparagus mixture aside.

Stir scrambled eggs, asparagus mixture, goat cheese and chives to combine. Garnish with reserved asparagus tips and serve.

Basic cheese omelet

ONCE YOU KNOW HOW TO MAKE SCRAMBLED EGGS, YOU'RE READY TO TRY THE OMELET, A SIMPLE THING CONSISTING OF EGGS THAT ARE COOKED, THEN FOLDED OR ROLLED WITH A FILLING INSIDE. PRACTICE IS ALL IT TAKES. AT THE END OF A DOZEN, YOU'LL HAVE THE TECHNIQUE DOWN.

6   large eggs

2   tablespoons (¼ stick) butter

1   cup grated cheese, such as cheddar or Swiss

   2 SERVINGS

Whisk 3 eggs in bowl. Season with salt and pepper. Melt 1 tablespoon butter in 7- to 8-inch nonstick skillet over medium heat. Pour eggs into skillet; stir with heat-resistant rubber spatula until eggs begin to set, about 1 minute. Sprinkle half of cheese over center of eggs. Cook until eggs are softly set, lifting edges and tilting skillet to let uncooked eggs flow underneath, about 2 minutes longer. Fold omelet in thirds; transfer to plate. Repeat with remaining ingredients.

If I don't have the sell-by date on the carton to go by, how can I test an egg for freshness?

First, the ideal egg will have an oval shape, few (if any) stains and no cracks, ridges or thin spots. Place the raw egg (in its shell) in a bowl of water. Generally, fresh eggs will lie flat on the bottom of the bowl; eggs that tilt with the large end up are older. Eggs that float are rotten. The tilting is caused by air pockets that increase in size as fluid evaporates through the porous shell and oxygen and other gases filter in.

Morel, ham and Brie omelet

CREATE YOUR OWN VARIATIONS ON THE BASIC OMELET BY ADDING DIFFERENT FILLING COMBINATIONS—OR MAKE THIS INDULGENT RECIPE.

4   tablespoons (½ stick) butter

1   3-ounce slice smoked ham (about ½ inch thick), cut into ½-inch cubes

6   ounces fresh morels, trimmed, cut into ¼-inch-thick slices

6   large eggs

2   ounces ripe Brie cheese, cut into small pieces

   2 SERVINGS

Melt 2 tablespoons butter in large nonstick skillet over medium-high heat. Add ham; sauté 3 minutes. Add morels; sauté until tender, about 5 minutes. Season with salt and pepper. Remove from heat.

Whisk 3 eggs in bowl. Season with salt and pepper. Melt 1 tablespoon butter in 7- to 8-inch nonstick skillet over medium heat. Pour eggs into skillet; stir with heat-resistant rubber spatula until eggs begin to set, about 1 minute. Sprinkle half of morel mixture and half of Brie over center of eggs. Cook until eggs are softly set, lifting edges and tilting skillet to let uncooked eggs flow underneath, about 2 minutes longer. Fold omelet in thirds; transfer to plate. Repeat with remaining ingredients.

Feta and green onion frittata

UNLIKE AN OMELET, WHICH IS COOKED QUICKLY OVER MODERATE HEAT AND THEN FOLDED TO ENCLOSE THE FILLING, AN ITALIAN FRITTATA IS COOKED SLOWLY OVER LOW HEAT AND SERVED OPEN-FACE.

3 tablespoons olive oil

1 bunch green onions, chopped

8 large eggs

6 ounces feta cheese, cut into small cubes

½ cup chopped fresh Italian parsley

2 tablespoons milk

½ teaspoon salt

½ teaspoon ground black pepper

6 SERVINGS

Heat 1 tablespoon oil in 12-inch-diameter broilerproof nonstick skillet over medium heat. Add green onions and sauté until tender, about 3 minutes. Transfer to large bowl and cool. Add eggs, cheese, parsley, milk, salt and pepper to onions and whisk until blended.

Preheat broiler. Heat remaining 2 tablespoons oil in same skillet over medium-high heat. Add egg mixture. Tilt and swirl pan to distribute evenly. Using heat-resistant rubber spatula, lift up edges of cooked egg to allow uncooked portion to flow underneath; cook until beginning to set. Reduce heat to low. Cover and cook until frittata is almost set, about 8 minutes. Transfer skillet to broiler; broil until frittata is set and top just begins to brown, about 3 minutes. Slide frittata onto plate. Cut into wedges. Serve warm or at room temperature.

Cheddar, vegetable and sausage strata

A KIND OF SAVORY ITALIAN BREAD PUDDING, A STRATA COMBINES THICK SLICES OF BREAD, AN EGG CUSTARD AND FLAVORINGS. MOST OF THE ASSEMBLY CAN BE DONE ONE DAY AHEAD.

9 1-inch-thick slices French bread (each about 3x5 inches)

5 large eggs

1 teaspoon Dijon mustard

1 teaspoon dried basil

½ teaspoon salt

1½ cups half and half

2 cups (packed) grated sharp cheddar cheese

½ green bell pepper, cut into 2x¼-inch strips

15 cherry tomatoes, halved

6 ounces smoked sausage (such as kielbasa), cut into ½-inch cubes

2 tablespoons minced onion

Chopped fresh parsley

6 TO 8 SERVINGS

Butter 13x9x2-inch glass baking dish. Fit 8 bread slices into prepared dish. Cut remaining bread slice into 1-inch cubes; fit cubes into any empty spaces. Whisk eggs, mustard, basil and salt in medium bowl to blend; whisk in half and half. Ladle custard over bread. Cover; chill at least 2 hours or overnight.

Preheat oven to 350°F. Sprinkle mixture in dish with ground black pepper. Top with half of cheese, then bell pepper, tomatoes, sausage, onion and remaining cheese. Cover loosely with foil. Bake 20 minutes. Remove foil. Bake until strata is set and springy to touch, about 20 minutes longer. Cool 5 minutes. Sprinkle with parsley.

Baked eggs with chive butter

SOMETIMES REFERRED TO AS SHIRRED OR CODDLED EGGS, BAKED EGGS ARE COOKED IN SMALL DISHES, SUCH AS RAMEKINS. FOR THE MOST EVEN COOKING, THEY ARE SET IN A HOT WATER BATH (*BAIN-MARIE*), THOUGH THAT'S NOT ABSOLUTELY ESSENTIAL. CHIVES ARE USED IN THE RECIPE HERE (PICTURED ON PAGE 11), BUT YOU CAN EXPERIMENT WITH DIFFERENT ADDITIONS, SUCH AS BACON OR CHEESE.

2 **tablespoons (¼ stick) butter, room temperature**

1½ **teaspoons minced fresh chives**

4 **large eggs**

2 TO 4 SERVINGS

Using wooden spoon, beat butter in small bowl until smooth. Mix in chives. Season generously with salt and pepper. (*Can be prepared 1 day ahead. Chill. Bring to room temperature before using.*)

Preheat oven to 400°F. Arrange four ⅔-cup or two 1-cup ramekins in roasting pan or large shallow baking dish. Pour boiling water into pan to come halfway up sides of ramekins. Add 1 teaspoon chive butter to each small ramekin or 2 teaspoons to each large one. Heat in oven until ramekins are very hot, about 2 minutes.

Break 1 egg into small bowl, then slide into hot ramekin, being careful not to break yolk. Repeat with remaining 3 eggs, adding 1 egg to each small ramekin or 2 to each large one. Dot ½ teaspoon chive butter on each egg. For very soft eggs, bake in water bath 5 minutes for small ramekins or 6 minutes for large. Check and continue cooking until eggs are set as desired. Carefully dry ramekins and set on plates. Serve baked eggs immediately.

Equipment

As one of the most basic of foods, the egg requires very little equipment. With just a stove and a skillet, the cook can create many wonderful combinations. From there, consider making that skillet nonstick. Add a timer to facilitate perfect hard-boiled eggs, a seasoned omelet pan and a good whisk. Finally, by the time you bring home an egg poacher with perforated cups to coax eggs into a uniform shape, an egg slicer to produce perfect slivers, and an aluminum or cast-iron griddle with a nonstick surface for scrambled eggs and frittatas, you have nearly every technique and recipe covered.

Also useful: a little imagination. The egg is wonderfully versatile.

Huevos rancheros verdes

FROM BAKED EGGS TO FRIED: THIS SOUTHWESTERN FAVORITE, ITS NAME IN SPANISH MEANING "RANCHER'S EGGS," CONSISTS OF FRIED TORTILLAS TOPPED WITH FRIED EGGS AND SALSA. GREEN TOMATILLO SALSA IS CALLED FOR, BUT ANY HOMEMADE OR PURCHASED RED OR GREEN SALSA WOULD BE FINE.

½ pound tomatillos, husked, rinsed

1½ cups (packed) fresh cilantro leaves

¾ cup diced peeled avocado

½ cup chopped onion

2 tablespoons fresh lime juice

4 teaspoons minced seeded serrano chilies

2 garlic cloves

1 teaspoon ground cumin

3 tablespoons (or more) butter

4 corn tortillas

8 large eggs

1½ cups (packed) grated Monterey Jack cheese (about 6 ounces)

4 SERVINGS

Cook tomatillos in large saucepan of simmering water until soft, about 20 minutes. Drain. Transfer tomatillos to blender; add 1 cup cilantro, avocado, onion, lime juice, chilies, garlic and cumin; puree. Season to taste with salt and pepper. Set sauce aside.

Melt 1 tablespoon butter in large nonstick skillet over medium-high heat. Add 2 tortillas; cook about 1 minute per side. Transfer to baking sheet. Repeat with remaining tortillas, adding more butter to skillet as necessary. Melt 1 tablespoon butter in same skillet over medium heat. Crack 4 eggs into skillet. Cover and cook eggs to desired doneness. Sprinkle fried eggs with salt and pepper. Using spatula, place 2 eggs on each of 2 fried tortillas. Repeat with remaining eggs and 1 tablespoon butter. Top eggs on each tortilla with ¼ of sauce and ¼ of cheese. Using spatula, return 2 huevos rancheros to same skillet. Cover and cook over medium heat until cheese melts, about 3 minutes. Transfer to 2 plates. Repeat with remaining huevos rancheros. Sprinkle with remaining ½ cup cilantro and serve.

Tips

FOR PERFECT hard-boiled eggs, place eggs in a single layer in a saucepan and add water to cover at least 1 inch above the eggs. Cover the pan; bring the water just to a boil. Turn off heat. Let the eggs stand, covered, about 15 minutes. Rinse under cold water or let stand in ice water until completely cooled. Refrigerate promptly; use within one week.

SOMETIMES a recipe calls for egg yolks or whites—but not both. What can be done with the leftovers? Yolks can be used in custards, puddings, homemade ice cream or sauces like hollandaise or béarnaise. Whites can be whisked to make a low-fat omelet, whipped to make an angel food cake, or beaten with sugar and baked to make meringues.

TO SEASON an omelet pan, pour vegetable oil into the pan to a depth of about half an inch. Heat the oil over medium-high heat until it's hot. Turn off the heat, and allow the oil to cool in the pan on the burner. Once it is cool, remove from the stove and let the pan sit with the oil in it for eight hours. Pour the oil out and wipe the pan with a cloth. Never wash with soap.

Double-salmon and sweet potato hash with poached eggs

POACHING EGGS IS ANOTHER TRADITIONAL PREPARATION. HERE, THEY ARE SERVED ATOP A SWEET POTATO AND LEEK HASH MADE WITH BOTH FRESH *AND* SMOKED SALMON. MAPLE SYRUP ACCENTS THE DISH. IT TAKES SOME TIME TO MAKE—BUT IT'S WORTH THE EFFORT.

¼ cup white wine vinegar

6 large eggs

4 tablespoons (½ stick) butter

2 pounds red-skinned sweet potatoes (yams), peeled, cut into ½-inch cubes

3 cups chopped leeks (white and pale green parts only)

1 large red bell pepper, diced

2 teaspoons dried thyme

1 12-ounce skinless salmon fillet, cut into ½-inch cubes

3 tablespoons pure maple syrup

2½ teaspoons chopped fresh sage

5 ounces thinly sliced smoked salmon, chopped

Paprika

Chopped fresh chives

6 SERVINGS

Fill large bowl with cold water. Add enough water to large pot to measure 3 inches in depth; add vinegar and bring to simmer. Reduce heat to medium-low. Crack eggs open 1 at a time over simmering water and drop in. Poach eggs until whites are set, about 4 minutes. Using slotted spoon, transfer eggs to bowl of cold water to stop cooking; reserve pot of vinegar water.

Melt half of butter in each of 2 large nonstick skillets over low heat. Add half of sweet potatoes, leeks, bell pepper and thyme to each skillet; stir to coat with butter. Cover skillets; cook until potatoes are tender, stirring occasionally, about 8 minutes. Increase heat to medium-high. Uncover; cook without stirring until potatoes are golden on bottom, about 3 minutes. Using spatula, turn hash over in sections and cook without stirring until potatoes are golden on bottom, about 3 minutes longer. Fold half of fresh salmon, maple syrup and sage into hash in each skillet. Cook until salmon is just opaque in center, stirring occasionally, about 3 minutes. Mix half of smoked salmon into hash in each skillet. Season to taste with salt and pepper. Remove hash from heat.

Meanwhile, bring reserved vinegar water to simmer; turn off heat. Transfer eggs to hot water 1 minute to rewarm.

Spoon hash onto plates. Remove eggs from water and place atop hash. Sprinkle with paprika and chives.

Goat cheese and herb soufflé

SIMPLER THAN MIGHT BE IMAGINED, THIS SOUFFLÉ (PICTURED OPPOSITE) IS REALLY JUST BEATEN EGG WHITES MIXED WITH A FLAVORED BASE AND BAKED. SOUFFLÉS ARE SENSITIVE TO TEMPERATURE CHANGES, SO DON'T OPEN THE OVEN DOOR TO CHECK THEM UNTIL JUST A FEW MINUTES BEFORE THEY SHOULD BE DONE.

2 tablespoons minced fresh thyme

¼ cup extra-virgin olive oil

5 tablespoons all purpose flour

1 large garlic clove, minced

1¼ cups whole milk

¼ cup dry white wine

6 large egg yolks

1 teaspoon salt

1 tablespoon minced fresh basil

1 teaspoon minced fresh rosemary

1 cup crumbled chilled soft fresh goat cheese

½ cup (packed) grated Gruyère cheese (about 2 ounces)

8 large egg whites

4 TO 6 SERVINGS

Position rack in center of oven and preheat to 400°F. Generously butter one 10-cup soufflé dish or six 1¼-cup soufflé dishes; sprinkle with 1 tablespoon thyme to coat. (If using 1¼-cup dishes, place all 6 on rimmed baking sheet.) Heat oil in heavy large saucepan over medium heat. Add flour and garlic. Cook without browning until mixture begins to bubble, whisking constantly, about 1 minute. Gradually whisk in milk, then wine. Cook until smooth, thick and beginning to boil, whisking constantly, about 2 minutes. Remove from heat. Mix egg yolks and salt in small bowl. Add yolk mixture all at once to sauce; whisk quickly to blend. Mix in basil, 1 tablespoon thyme and rosemary. Fold in chilled goat cheese and Gruyère cheese (cheeses do not need to melt).

Using electric mixer, beat egg whites in large bowl until stiff but not dry. Gently fold ¼ of whites into lukewarm soufflé base to lighten. Fold in remaining whites. Transfer soufflé mixture to prepared dish or dishes. Sprinkle with ground black pepper.

Place soufflé in oven; reduce heat to 375°F. Bake until puffed, golden and gently set in center, 35 minutes for large soufflé (or 25 minutes for small soufflés). Transfer soufflé to platter; serve immediately.

MAKING A SOUFFLÉ:

STEP 1: After adding milk and white wine to the roux (a cooked combination of flour and oil), whisk the sauce constantly until it is smooth, thick and beginning to bubble.

STEP 2: The air that is whipped into the egg whites will make the soufflé rise. Enough air has been beaten into the whites when they form stiff peaks but still look moist.

STEP 3: To retain as much air in the whites as possible, fold one-fourth of the whites into the base to loosen its texture. That way, the rest of the whites will be easier to incorporate.

2

Who doesn't love homemade soup? It's comforting in winter, refreshing in summer; it can be an elegant first course or a hearty meal-in-a-bowl. Best of all—how easy it is to make.

Every soup starts with stock, whether meat, chicken or vegetable. Making stock is a great job for a lazy weekend afternoon, but purchased stock (with a few additions) works just fine, too. What you add next is up to you: maybe a flavorful mix of wild mushrooms, or the makings of that French classic, onion soup.

That's the way soups are—simple, versatile and completely satisfying. In the following recipes, you'll learn techniques that will make you a master of the soup pot in no time.

Soups

Split Pea Soup with Bacon and Rosemary (page 28)

Basic chicken stock

HOMEMADE CHICKEN STOCK IS THE FOUNDATION FOR MANY SOUPS, SAUCES AND STEWS. THIS VERSATILE SOUP BASE CAN BE USED IN ANY RECIPE THAT CALLS FOR CHICKEN STOCK OR CANNED BROTH.

2   medium leeks (white and pale green parts only)

4   pounds chicken wings, rinsed

3   quarts plus 3 cups cold water

2   carrots, cut into 1-inch pieces

1   large onion, cut into 1-inch pieces

6   fresh thyme sprigs

12 whole black peppercorns

2   bay leaves

MAKES 8 CUPS

Cut leeks lengthwise in half. Using cold water, rinse any dirt from leeks. Cut halves into 1-inch pieces. Place in 8- to 10-quart pot. Add chicken wings, 3 quarts plus 3 cups water, carrots, onion, thyme, peppercorns and bay leaves to pot. Bring to boil. Reduce heat to medium-low and simmer 2 hours 15 minutes, occasionally skimming foam from surface. Strain stock through fine sieve into large bowl. Measure stock. If necessary, simmer in large saucepan until reduced to 8 cups.

Chill stock until fat hardens on surface, about 2 hours. Spoon off fat and discard. (*Stock can be prepared ahead. Cover and refrigerate up to 2 days or freeze up to 3 months.*)

MAKING CHICKEN STOCK:

STEP 1: To ensure that the stock will be clear, remove the foam that bubbles to the top: Partially submerge a spoon into the liquid and skim the surface clean.

STEP 2: Simmer the stock for about two hours to draw out the best flavor from the chicken and vegetables. Then strain it by ladling the liquid through a fine sieve set over a large bowl.

STEP 3: Degreasing the stock is easy: As the strained stock chills, the fat will rise to the surface and solidify. Simply spoon off the hardened fat and discard it.

Wild mushroom soup with vegetable confetti

START WITH THE BASIC CHICKEN STOCK AND ADD AN ASSORTMENT OF WILD MUSHROOMS AND A VEGETABLE GARNISH FOR A RICH AND ELEGANT SOUP.

6½ cups Basic Chicken Stock (see recipe opposite) or canned low-salt chicken broth

½ teaspoon saffron threads

2 tablespoons vegetable oil

6 tablespoons minced shallots

2 tablespoons finely chopped garlic

15 ounces assorted fresh wild mushrooms (such as crimini, chanterelle, oyster, morel and stemmed shiitake), sliced

6 ounces button mushrooms, sliced

⅛ teaspoon curry powder

⅓ cup finely diced leek

⅓ cup finely diced peeled carrot

⅓ cup finely diced peeled turnip

2 tablespoons (¼ stick) butter

4 SERVINGS

Bring ½ cup stock to simmer in saucepan. Add saffron; set aside to steep.

Heat oil in heavy large saucepan over medium-low heat. Add shallots and garlic; stir 1 minute. Add ⅓ of wild mushrooms and all of button mushrooms. Sauté until mushrooms release liquid, about 8 minutes. Add curry powder; sauté until mushrooms are tender, about 4 minutes. Add saffron mixture and remaining 6 cups stock. Simmer about 15 minutes to blend flavors. Remove from heat.

Puree cooked mushrooms and 1 cup mushroom broth in processor until almost smooth. Return mushroom puree to saucepan with broth. Simmer soup 15 minutes. Season to taste with salt and pepper. (Can be prepared 1 day ahead. Cool slightly. Refrigerate uncovered until cold, then cover and keep refrigerated.)

Cook leek, carrot and turnip in saucepan of boiling salted water until just tender, about 1 minute. Drain. Rinse under cold water; drain again. (Vegetable confetti can be prepared up to 2 hours ahead. Pat dry; cover and let stand at room temperature.)

Melt butter in large skillet over medium-high heat. Add remaining ⅔ of wild mushrooms; sauté until tender, about 8 minutes. Season mushrooms to taste with salt and pepper.

Rewarm soup. Ladle into 4 shallow bowls. Top with sautéed mushrooms and vegetable confetti and serve.

Do some soups freeze better than others?

Many soups freeze well. Homemade stock can be frozen for two to four months; just be sure to store it in a labeled and dated airtight container. On the other hand, milk-, cream- or yogurt-based soups don't freeze well; instead, prepare them up to the point before the dairy products are added, then freeze them. When you're ready to finish preparing the soup, defrost it first and then add the dairy ingredients.

Basic beef stock

A RICH AND CLASSIC BEEF STOCK. THIS RECIPE CAN ALSO BE CALLED A "BROWN STOCK" BECAUSE THE MEAT BONES ARE BROWNED BEFORE THEY ARE SIMMERED IN THE LIQUID.

5 pounds meaty beef knuckle, shank or neck bones, cut into small pieces

2 medium unpeeled onions, trimmed, quartered

2 medium unpeeled carrots, halved crosswise

4½ quarts (about) water

2 celery stalks, cut into 3-inch pieces

2 bay leaves

10 parsley stems

4 large unpeeled garlic cloves

10 whole black peppercorns

2 fresh thyme sprigs or ½ teaspoon dried

MAKES ABOUT 8 CUPS

Preheat oven to 450°F. Arrange beef bones in large roasting pan. Bake until browned, turning occasionally, about 30 minutes. Add onions and carrots and cook until browned, about 30 minutes.

Using slotted spoon, transfer bones, onions and carrots to stockpot. Pour off drippings from pan. Set pan over high heat. Add 1 cup water and bring to boil, scraping up browned bits. Add to stockpot. Add celery, bay leaves, parsley and garlic. Pour in enough water to cover ingredients. Bring to simmer, skimming foam from surface. Add peppercorns and thyme. Cover partially; simmer gently 8 hours, skimming surface occasionally and adding more hot water if necessary to keep bones submerged. Strain stock. Cool slightly. Chill uncovered until cold, then cover and keep chilled. Remove fat from surface. *(Can be prepared ahead. Cover and refrigerate up to 2 days or freeze up to 3 months.)*

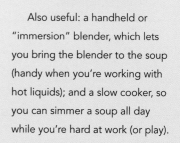

Equipment

Take one stockpot (8 to 22 quarts, with 12 quarts being a good size for most stocks), a heavy-bottomed pot (for even browning), a knife (for chopping), a spoon (for stirring—and tasting) and a ladle (for serving), and you're equipped to make any simple, hearty soup. For a pureed soup, you'll need a blender with a glass container (plastic containers are easily scratched, and food processors don't always achieve the smoothest result).

Also useful: a handheld or "immersion" blender, which lets you bring the blender to the soup (handy when you're working with hot liquids); and a slow cooker, so you can simmer a soup all day while you're hard at work (or play).

Onion soup gratinée

THE TERM *GRATINÉE* REFERS TO ANY DISH THAT IS TOPPED WITH CHEESE OR BREADCRUMBS, THEN HEATED IN THE OVEN OR UNDER A BROILER UNTIL THE TOPPING IS BROWN AND CRISPY. BEGIN PREPARING THIS TRADITIONAL FRENCH SOUP A DAY AHEAD: IT NEEDS TO CHILL OVERNIGHT FOR MAXIMUM FLAVOR.

2	tablespoons olive oil
2	pounds onions, thinly sliced
½	teaspoon sugar
3	tablespoons all purpose flour
8	cups Basic Beef Stock (see recipe opposite) or canned beef broth
½	cup dry white wine
1	tablespoon minced fresh thyme
2	bay leaves
3	tablespoons brandy
4	3x2x½-inch slices French bread
1½	cups grated Gruyère cheese
	Fresh thyme leaves

4 SERVINGS

Heat oil in heavy large saucepan over medium-low heat. Add onions. Cover and cook 15 minutes, stirring occasionally. Add sugar; increase heat to medium and cook uncovered until onions are deep golden brown, stirring frequently, about 40 minutes.

Add flour to onions and stir 2 minutes. Gradually mix in stock and wine. Add minced thyme and bay leaves. Simmer 40 minutes. Stir in brandy. Remove bay leaves from soup. Cool slightly. Refrigerate uncovered until cold, then cover and refrigerate overnight. *(Can be prepared 3 days ahead; keep chilled.)*

Preheat oven to 325°F. Arrange bread in single layer on baking sheet. Bake until croutons are dry and light brown, about 30 minutes.

Increase heat to 450°F. Bring soup to boil. Ladle into deep ovenproof bowls. Top each with crouton. Cover with cheese. Bake until cheese begins to melt, about 5 minutes. Sprinkle with thyme leaves and serve.

Which type of onion—yellow, white, or red—is best for soups?

Yellow onions generally are highly flavored and somewhat sharp in taste. They hold up well in soups and stews. Consider them all-purpose onions, and use them in recipes that do not specify a particular type. White onions have a milder flavor, and a hint of sweetness. They are excellent for sautéing and work well in fresh salsas. Red onions are the sweetest and are best used raw, since they tend to lose their vibrant color when cooked. Add them to a variety of salads, sandwiches and burgers, but not to soups.

Basic vegetable stock

MANY SOUPS CALL FOR VEGETABLE STOCK. THE KEY TO GOOD FLAVOR IS ROASTING THE VEGETABLES FIRST (ALWAYS ROAST THEM IN THE BOTTOM THIRD OF THE OVEN FOR BETTER BROWNING).

1 **cup chopped onion**

1 **cup quartered crimini mushrooms**

1 **cup sliced carrots**

½ **cup chopped parsnips**

½ **cup sliced celery**

4 **large garlic cloves, crushed, peeled**

1 **tablespoon olive oil**

8 **cups water**

1 **cup coarsely chopped Swiss chard (including stems)**

½ **cup thinly sliced leek (white and pale green parts only)**

¼ **cup chopped fresh parsley (including stems)**

1 **teaspoon salt**

1 **bay leaf**

1 **large fresh thyme sprig**

MAKES ABOUT 8 CUPS

Preheat oven to 400°F. Combine first 6 ingredients in 13x9x2-inch roasting pan. Drizzle 1 tablespoon oil over; toss to coat. Sprinkle with salt. Roast vegetables until tender and golden, stirring occasionally, about 40 minutes. Remove from oven.

Add 2 cups water to roasting pan; stir vegetables, scraping up any browned bits. Transfer vegetable mixture to large pot. Add remaining 6 cups water and all remaining ingredients. Bring to boil. Reduce heat, cover and simmer 30 minutes. Strain, discarding vegetables. *(Can be prepared ahead. Cool slightly. Refrigerate uncovered until cold, then cover and keep refrigerated 2 days or freeze up to 3 months.)*

Tips

TO MAKE fast work of degreasing stock, refrigerate, then scoop the congealed fat off the top.

TO RID a cutting board of the lingering aromas of onion or garlic—ingredients essential to soups—rub a cut lemon over the board before washing it with hot, soapy water, or scrub the board with a little baking soda and water. Better yet, use a plastic board for strongly scented foods; smells tend to cling to wooden boards.

WHEN hot soup is pureed in a blender, steam can push the top off the blender. To avoid this, work in batches or use a handheld (immersion) blender.

FOR AN elegant presentation, dice a little extra of one of the fresh ingredients in the soup recipe and sprinkle it across the surface. Or add a dollop of sour cream or yogurt; garnish with fresh herbs.

Minestrone with yellow squash

THIS LIGHT SOUP CALLS FOR VEGETABLE STOCK. FOR A THICKER, MORE TRADITIONAL MINESTRONE, REPLACE ALL THE GREEN PEAS WITH HALF A CUP OF DRAINED CANNED WHITE BEANS.

8 cups Basic Vegetable Stock (see recipe opposite) or canned vegetable broth

2 cups chopped onions

2 cups chopped parsnips

¾ cup elbow macaroni

1 14½-ounce can diced tomatoes, drained

1 cup sliced green beans

¾ cup chopped yellow crookneck squash

1 cup frozen green peas

½ cup chopped fresh basil

¼ cup grated Parmesan cheese

6 SERVINGS

Bring stock to boil in large pot. Add onions and parsnips; boil 5 minutes. Add macaroni; reduce heat and simmer 5 minutes. Add tomatoes, green beans and squash; simmer 5 minutes. Add peas and simmer until macaroni and all vegetables are tender, about 5 minutes. Stir in basil. Season with salt and pepper. Sprinkle soup with cheese.

Potato soup with caramelized shallots

HERE'S A PUREED POTATO SOUP THAT CAN BE MADE WITH EITHER VEGETABLE STOCK OR CHICKEN STOCK.

2 heads of garlic

8 tablespoons olive oil

2 cups chopped leeks (white and pale green part only)

2 cups chopped onions

⅓ cup chopped celery

4 teaspoons ground coriander

3¼ pounds russet potatoes, peeled, cut into ¾-inch pieces

8 cups (or more) Basic Vegetable Stock (see recipe opposite) or Basic Chicken Stock (see recipe on page 22) or canned broth

2 cups sliced shallots (about 10 large)

12 SERVINGS

Preheat oven to 350°F. Rub heads of garlic with 1 tablespoon oil. Place in small baking dish; cover with foil. Bake until garlic is tender, about 1 hour. Cut tops off garlic; squeeze out roasted garlic and reserve.

Heat 4 tablespoons oil in heavy large pot over medium-low heat. Add leeks, onions and celery; sauté until tender but not brown, about 20 minutes. Add coriander; stir 2 minutes. Add potatoes; stir 2 minutes. Add roasted garlic and 8 cups stock; bring to boil. Reduce heat; simmer until potatoes are very tender, about 20 minutes. Cool slightly. Working in batches, puree soup in blender.

Heat remaining 3 tablespoons oil in heavy large skillet over medium heat. Add shallots; sauté until deep golden, about 15 minutes.

Bring soup to simmer in large pot. Thin with more stock, if desired. Season with salt and pepper. Ladle into bowls. Top with shallots.

Creamy zucchini soup

THIS SIMPLE RECIPE IS ANOTHER DELICIOUS EXAMPLE OF A PUREED SOUP. NUTMEG ADDS NICE FLAVOR, WHILE CREAM GIVES IT A GREAT TEXTURE. USE CHICKEN STOCK—OR EVEN EASIER, CANNED BROTH.

1½   pounds zucchini, cut into ½-inch pieces

1½   cups Basic Chicken Stock (see recipe on page 22) or canned low-salt chicken broth

¼   cup whipping cream

¼   teaspoon ground nutmeg

1   tablespoon grated Parmesan cheese

4 SERVINGS

Bring zucchini and chicken stock to boil in heavy medium saucepan. Reduce heat to medium-low, cover and simmer until zucchini is very tender, about 15 minutes.

Working in batches, puree soup in blender until almost smooth. Return soup to same saucepan. Add cream, nutmeg and cheese; stir over medium heat until warm. Season with salt and pepper.

Split pea soup with bacon and rosemary

BEAN SOUPS ARE HEARTY AND SATISFYING. SPLIT PEAS DON'T REQUIRE PRE-SOAKING BEFORE THEY ARE COOKED, WHICH MAKES THIS SOUP (PICTURED ON PAGE 21) A REAL TIME-SAVER. TOP EACH BOWL OF SOUP WITH A DOLLOP OF SOUR CREAM OR CRÈME FRAÎCHE, IF YOU LIKE.

4   bacon slices, chopped

1   small onion, chopped

1   medium leek (white and pale green parts only), sliced

1   large carrot, peeled, chopped

2   garlic cloves, minced

8   cups Basic Chicken Stock (see recipe on page 22) or canned low-salt chicken broth

1¼   cups green split peas, rinsed

2   bay leaves

½   teaspoon chopped fresh rosemary

4 TO 6 SERVINGS

Sauté bacon in heavy large pot over medium-high heat until crisp and brown. Add onion, leek, carrot and garlic; sauté until vegetables begin to soften, about 6 minutes. Add stock, peas, bay leaves and rosemary; bring soup to boil. Reduce heat to medium-low, cover and simmer until peas are tender, stirring occasionally, about 1 hour. Season soup to taste with salt and pepper. *(Can be prepared 1 day ahead. Cool slightly. Chill uncovered until cold, then cover and keep chilled. Bring to simmer before serving.)* Discard bay leaves and serve.

Black bean soup with cumin

HERE'S ANOTHER TYPE OF BEAN SOUP; THIS ONE IS MADE WITH BLACK BEANS. BECAUSE THE DRIED BEANS FOR THIS LATIN-INSPIRED SOUP ARE NOT PRE-SOAKED, THEY REQUIRE A LONGER COOKING TIME TO BECOME TENDER.

2	tablespoons olive oil
1½	cups chopped onion
8	garlic cloves, chopped
¼	cup chopped jalapeño chilies with seeds
2	cups dried black beans (about 13 ounces)
1	tablespoon ground cumin
2	teaspoons ground coriander
8	cups (or more) Basic Vegetable Stock (see recipe on page 26) or canned vegetable broth
1	cup coarsely chopped fresh cilantro
	Lime wedges

8 SERVINGS

Heat oil in heavy large pot over medium-high heat. Add onion, garlic and jalapeños; sauté 5 minutes. Mix in beans and spices. Add 8 cups stock and bring to boil. Reduce heat, cover and simmer until beans are tender, stirring occasionally, about 2 hours 15 minutes. Working in batches, puree soup with cilantro in blender. Return soup to pot. Season to taste with salt and pepper. *(Can be prepared 1 day ahead. Cool slightly. Refrigerate uncovered until cold, then cover and keep chilled.)*

Bring soup to simmer, thinning with more stock if necessary. Ladle into bowls. Serve, passing lime wedges separately.

Lentil soup with thyme

LIGHTLY CARAMELIZING THE ONIONS AND CARROTS GIVES THIS LENTIL SOUP A NICE SWEETNESS. FOR CONVENIENCE, YOU CAN MAKE IT UP TO ONE DAY AHEAD.

1	tablespoon olive oil
2	cups chopped onions
¾	cup chopped peeled carrots
¼	cup chopped celery
½	16-ounce package lentils
5	cups (or more) Basic Vegetable Stock (see recipe on page 26) or canned vegetable broth
¼	cup canned tomato puree
2	teaspoons chopped fresh thyme

4 TO 6 SERVINGS

Heat oil in heavy large pot over medium-high heat. Add onions; sauté until brown, about 10 minutes. Add carrots and celery; sauté 5 minutes. Stir in lentils. Add 5 cups stock, tomato puree and 1½ teaspoons thyme. Bring to boil. Reduce heat to medium. Cover; simmer until lentils are tender, stirring soup occasionally, about 1 hour.

Puree 1 cup soup in blender until smooth. Return to pot. Stir in ½ teaspoon thyme. Season soup with salt and pepper. *(Can be made 1 day ahead. Chill uncovered until cold; cover and keep chilled. Bring to simmer before serving, thinning with more broth if too thick.)*

Gazpacho with jalapeño and cilantro

A COLD, UNCOOKED SOUP FROM SOUTHERN SPAIN, GAZPACHO TRADITIONALLY INCLUDES PUREED TOMATOES, BELL PEPPERS, ONIONS, CUCUMBER, BREADCRUMBS AND GARLIC. THE VERSION HERE (PICTURED OPPOSITE) GETS EXTRA FLAVOR FROM JALAPEÑO AND CILANTRO.

3½ cups (or more) tomato juice

8 plum tomatoes (about 18 ounces), seeded, cut into ¼-inch pieces

1 English hothouse cucumber, cut into ¼-inch pieces (about 7 ounces)

1 red bell pepper, cut into ¼-inch pieces (about 1 cup)

1 medium onion, chopped

¼ cup chopped fresh cilantro

¼ cup chopped fresh parsley

3 tablespoons fresh lemon juice

1 green onion, minced

1½ teaspoons minced seeded jalapeño chili

2 garlic cloves, minced

6 TO 8 SERVINGS

Combine 1 cup tomato juice, half of tomatoes, half of cucumber and half of bell pepper in blender. Puree until smooth. Pour into large bowl. Stir in remaining tomatoes, cucumber and bell pepper; add onion, cilantro, parsley, lemon juice, green onion, jalapeño and garlic. Transfer 1 cup mixture to blender. Add 2½ cups tomato juice to blender and puree. Pour back into remaining soup and stir to combine. Thin with additional tomato juice, if desired. Season to taste with salt and pepper. Cover; refrigerate 2 hours. *(Can be prepared 1 day ahead. Keep refrigerated.)* Serve cold.

Chilled beet and buttermilk soup

ANOTHER COLD SOUP TO ADD TO YOUR REPERTOIRE, THIS RECIPE IS THE PERFECT BALANCE OF SWEET AND SOUR: COOKED BEETS AND HONEY ARE COMBINED WITH SOUR CREAM AND BUTTERMILK. ORANGE JUICE AND RASPBERRY VINEGAR LEND EXTRA TANG.

1¼ pounds medium beets, trimmed

1 cup sour cream

½ cup (or more) fresh orange juice

¼ cup raspberry vinegar or red wine vinegar

1 tablespoon honey

Ground white pepper

1 cup buttermilk

1 apple, peeled, diced (optional)

6 SERVINGS

Cook beets in large pot of boiling water until very tender and knife pierces center easily, about 50 minutes. Drain beets; cool slightly. Peel and chop coarsely. Transfer beets to food processor. Add sour cream, ½ cup orange juice, vinegar and honey and blend until smooth. Season to taste with salt and white pepper. Pour into large bowl and whisk in buttermilk. Thin soup with more orange juice, if desired. Cover and refrigerate until cold, about 2 hours. *(Can be prepared 2 days ahead. Keep refrigerated.)* Ladle into bowls. Garnish soup with diced apple, if desired, and serve.

3

The person who invented washed and bagged salad greens is a charter member of the Keep It Simple Hall of Fame. Gone are the days of wilted lettuce and gritty spinach. Now getting a salad on the table is often the easiest part of the meal.

Of course, we're not suggesting you ignore the rest of the produce section—or the farmers' market if you're lucky enough to live near one. The best salads are seasonal: Add some pears in autumn, artichoke hearts in spring, ripe tomatoes in summer. As long as the ingredients are in their prime, you really can't go wrong, no matter what you choose.

And don't forget those picnic favorites: potato salad, coleslaw and pasta salad. Once you see how easy it is to make your own, you'll never go back to the deli kind again.

Salads

Tomato and Bread Salad with Basil and Red Onion (page 35)

Basic vinaigrette

IN ITS SIMPLEST FORM, A VINAIGRETTE IS A COMBINATION OF OIL AND VINEGAR IN A RATIO OF THREE PARTS OIL TO ONE PART VINEGAR. SALT AND PEPPER ARE USED FOR SEASONING. THIS RECIPE IS A STRAIGHTFORWARD VERSION WITH A FEW EXTRA INGREDIENTS ADDED FOR INTEREST. WHEN MAKING AN OIL-AND-VINEGAR DRESSING, ALWAYS WHISK IN THE OIL LAST TO HELP KEEP THE INGREDIENTS FROM SEPARATING.

6   tablespoons apple cider vinegar

1   shallot, minced

1   teaspoon Dijon mustard

1   teaspoon honey

¾   cup extra-virgin olive oil

MAKES ABOUT 1¼ CUPS

Whisk first 4 ingredients in small bowl to blend. Gradually whisk in oil. Season to taste with salt and pepper.

Why do vinaigrette recipes recommend gradually whisking the oil into the vinegar?

By whisking the oil into the vinegar, you create an "emulsion"—a well-blended mixture of two liquids that don't usually combine smoothly. The vinegar gets evenly dispersed throughout the oil—and stays that way longer. An emulsified vinaigrette tastes better, too, because the flavor is more consistent throughout the salad.

Mixed green salad with pumpkin seeds and Asiago cheese

THE BASIC VINAIGRETTE IS USED TO DRESS THIS MIXED GREEN SALAD. *PEPITAS*, COMMONLY KNOWN AS PUMPKIN SEEDS, ARE A POPULAR INGREDIENT IN MEXICAN COOKING AND ARE AN INTRIGUING ADDITION TO THIS SALAD. IF UNAVAILABLE, TOASTED PINE NUTS MAKE A FINE SUBSTITUTE.

1   large head of red leaf lettuce, torn into bite-size pieces

1   large head of butter lettuce, torn into bite-size pieces

3   bunches watercress, trimmed

Basic Vinaigrette (see recipe above)

¾   cup roasted salted pumpkin seeds (pepitas)

1   6-ounce piece Asiago cheese

12 SERVINGS

Combine lettuces and watercress in large bowl. Add vinaigrette and toss to coat. Sprinkle with pumpkin seeds. Using vegetable peeler, shave cheese atop salad and serve.

Tomato and bread salad with basil and red onion

THERE ARE SEVERAL VERSIONS OF THE ITALIAN TOMATO-AND-BREAD SALAD CALLED *PANZANELLA*. BUT NO MATTER HOW THE SALAD IS MADE, THE BREAD SHOULD BE A FEW DAYS OLD AND COARSE IN TEXTURE. THIS RECIPE (PICTURED ON PAGE 33), WITH ITS SIMPLE OIL-AND-VINEGAR DRESSING, IS A REAL WINNER.

8 ounces stale Italian bread, cut into 2-inch pieces

8 cups (about) cold water

2 pounds ripe plum tomatoes, coarsely chopped (about 5 cups)

1 small red onion, thinly sliced

1 cup (loosely packed) fresh basil leaves, torn into bite-size pieces

⅓ cup red wine vinegar

½ cup extra-virgin olive oil

6 SERVINGS

Place bread in large bowl. Pour in enough cold water (about 8 cups) to cover bread. Soak 5 minutes. Drain well; squeeze bread to remove as much liquid as possible. Coarsely crumble bread into same bowl. Add tomatoes, onion and basil. Pour vinegar into small bowl. Gradually whisk in oil. Season vinaigrette to taste with salt and pepper. Toss salad with enough vinaigrette to coat. Season generously with salt and pepper. *(Can be prepared 8 hours ahead. Cover and refrigerate. Let stand 1 hour at room temperature before serving.)*

Equipment

A salad spinner—crank, pull-cord or pump—makes fast work of drying lettuce, so it's a useful piece of equipment. In addition, a good sharp knife, a food processor or a hand grater is needed to shred cheese and any vegetables that will go into the salad.

Also useful for salad dressings: a blender or whisk and a self-cleaning garlic press (the handle swings backward and tiny teeth on the handle back nudge garlic out of the holes). And for that dramatic flourish, you'll need a pepper mill—classic knob

style, crank-driven, or the newfangled kind you squeeze to set the grinding blade in action.

Pear, arugula and endive salad with candied walnuts

ANOTHER EXAMPLE OF A VINAIGRETTE-DRESSED SALAD, THIS ELEGANT PEAR AND BITTER GREENS SALAD (PICTURED OPPOSITE) IS TOPPED WITH CANDIED WALNUTS. THE WALNUTS ARE COATED WITH A MIXTURE OF SPICES AND CORN SYRUP, THEN BAKED UNTIL THEY ARE DEEP GOLDEN BROWN.

CANDIED WALNUTS

    Nonstick vegetable oil spray
1   cup walnuts (about 3½ ounces)
2   tablespoons light corn syrup
1   tablespoon sugar
½   teaspoon salt
¼   teaspoon ground black pepper
    Generous pinch of cayenne
    pepper

DRESSING

2   tablespoons Sherry
    wine vinegar
2   tablespoons fresh lemon juice
1   tablespoon chopped
    fresh parsley
2   teaspoons Dijon mustard
6   tablespoons walnut oil or
    olive oil
6   tablespoons extra-virgin
    olive oil

SALAD

12 cups arugula, torn into pieces
    (about 12 ounces)
4   heads of Belgian endive,
    trimmed, leaves separated
2   firm but ripe pears, halved,
    cored, thinly sliced lengthwise

10 SERVINGS

FOR CANDIED WALNUTS: Preheat oven to 325°F. Spray rimmed baking sheet with nonstick spray. Combine walnuts and next 5 ingredients in medium bowl; toss to coat. Spread nut mixture on prepared baking sheet (some nuts may clump together). Bake until nuts are deep golden and sugar mixture is bubbling, stirring occasionally to break up clumps, about 15 minutes. Cool completely on baking sheet. *(Can be prepared 3 days ahead. Store at room temperature in airtight container.)*

FOR DRESSING: Whisk vinegar and next 3 ingredients in medium bowl to blend. Add walnut oil and extra-virgin olive oil; whisk until well blended. Season dressing to taste with salt and pepper. *(Can be prepared 1 day ahead. Cover and chill. Let stand at room temperature 1 hour and rewhisk before continuing.)*

FOR SALAD: Toss arugula in large bowl with enough dressing to coat. Divide among 10 plates. Arrange endive leaves and pear slices atop arugula on each. Drizzle with more dressing. Sprinkle with walnuts; serve.

Caesar salad

WITH A DRESSING THAT'S A CROSS BETWEEN A VINAIGRETTE AND A CREAM-BASED ONE, THE TRADITIONAL VERSION OF THIS SALAD, CREATED IN 1924 BY CAESAR CARDINI IN TIJUANA, MEXICO, CONTAINED RAW EGGS. THIS NEWER TAKE USES MAYONNAISE INSTEAD, AND IT'S AS GOOD AS EVER.

7   garlic cloves

¾   cup mayonnaise

4   canned rolled anchovy fillets with capers, drained

2   tablespoons plus ⅓ cup freshly grated Parmesan cheese

1   tablespoon fresh lemon juice

1   teaspoon Worcestershire sauce

1   teaspoon Dijon mustard

¼   cup olive oil

4   cups ¾-inch bread cubes (made from day-old bread, crusts trimmed)

1   large head of romaine lettuce, cut into bite-size pieces

4 SERVINGS

Mince 3 garlic cloves in processor. Add mayonnaise, anchovies with capers, 2 tablespoons cheese, juice, Worcestershire sauce and mustard; process until blended. Transfer to medium bowl. Season dressing with salt and pepper. *(Can be made 1 day ahead. Cover; chill.)*

Heat oil in heavy large skillet over low heat. Cut remaining 4 garlic cloves in half. Add to skillet and cook until garlic is golden brown, stirring frequently, about 8 minutes. Using slotted spoon, remove garlic and discard. Add bread cubes to skillet and cook over low heat until golden brown, stirring frequently, about 15 minutes. Remove from heat. Season with salt and pepper. Cool to room temperature.

Place lettuce in large bowl. Toss with enough dressing to coat. Add remaining ⅓ cup cheese and croutons and toss gently to blend. Divide salad among 4 plates and serve.

Creamy blue cheese dressing

CREAMY DRESSINGS OFTEN INCLUDE CHEESE. HERE'S A BASIC RECIPE FOR A BLUE CHEESE DRESSING (USE ANY TYPE OF BLUE CHEESE YOU LIKE) THAT WILL COMPLEMENT A VARIETY OF SALADS.

1   cup mayonnaise

½   cup plus 2 tablespoons sour cream

½   cup buttermilk

2   tablespoons freshly grated Parmesan cheese

1   teaspoon Worcestershire sauce

½   teaspoon distilled white vinegar

    Dash of hot pepper sauce

1   cup crumbled blue cheese (about 4 ounces)

2   tablespoons chopped fresh parsley

MAKES ABOUT 2½ CUPS

Whisk first 3 ingredients in medium bowl until smooth. Add Parmesan, Worcestershire sauce, vinegar and hot pepper sauce and stir until well blended. Fold in blue cheese and parsley. Season with salt, pepper and additional hot pepper sauce, if desired. Cover and refrigerate dressing 1 hour. *(Can be prepared 3 days ahead. Keep refrigerated.)*

Butter lettuce, celery and mushroom salad with blue cheese dressing

WHEN MAKING THIS SALAD, LOOK FOR WHOLE HEADS OF BUTTER LETTUCE PACKAGED IN PLASTIC CONTAINERS AT YOUR LOCAL GROCERY STORE. THESE LETTUCES ARE GROWN HYDROPONICALLY (IN WATER, WITHOUT SOIL); THEY ARE SOLD WHILE STILL GROWING—AND SUPREMELY FRESH.

1 head of butter lettuce, separated into leaves

4 celery stalks, trimmed, very thinly sliced

1 cup sliced mushrooms

4 green onions, thinly sliced

Creamy Blue Cheese Dressing (see recipe opposite)

8 cherry tomatoes, halved

4 SERVINGS

Divide butter lettuce leaves equally among 4 plates. Top each with celery, mushrooms and green onions, dividing equally. Spoon 2 generous tablespoons dressing over each salad. Garnish each with 2 cherry tomatoes and serve, passing additional dressing separately.

What's the best way to keep lettuce fresh in the refrigerator?

Soak the leaves for five to ten minutes in cold water right after you buy them (this fills the lettuce cells with water, promoting maximum crispness). Then dry them thoroughly, using a salad spinner or rolling the leaves between cotton towels. When the leaves are dry, wrap them loosely in paper towels, and seal in a plastic bag. Always store lettuce in the most humid part of the refrigerator, which is generally the crisper. It should stay fresh for four to five days.

Basic potato salad

POTATO SALAD IS A VERSATILE SIDE DISH. IT CAN BE MADE CREAMY BY FOLDING IN MAYONNAISE (AS HERE) OR LIGHTER BY TOSSING WITH A VINAIGRETTE (AS IN THE NEXT RECIPE). TRY MIXING IN CHOPPED HARD-BOILED EGGS WITH PICKLES; SMOKED SALMON WITH RED ONION; OR AVOCADO WITH TOMATO AND CILANTRO.

2 pounds small white-skinned potatoes

2 tablespoons dry white wine

2 tablespoons minced green onions or chives

¾ to 1¼ cups mayonnaise

4 TO 6 SERVINGS

Cook potatoes in large pot of boiling salted water until tender, about 25 minutes. Drain; peel. Cut potatoes into ½-inch cubes. Transfer to medium bowl. Pour wine over potatoes. Toss gently to coat. Mix in onions. Cool to room temperature. Toss with mayonnaise to taste. Season with salt and pepper. (Can be made 1 day ahead. Cover; chill.) Serve potato salad chilled or at room temperature.

Potato salad with fresh herbs and lemon

ANOTHER COMMON TYPE OF POTATO SALAD IS THE OIL-AND-VINEGAR VERSION: IN THIS RECIPE, THE ACID IN THE DRESSING COMES NOT FROM VINEGAR, BUT FROM ¼ CUP OF FRESH LEMON JUICE. LIKE THE CREAMY POTATO SALAD ON PAGE 39, THIS VERSION LENDS ITSELF TO A NUMBER OF VARIATIONS.

¾ cup olive oil

¼ cup fresh lemon juice

1½ teaspoons grated lemon peel

1 green bell pepper, diced

1 cup chopped onion

¼ cup finely chopped fresh cilantro

¼ cup finely chopped fresh basil

¼ cup finely chopped fresh mint

2¼ pounds small red-skinned new potatoes, unpeeled

6 TO 8 SERVINGS

Whisk oil, lemon juice and lemon peel in small bowl to blend. Season dressing with salt and pepper. Place ½ cup dressing in large bowl. Mix in green pepper, onion, cilantro, basil and mint.

Cook potatoes in large pot of boiling salted water until tender, about 25 minutes. Drain; cool 15 minutes. Cut potatoes into ½-inch cubes. Add potatoes to bowl with dressing and toss to blend well. Let stand 10 minutes. Season to taste with salt and pepper, adding more dressing if desired. Serve at room temperature.

Yukon Gold potato and artichoke salad

HERE'S ANOTHER LEMON-AND-OIL-DRESSED POTATO SALAD, THIS ONE WITH ARTICHOKES. (FOR TIPS ON PREPARING ARTICHOKES FOR COOKING, SEE THE STEP-BY-STEP PHOTOS OPPOSITE.) IF YOU CAN'T GET YUKON GOLDS, REGULAR WHITE-SKINNED POTATOES WILL DO FINE.

SALAD

8 medium Yukon Gold potatoes (about 2¾ pounds)

1 lemon, halved

4 large artichokes

1⅔ cups water

⅓ cup olive oil

⅓ cup dry white wine

6 whole black peppercorns

6 coriander seeds

2 fresh thyme sprigs or ½ teaspoon dried

FOR SALAD: Cook potatoes in large pot of boiling salted water until just tender, about 22 minutes. Drain well. Cool. Cut into 1-inch pieces.

Halfway fill large bowl with cold water. Squeeze in juice from half of lemon. Cut second lemon half in half. Cut off stem from 1 artichoke; rub exposed area with cut side of lemon piece. Starting from base of artichoke, bend back each leaf and snap off where leaf breaks naturally. Continue until light green leaves are exposed. Using small sharp knife, cut off all dark green areas. Cut artichoke heart into quarters. Rub all cut surfaces with lemon. Cut out choke and pink inner leaves from each section; discard. Place artichoke heart sections in water with lemon juice. Cut off top 2 inches of artichoke. Repeat with remaining artichokes.

½ red onion, very thinly sliced

3 green onions, thinly sliced
diagonally

1 tomato, peeled, seeded,
chopped

10 black brine-cured olives (such
as Niçois or Kalamata), pitted,
chopped

6 fresh basil leaves, thinly sliced

DRESSING

¼ cup fresh lemon juice

2 tablespoons Dijon mustard

¾ cup olive oil

6 TO 8 SERVINGS

Combine 1⅔ cups water, olive oil, wine, peppercorns, coriander and thyme in heavy large saucepan and bring to boil. Drain artichokes. Add to saucepan. Cook until tender, about 15 minutes. Drain. Cool. Cut into slices. *(Potatoes and artichokes can be made 1 day ahead. Cover separately; chill.)* Mix potatoes, artichoke slices, red onion, green onions, tomato, olives and basil in large bowl to blend well.

FOR DRESSING: Mix lemon juice and mustard in medium bowl. Gradually whisk in oil. Mix into salad. Season with salt and pepper.

PREPARING ARTICHOKES:

STEP 1: To prepare an artichoke for cooking, cut off the stem. Remove the tough dark green outer leaves by bending them backward until they snap off near the bottom.

STEP 2: Use a small sharp knife to cut off the dark green parts of the base and the leaf bottoms until the base is smooth and pale green.

STEP 3: Cut the artichoke into quarters, then cut out the choke. Trim the tougher leaf tops from each quarter so all that remains is the choicest, most tender portion of the artichoke.

Basic oil-and-vinegar coleslaw

LIKE POTATO SALAD, COLESLAW IS USUALLY PREPARED ONE OF TWO WAYS: WITH OIL-AND-VINEGAR DRESSING
OR WITH A MAYONNAISE-BASED ONE. HERE'S A SIMPLE AND DELICIOUS VERSION OF THE FORMER.

½	cup distilled white vinegar
6	tablespoons sugar
6	tablespoons vegetable oil
2½	teaspoons dry mustard
1	teaspoon celery seeds
1	1¼-pound cabbage (about 1 medium), thinly sliced
1	large onion, thinly sliced
1	large green bell pepper, thinly sliced

6 TO 8 SERVINGS

Combine vinegar, sugar, oil, mustard and celery seeds in heavy non-reactive medium saucepan. Stir over medium heat until sugar dissolves and dressing comes to boil. Remove from heat. Season dressing with salt and pepper. Cool completely.

Combine cabbage, onion and green pepper in large bowl. Add dressing; toss to coat. Cover; refrigerate until cold, tossing occasionally, at least 2 hours. *(Can be prepared 1 day ahead. Cover; keep chilled.)*

Creamy coleslaw with chives and shallots

THIS CREAMY TAKE ON COLESLAW CALLS FOR SHALLOTS AND FRESH CHIVES; IF NEITHER IS READILY AVAILABLE,
USE CHOPPED GREEN ONIONS.

1	cup sour cream
6	tablespoons mayonnaise
¼	cup finely chopped fresh chives
3½	tablespoons white wine vinegar
3	tablespoons minced shallots
3	tablespoons sugar
1	teaspoon salt
1	teaspoon paprika
½	teaspoon ground black pepper
1	2-pound green cabbage, thinly sliced (about 14 cups)

6 TO 8 SERVINGS

Puree first 9 ingredients in blender. Place cabbage in large bowl. Pour dressing over cabbage and toss to coat. Cover and refrigerate at least 3 hours and up to 8 hours, tossing occasionally.

Pasta salad with tomatoes and corn

THIS SIMPLE PASTA SALAD COMES TOGETHER QUICKLY. THE RECIPE USES PENNE, BUT ROTINI, FARFALLE OR SMALL SHELL-SHAPED PASTA WOULD BE JUST AS GOOD.

5	tablespoons olive oil
5	tablespoons red wine vinegar
½	cup chopped fresh basil
2	large garlic cloves, chopped
1½	cups fresh corn kernels (cut from 3 ears) or frozen, thawed
1¼	pounds plum tomatoes, chopped
8	ounces penne pasta, freshly cooked
½	cup grated Parmesan cheese

4 TO 6 SERVINGS

Whisk 4 tablespoons oil, vinegar, basil and garlic in large bowl to blend. Heat remaining 1 tablespoon oil in heavy large skillet over medium heat. Add corn; sauté 3 minutes. Add corn to dressing in bowl. Add tomatoes, pasta and cheese to bowl and toss to blend. Season salad with salt and pepper.

Rice salad with pine nuts and olives

COOKING THE RICE IN CHICKEN BROTH GIVES THE SALAD MORE FLAVOR. IF YOU DON'T HAVE ROMANO CHEESE ON HAND, SUBSTITUTE GRATED PARMESAN.

3	cups Basic Chicken Stock (see recipe on page 22) or canned low-salt chicken broth
2	cups long-grain white rice
5	tablespoons olive oil
¾	cup slivered pitted Kalamata olives or other brine-cured black olives (about 4 ounces)
2	tablespoons fresh lemon juice
1	½-ounce package fresh arugula, stemmed, chopped
3	green onions, minced
½	cup pine nuts, toasted
⅓	cup freshly grated Romano cheese

8 SERVINGS

Bring chicken stock to boil in heavy medium saucepan. Add rice. Return to boil; reduce heat to low, cover and cook until chicken stock is absorbed, about 20 minutes. Turn off heat and let stand 5 minutes.

Fluff rice with fork. Transfer to large bowl. Mix in olive oil, then all remaining ingredients. Season salad to taste with pepper. *(Salad can be prepared 2 hours ahead. Let stand at room temperature.)*

Tabbouleh with avocado and feta cheese

ANOTHER TYPE OF GRAIN SALAD, TABBOULEH IS A MIDDLE EASTERN DISH THAT BLENDS BULGUR (CRACKED WHEAT) WITH PARSLEY, CHOPPED VEGETABLES AND LEMON JUICE. THIS VERSION INCLUDES CUCUMBER AND RADISHES.

1½ cups hot water

½ cup bulgur*

12 ounces plum tomatoes, seeded, chopped

1 cup chopped fresh Italian parsley

4 green onions, chopped

½ cucumber, peeled, seeded, finely chopped

4 radishes, chopped

½ cup crumbled feta cheese

¼ cup chopped fresh mint

1 tablespoon grated lemon peel

6 tablespoons olive oil

3 tablespoons fresh lemon juice

2 avocados, pitted, peeled, sliced

4 TO 6 SERVINGS

Combine 1½ cups hot water and bulgur in large bowl. Cover tightly and let stand until bulgur is tender, about 45 minutes. Strain bulgur in colander. Place bulgur in clean dry towel and squeeze out any excess liquid. Return bulgur to bowl.

Add tomatoes, parsley, green onions, cucumber, radishes, cheese, mint and lemon peel to bulgur. Stir to combine.

Whisk oil and lemon juice in medium bowl to blend. Season dressing to taste with salt and pepper. Add all but 2 tablespoons dressing to bulgur mixture. Toss to combine. Season with salt and pepper.

Add avocado slices to remaining dressing; toss to coat. Mound tabbouleh on platter. Garnish with avocado slices.

*Also called cracked wheat; available at natural foods stores and supermarkets.

Tips

NUT OILS (walnut, hazelnut, peanut) should be stored in the refrigerator, but other oils (olive, canola, corn, sesame) can be kept in a cool, dark place. Most will keep for approximately a year.

MAKING homemade croutons is an easy way to add character to bagged salad. Brush fresh bread slices with olive oil combined with minced fresh garlic; toast in a 350°F oven until golden, about 15 minutes, turning over after 4 minutes. Cut into cubes; cool.

USING a flavored vinegar is a great way to enhance a basic vinaigrette. Try a mild-tasting variety such as Champagne (or rice vinegar for an Asian twist) with delicate lettuces. Stronger vinegars (like apple cider or balsamic) are a good complement for heartier greens. In addition, citrus juices add a fresh, clean flavor; they pair well with many vinegars or, in some dressing recipes, can be substituted for vinegar.

Warm spinach salad with Parmesan toasts

THIS VARIATION ON A CLASSIC—WARM SPINACH SALAD—HAS RADICCHIO AND TOASTED PINE NUTS. CRISP PARMESAN TOASTS (WHICH CAN BE MADE A DAY AHEAD) LEND EXTRA CRUNCH.

PARMESAN TOASTS

- 1 French-bread baguette
- ¼ cup (½ stick) butter
- ⅓ cup extra-virgin olive oil
- 1 garlic clove, pressed
- ¾ cup (packed) freshly grated Parmesan cheese (about 2½ ounces)

SALAD

- 2 6-ounce packages fresh baby spinach
- 1 small head of radicchio, thinly sliced
- ⅓ cup extra-virgin olive oil
- ¼ cup balsamic vinegar
- ¼ cup dry red wine
- 1 shallot, minced
- ½ cup pine nuts, toasted

6 SERVINGS

FOR PARMESAN TOASTS: Preheat oven to 350°F. Slice baguette on sharp diagonal to make about twenty 6- to 7-inch-long, ¼-inch-thick slices. Melt butter with oil and garlic in small saucepan over medium heat. Remove from heat. Brush butter mixture over both sides of bread slices. Arrange bread in single layer on 2 baking sheets. Sprinkle cheese over bread. Sprinkle with salt and pepper. Bake bread until crisp, about 13 minutes. *(Can be made 1 day ahead. Store airtight at room temperature. Rewarm in 350°F oven 3 minutes.)*

FOR SALAD: Combine spinach and radicchio in large bowl. Bring ⅓ cup oil, vinegar, wine and shallot to simmer in large saucepan. Season with salt and pepper. Immediately pour dressing over salad. Cover with aluminum foil and let stand 5 minutes. Toss salad to coat. Divide among plates. Sprinkle with nuts; serve with warm toasts.

How can I tell if oil is still fresh?

Oil that is spoiled (rancid) will have a strong aroma and flavor reminiscent of plastic or petroleum. Be sure to check oil before each use; even a small amount of rancid oil can ruin an entire dish. Because contact with water during storage can encourage rancidity, be careful not to allow any condensation from the refrigerator or the bottle to come into contact with the oil.

4

"Too many veggies, too little time" could be the mantra of today's busy cook. Sometimes, when you're faced with a market full of produce, it's tempting to take the path of least resistance. That often means frozen peas or simply raw carrot sticks.

But it doesn't have to be like that. Not only is a diet full of fresh, seasonal produce healthful, but it really is delicious. The simple techniques outlined in this chapter will open up a world of vegetable preparations. From stir-frying and steaming to grilling, roasting and mashing (no, we haven't ignored potatoes), there's plenty of inspiration here. You'll never avoid the produce aisle again.

Vegetables

Roasted Vegetables with Garlic-Tarragon Butter (page 52)

Sautéed zucchini with basil and olive oil

SAUTÉING IS A QUICK AND TASTY WAY TO PREPARE ANY NUMBER OF VEGETABLES. HERE, ZUCCHINI IS SAUTÉED SIMPLY IN OLIVE OIL AND TOSSED WITH SLICED FRESH BASIL.

2 tablespoons olive oil

1¼ pounds zucchini, cut into 2-inch-long pieces, then 2x½-x½-inch strips

¼ cup thinly sliced fresh basil

4 SERVINGS

Heat oil in large deep skillet over high heat. Add zucchini and sauté until crisp-tender, about 5 minutes. Transfer to large bowl. Toss with basil. Season to taste with salt and pepper and serve.

Is there a quick way to trim green beans?

Removing the tough ends of green beans before cooking can be a chore. Here are two ways to get the job done quickly and efficiently:

ALIGN the stem ends of a handful of beans and trim them simultaneously with a chef's knife.

USE kitchen shears to snip off the stem ends of a few beans at a time.

Sautéed green beans with shallots

SOME VEGETABLES ARE BEST BOILED FIRST, THEN SAUTÉED. THAT'S TRUE OF GREEN BEANS, WHICH ARE SAUTÉED HERE IN A BALSAMIC-SHALLOT BUTTER AFTER BOILING UNTIL CRISP-TENDER.

½ cup balsamic vinegar

2 large shallots, finely chopped

4 tablespoons (½ stick) butter, room temperature

2 pounds green beans, trimmed

8 SERVINGS

Combine vinegar and shallots in heavy small saucepan. Boil over medium heat until almost all vinegar is absorbed (about 1 tablespoon liquid should remain in pan), stirring frequently, about 6 minutes. Transfer vinegar mixture to small bowl; cool completely. Add butter; mix with fork until well blended.

Cook beans in large pot of boiling salted water until crisp-tender, about 6 minutes. Drain. Rinse under cold water; drain well. Pat dry with paper towels. (*Balsamic-shallot butter and beans can be prepared 1 day ahead. Cover separately; chill.*)

Combine beans and balsamic-shallot butter in large nonstick skillet. Toss over medium heat until beans are heated through, about 5 minutes. Season to taste with salt and pepper and serve.

Whipped carrots and parsnips

MANY VEGETABLES TAKE WELL TO PUREEING AFTER THEY ARE BOILED. ROOT VEGETABLES, LIKE THE CARROTS AND PARSNIPS USED IN THIS RECIPE, ARE ESPECIALLY WELL SUITED TO THE TECHNIQUE.

1½ pounds carrots (about 6 medium), peeled, cut into ½-inch pieces

2 pounds parsnips, peeled, cut into ½-inch pieces

½ cup (1 stick) butter, cut into pieces, room temperature

Ground nutmeg

8 SERVINGS

Bring large pot of salted water to boil. Add carrots; cover partially and simmer 5 minutes. Add parsnips; cover partially and simmer until vegetables are very tender, about 15 minutes. Drain well. Return vegetables to same pot; stir over medium heat until any excess moisture evaporates. Transfer to processor. Add butter; process until smooth. Season with nutmeg, salt and pepper. *(Can be made 4 hours ahead. Rewarm over low heat, stirring often.)* Transfer to bowl; serve.

Broccoli with fennel and red bell pepper

THIS COLORFUL MÉLANGE OF BROCCOLI, FENNEL AND RED BELL PEPPER IS FIRST SAUTÉED AND THEN SIMMERED BRIEFLY IN CHICKEN BROTH.

4 tablespoons extra-virgin olive oil

1 teaspoon chopped fennel seeds

2 shallots, chopped

1 fresh fennel bulb (about 1 pound), halved lengthwise, thinly sliced crosswise

1 large red bell pepper, cut into long strips

3 large heads of broccoli, cut into florets (about 7 cups)

1 teaspoon herbes de Provence*

⅔ cup Basic Chicken Stock (see recipe on page 22) or canned low-salt chicken broth

6 TO 8 SERVINGS

Heat 2 tablespoons oil in heavy large skillet over medium heat. Add fennel seeds and stir until toasted, about 3 minutes. Add shallots and sauté until golden, about 3 minutes. Add sliced fennel bulb and red bell pepper and sauté until just tender, about 3 minutes. Add broccoli. Drizzle remaining 2 tablespoons oil over vegetables. Stir in herbes de Provence. Pour stock over. Simmer until broccoli is crisp-tender and liquid evaporates, about 6 minutes. Season with salt and pepper.

*A dried herb mixture available at specialty foods stores and in the spice section of some supermarkets. If unavailable, a combination of dried thyme, basil, savory and fennel seeds can be substituted.

Steamed asparagus with almond butter

FOR VEGETABLES THAT NEED MINIMAL COOKING, STEAMING IS AN EXCELLENT METHOD OF PREPARATION. IT HELPS THEM RETAIN FLAVOR, SHAPE AND TEXTURE.

8 tablespoons (1 stick) unsalted butter, room temperature

3 tablespoons finely chopped shallots

1 large garlic clove, minced

3 tablespoons chopped fresh parsley

2 teaspoons fresh lemon juice

2 teaspoons grated lemon peel

2 pounds asparagus, trimmed

½ cup sliced almonds

8 SERVINGS

Melt 2 tablespoons butter in heavy small skillet over low heat. Add shallots and garlic and sauté until tender, about 5 minutes. Pour into medium bowl. Add remaining 6 tablespoons butter, parsley, lemon juice and peel to shallot mixture and whisk to blend. Season with salt and pepper. Steam asparagus until crisp-tender. *(Can be made 1 day ahead. Cover butter mixture and asparagus separately; chill.)*

Place butter mixture in heavy large skillet over medium heat. Add almonds and cook until butter browns, stirring occasionally, about 3 minutes. Add asparagus and stir until heated through. Season to taste with salt and pepper. Divide asparagus among plates.

Is there a good condiment to serve with steamed vegetables?

As an accompaniment to steamed artichokes or asparagus, or even grilled vegetables, make aioli (the garlicky French mayonnaise-like sauce) by stirring ¼ cup extra-virgin olive oil into ¾ cup mayonnaise, then adding 2 minced garlic cloves and minced fresh thyme.

Wilted greens

HERE, A COMBINATION OF SWISS CHARD, MUSTARD GREENS AND SPINACH IS ADDED TO A POT AND COOKED WITH A SMALL AMOUNT OF BUTTER AND CHICKEN STOCK UNTIL WILTED.

3 tablespoons butter

1 large bunch Swiss chard, stems cut from leaves and discarded, leaves torn

1 large bunch mustard greens, stems trimmed, leaves torn

1 10-ounce bag spinach leaves

⅓ cup Basic Chicken Stock (see recipe on page 22) or canned low-salt chicken broth

4 SERVINGS

Melt butter in heavy large pot over medium-high heat. Add all greens and stock. Cover and cook until greens wilt, stirring occasionally, about 3 minutes. Uncover; cook until juices thicken slightly, about 4 minutes. Season with salt and pepper.

Stir-fried sugar snap peas and cherry tomatoes

WHEN STIR-FRYING VEGETABLES, THE TRICK IS TO COOK QUICKLY, SO FLAVORS AND JUICES ARE SEALED IN. TO SAVE TIME, PREP THE VEGETABLES FOR THIS RECIPE (PICTURED BELOW) UP TO TWO DAYS AHEAD. STORE THEM IN RESEALABLE PLASTIC BAGS IN THE REFRIGERATOR UNTIL NEEDED.

2 teaspoons olive oil

6 ounces sugar snap peas, stems and strings removed

10 small cherry tomatoes, stemmed

1 large shallot, thinly sliced

1 teaspoon white wine vinegar

2 SERVINGS

Heat oil in heavy medium skillet over medium-high heat. Add peas, tomatoes and shallot. Stir-fry until peas are bright green and tomatoes are heated through, about 3 minutes. Sprinkle with vinegar and toss to coat. Season with salt and pepper and serve.

Roasted vegetables with garlic-tarragon butter

ROASTING ADDS GREAT TASTE WHILE MAINTAINING NUTRIENTS. THIS MIX OF ONIONS, BELL PEPPERS, SQUASH AND MUSHROOMS (PICTURED ON PAGE 47) IS BRUSHED WITH A SEASONED BUTTER BEFORE ROASTING.

2 medium-size red onions, cut into ½-inch-thick rounds

2 red bell peppers, quartered lengthwise, seeded

4 zucchini or yellow crookneck squash, cut on diagonal into ½-inch-thick slices

2 large portobello mushrooms, dark gills scraped away, quartered

1 head of radicchio, cut into 6 wedges

6 tablespoons (¾ stick) butter

6 small garlic cloves, minced

2 teaspoons dried tarragon

3 tablespoons dry white wine

1 tablespoon olive oil

Lemon wedges

6 SERVINGS

Position 1 rack in top third and 1 rack in bottom third of oven and preheat to 500°F. Arrange vegetables in single layer on 2 large baking sheets. Stir butter, garlic and tarragon in heavy small saucepan over low heat until butter melts. Whisk in wine and oil. Brush vegetables with all of butter mixture; sprinkle generously with salt and pepper.

Roast vegetables 10 minutes. Turn vegetables over, reverse position of baking sheets and roast until vegetables are tender and browned in spots, about 10 minutes longer. Transfer vegetables to large platter. Serve with lemon wedges.

Equipment

At a few dollars a pop, an inexpensive vegetable peeler becomes one of the kitchen's most essential tools. (It also happens to produce great chocolate curls.) Go for a stationary-blade peeler with a high-tech handle, and/or a swivel-blade model; they're easiest on the wrist. Don't forget to change peelers every year or so, since the blades eventually wear out and can't be sharpened.

For the best mashed potatoes, forget the food processor, which can make potatoes gluey. Instead, use a handheld potato masher or ricer. The masher makes lovely, not-too-lumpy potatoes; the ricer produces light, fluffy ones. After the hot potatoes are mashed into small pellets by the ricer, use a fork to fluff them with butter or cream—or both.

Also useful: a steamer or steamer basket (stove-top and/or microwave); a good, sharp paring knife; a slotted spoon; a strainer; a vegetable scrubber; and a blender or food processor for making purees.

Basic grilled vegetables

GRILLING IS ANOTHER FLAVOR-ENHANCING—AND FAST—WAY TO PREPARE VEGETABLES. THESE CAN BE SERVED RIGHT OFF THE GRILL OR DRIZZLED WITH A FAVORITE SAUCE OR DRESSING.

2　large ears fresh corn, husked, each cut crosswise into 4 pieces

1　small eggplant, cut crosswise into ½-inch-thick rounds

1　large red onion, cut into ¾-inch-thick wedges

1　large red bell pepper, seeded, cut lengthwise into 6 strips

1　large yellow or green bell pepper, seeded, cut lengthwise into 6 strips

1　large zucchini, trimmed, quartered lengthwise

8　asparagus spears, trimmed

1　large carrot, peeled, cut on deep diagonal into ¼-inch-thick slices

　　Olive oil

6 SERVINGS

Prepare barbecue (medium-high heat). Arrange corn pieces, eggplant rounds and onion wedges in single layer on large baking sheet. Arrange bell pepper strips, zucchini spears, asparagus spears and carrot slices in single layer on another large baking sheet. Brush vegetables with oil; sprinkle with salt and pepper.

Arrange corn, eggplant and onion oiled side down on grill. Brush with olive oil; sprinkle with salt and pepper. Grill until tender and lightly charred, brushing occasionally with oil and turning with tongs, about 6 minutes. Transfer vegetables to small platter as vegetables finish grilling. Tent with foil to keep warm.

Arrange peppers, zucchini, asparagus and carrot oiled side down on grill. Brush with oil; sprinkle with salt and pepper. Grill until tender and lightly charred, brushing occasionally with oil and turning with tongs, about 6 minutes. Transfer vegetables to same platter; serve.

GRILLING VEGETABLES:

STEP 1: A soft, wide pastry brush is the best tool for applying an even coating of olive oil. The vegetables are cut into pieces that are small enough to cook through properly and pick up a smoky flavor quickly.

STEP 2: Turn the vegetables over to finish cooking when they are almost tender, lightly charred and striped from the grill pattern. Use tongs to lift and reposition them (a fork can tear the vegetables).

STEP 3: Long, slender vegetables need to be placed crosswise on the grill so that they don't fall through. Barbecue utensils with extra-long handles, like the brush used here, make basting a cooler procedure.

Eggplant, mozzarella and pesto gratins

THIS LAYERED GRATIN WILL SERVE FOUR AS A MEATLESS MAIN COURSE. TO SERVE EIGHT AS A SIDE DISH, SIMPLY LAYER THE INGREDIENTS IN A 13X9X2-INCH BAKING DISH, THEN BAKE AND BROIL AS DIRECTED.

¼ cup plus 6 tablespoons (about) olive oil

1 18-ounce eggplant, sliced lengthwise into eight ¼-inch-thick slices

1 pound plum tomatoes

½ onion, diced

1 carrot, peeled, diced

2 garlic cloves, minced

4 thyme sprigs

2 tablespoons water

1 bay leaf

½ bunch fresh basil, stemmed, torn into pieces (about 2 ounces)

1 tablespoon pine nuts, toasted

1 tablespoon plus 1 cup grated Parmesan cheese

2 8-ounce balls buffalo milk mozzarella cheese, each cut into six ¼-inch-thick slices

4 SERVINGS

Heat ¼ cup oil in heavy large nonstick skillet over medium-high heat. Working in batches, add eggplant to oil and sauté until light brown, turning once and adding up to 2 tablespoons more oil as necessary, about 1 minute per side. Transfer eggplant to paper-towel-lined plate to drain. Sprinkle with salt and pepper.

Cook tomatoes in boiling water 1½ minutes. Peel, seed and chop into ½-inch pieces. Heat 1 tablespoon oil in heavy small saucepan over medium-high heat. Add onion, carrot and half of garlic; sauté 5 minutes. Add tomatoes, thyme, 2 tablespoons water and bay leaf; reduce heat to low and simmer until slightly thickened, about 15 minutes. Discard bay leaf. Season tomato mixture with salt and pepper.

Place basil, 3 tablespoons oil, pine nuts, 1 tablespoon Parmesan cheese and remaining half of garlic in processor; puree. Set pesto aside.

Preheat oven to 350°F. Place 4 individual gratin dishes (each about 7x4¾ inches) on rimmed baking sheet. Place 2 slices eggplant in 1 dish. Top with ¼ of tomato mixture, 3 slices mozzarella cheese, 2 tablespoons pesto and ¼ cup Parmesan cheese. Repeat layering of remaining ingredients in 3 more gratin dishes. Bake gratins until heated through, about 8 minutes. Preheat broiler. Broil until cheese bubbles, about 3 minutes. Serve gratins hot.

How do I select a good eggplant?

Although eggplant is commonly considered a vegetable, it is actually a fruit. Be sure to choose a smooth-skinned one that is firm and feels heavy. It should not have any soft or brown spots on the skin. Eggplants should be stored in a cool, dry place and used within two days of purchase.

Basic baked potatoes

RUSSET POTATOES ARE IDEAL FOR BAKING BECAUSE OF THEIR LOW MOISTURE AND HIGH STARCH CONTENT. A WORD OF ADVICE: DON'T WRAP POTATOES IN FOIL TO BAKE THEM, SINCE THE FOIL CAUSES THEM TO STEAM AND LEAVES THE POTATO SKINS LIMP RATHER THAN CRUSTY.

4 large russet potatoes, rinsed, dried

Assorted toppings (such as sour cream, butter and chopped green onions or chives)

4 SERVINGS

Preheat oven to 400°F. Pierce potatoes several times with toothpick or fork. Place potatoes on oven rack and bake until cooked through, about 1 hour. Transfer potatoes to platter. Using small sharp knife, cut lengthwise slit in top of each potato; press in ends to open top. Serve, allowing guests to garnish potatoes as desired.

Twice-baked potatoes with three cheeses

FOR THIS RECIPE, POTATOES ARE FIRST BAKED, AND THEN THE INSIDES ARE SCOOPED OUT OF THE SKINS AND COMBINED WITH GORGONZOLA AND CREAM CHEESE. THE MIXTURE IS RETURNED TO THE POTATO SKINS, TOPPED WITH PARMESAN CHEESE AND BAKED UNTIL HEATED THROUGH.

8 large russet potatoes, rinsed, dried

3 cups crumbled Gorgonzola cheese (about 12 ounces)

4 ounces cream cheese, room temperature

¾ cup milk

1 bunch green onions, finely chopped

½ cup freshly grated Parmesan cheese (about 1½ ounces)

8 SERVINGS

Preheat oven to 400°F. Pierce potatoes several times with toothpick or fork. Place potatoes on oven rack and bake until cooked through and tender, about 1 hour.

Transfer potatoes to large baking sheet and cool 5 minutes. Cut off top ⅓ of potatoes. Scoop out potato bottoms and place potato flesh in large mixing bowl, leaving ¼-inch-thick shell. Scoop out potato flesh from tops and place in same bowl; discard tops. Using electric mixer, beat potato until flesh is almost smooth. Add Gorgonzola, cream cheese and milk and beat just until mixture is well blended and almost smooth. Stir in green onions. Season with salt and pepper. Spoon mixture into potato shells, mounding high. (*Potatoes can be prepared 1 day ahead. Cover and refrigerate.*)

Reheat oven, if necessary, to 400°F. Sprinkle each potato with Parmesan cheese. Bake until heated through and lightly browned on top, about 20 minutes if not chilled and 30 minutes if chilled.

Yams with spiced honey-molasses butter

LIKE RUSSET POTATOES, YAMS LEND THEMSELVES WELL TO BAKING. SWEET AS THEY MAY BE ON THEIR OWN, THEY TASTE EVEN BETTER WITH THE HONEY-MOLASSES BUTTER ADDED HERE.

1 cup (2 sticks) unsalted butter, room temperature

½ cup clover honey

1 tablespoon robust-flavored (dark) molasses

1 teaspoon ground cinnamon

½ teaspoon ground cloves

Large pinch of cayenne pepper

8 10- to 11-ounce yams (red-skinned sweet potatoes)

8 SERVINGS

Beat butter, honey, molasses, cinnamon, cloves and cayenne in medium bowl to blend; season to taste with salt. *(Honey-molasses butter can be prepared 5 days ahead. Cover and refrigerate. Bring mixture to room temperature before using.)*

Preheat oven to 375°F. Rinse potatoes; pat dry. Pierce each potato several times with fork; place on baking sheet. Bake potatoes until tender, about 1 hour. Cut lengthwise slit in top of each potato; press in ends to open top. Spoon some honey-molasses butter into opening of each potato and serve.

Tips

BUY the freshest possible vegetables; you'll get the best quality and price for vegetables at the peak of their season. Although characteristic signs of freshness vary, look for bright color and crispness or firmness. Most fresh vegetables can be stored for two to five days; root vegetables maintain quality for one to several weeks.

TOP steamed green beans, grilled corn or mashed potatoes with pats of flavorful do-ahead herb butters. Just mix butter (either by hand or in the blender or food processor) with minced shallots and your favorite fresh herbs. Roll the compound butter in plastic wrap, seal in an airtight container and store in the freezer for up to six months.

CHOOSE potatoes best suited to the preparation you have in mind. Russets—often labeled "baking potatoes" or "Idaho potatoes"— have a high starch content and flaky consistency that make them a good choice for baked or mashed potatoes. If you want creamier mashed potatoes, try a waxy, lower-starch variety like Yukon Gold, white-skinned or red-skinned potatoes. Small red- or white-skinned potatoes are ideal for boiling; russets produce great hash browns and french fries; and just about all types are delicious when oven-roasted.

Basic mashed potatoes

USE THIS BASIC RECIPE FOR MASHED POTATOES AS THE STARTING POINT FOR ANY NUMBER OF VARIATIONS.

4 pounds russet potatoes, peeled, cut into 1-inch pieces

1 cup half and half or whipping cream

6 tablespoons (¾ stick) butter, cut into pieces

6 SERVINGS

Cook potatoes in large pot of boiling salted water until tender, about 25 minutes. Drain. Return potatoes to pot and mash. Add half and half and butter and stir over low heat until butter melts. Season potatoes to taste with salt and pepper and serve.

Are sprouted potatoes safe to use in cooking?

Yes, sprouted potatoes are edible, but the sprouts themselves must be dug out and discarded before cooking. The sprouts contain an alkaloid called solanine, which is toxic when consumed in large amounts.

Garlic, white cheddar and chipotle mashed potatoes

THIRTY-SIX GARLIC CLOVES MAY SOUND LIKE A LOT, BUT THE GARLIC IS ROASTED UNTIL MELLOW IN FLAVOR BEFORE BEING MIXED INTO MASHED POTATOES, ALONG WITH WHITE CHEDDAR CHEESE AND CHIPOTLE CHILIES.

36 garlic cloves (unpeeled)

⅓ cup olive oil

5 pounds russet potatoes, peeled, cut into 1-inch pieces

2 cups (packed) grated sharp white cheddar cheese (about 8 ounces)

4 ounces cream cheese, room temperature

¼ cup (½ stick) unsalted butter, room temperature

1⅓ teaspoons minced canned chipotle chilies*

8 TO 10 SERVINGS

Preheat oven to 350°F. Toss garlic with oil in baking pan. Cover with foil; bake 30 minutes. Uncover; bake until garlic is tender, about 15 minutes longer. Cool, peel and chop garlic.

Cook potatoes in large pot of boiling salted water until tender, about 25 minutes. Drain. Transfer potatoes to large bowl. Add garlic and remaining ingredients. Using electric mixer, beat mixture until smooth. Season mashed potatoes to taste with salt and pepper. *(Can be prepared up to 2 hours ahead. Cover; let stand at room temperature. Rewarm, stirring constantly, before serving.)*

*Chipotle chilies canned in a spicy tomato sauce, sometimes called *adobo*, are available at Latin American markets, specialty foods stores and some supermarkets.

5

Beans, rice, polenta and other grains have lots going for them. They are inherently comforting, inexpensive, easily stored and highly nutritious.

Need another reason to keep these foods in your pantry? They are super-adaptable. Start with beans, either dried or canned, using them as the building blocks for a multitude of stews, soups and salads. As for rice, keep a few varieties on hand, and you can whip up a rustic pilaf or a sophisticated risotto in less time than you would think.

You'll want to stock up on a mix of different grains and legumes too, since they are every bit as versatile as beans and rice. Try bulgur and couscous, to name just two.

Beans & Grains

White Beans with Bacon and Endive (page 66)

Rice with parsley

COOKING THE RICE IN CHICKEN STOCK INSTEAD OF WATER LENDS ADDITIONAL FLAVOR TO THIS DISH. IF YOU LIKE, TRY OTHER LONG-GRAIN VARIETIES, SUCH AS BASMATI OR BROWN RICE, FOLLOWING INSTRUCTIONS FOR COOKING TIMES AND PROPORTIONS AS DIRECTED ON THE PACKAGE.

3 cups Basic Chicken Stock (see recipe on page 22) or canned low-salt chicken broth

1 teaspoon salt

1½ cups long-grain white rice

¼ cup chopped fresh Italian parsley

¼ cup (½ stick) butter

4 TO 6 SERVINGS

Combine stock and salt in medium saucepan. Bring to boil. Add rice. Return to boil. Reduce heat to low, cover and cook until liquid is absorbed, about 20 minutes. Remove from heat. Mix in parsley and butter. Let stand, covered, until butter melts, about 5 minutes. Fluff rice with fork. Season with salt and pepper.

Rice pilaf with spinach and caramelized onions

FOR A PILAF, THE RICE IS FIRST SAUTÉED IN OIL SO THAT EACH GRAIN IS COATED BEFORE THE LIQUID IS ADDED. WILTED SPINACH AND CARAMELIZED ONIONS ENHANCE THE FLAVOR.

2 tablespoons olive oil

2 very large onions, halved, sliced (about 4 cups)

1 large carrot, coarsely grated

1 teaspoon ground cumin

1 garlic clove, minced

1½ cups arborio rice* or medium-grain white rice

4 cups Basic Chicken Stock (see recipe on page 22) or canned low-salt chicken broth

1 6-ounce bag fresh baby spinach

6 SERVINGS

Heat oil in heavy large wide pot over medium heat. Add onions; sauté until tender and deep brown, about 20 minutes. Transfer ½ cup onion slices to small bowl and reserve. Add carrot, cumin and garlic to onions in pot; stir 1 minute. Add rice and stir 1 minute. Add stock; bring to boil. Reduce heat to low, cover and simmer until rice is tender and most liquid is absorbed, about 15 minutes. Stir spinach into rice mixture; cover and cook until spinach wilts, about 2 minutes. Season with salt and pepper. Transfer pilaf to bowl; top with reserved onion.

*Arborio, an Italian short-grain rice, is available at Italian markets and at many supermarkets nationwide.

Wild mushroom risotto

IN A RISOTTO, SMALL QUANTITIES OF STOCK ARE GRADUALLY ADDED TO THE RICE MIXTURE, WHICH IS STIRRED CONSTANTLY. FOR THE CREAMIEST RISOTTO, BE SURE THE STOCK HAS BEEN ABSORBED BEFORE YOU ADD MORE.

6   cups Basic Vegetable Stock (see recipe on page 26) or canned vegetable broth

3   tablespoons butter

3   tablespoons olive oil

2   shallots, chopped

1   pound assorted wild mushrooms (such as oyster and crimini), sliced

1   cup arborio rice* or medium-grain rice

½   cup dry Sherry

½   cup freshly grated Parmesan cheese (about 2 ounces)

¾   teaspoon chopped fresh thyme

4 TO 6 SERVINGS

Bring vegetable stock to simmer in medium saucepan. Reduce heat to low; cover and keep stock hot.

Melt butter with olive oil in heavy large saucepan over medium heat. Add shallots; sauté 1 minute. Add wild mushrooms; cook until mushrooms are tender and juices are released, about 8 minutes. Add rice and stir 1 minute. Add Sherry and simmer until liquid is absorbed, stirring frequently, about 8 minutes. Add ¾ cup hot vegetable stock and simmer until absorbed, stirring frequently. Add remaining stock ¾ cup at a time, allowing liquid to be absorbed before adding more and stirring frequently, until rice is just tender and mixture is creamy, about 20 minutes. Stir in cheese and thyme. Serve warm.

*Arborio, an Italian short-grain rice, is available at Italian markets and at many supermarkets nationwide.

MAKING RISOTTO:

STEP 1: Soften the chopped shallots in olive oil and butter, being careful not to let the shallots brown. When adding the rice, stir until it's well coated with oil.

STEP 2: Add Sherry to the rice, and simmer until it is absorbed. Next, stir in ¾ cup of vegetable stock, and simmer until it, too, is absorbed. At this point the rice is still hard and in separate grains, as shown.

STEP 3: Stir in ¾ cup of hot stock every few minutes so that the rice softens and releases its starch gradually, creating a creamy texture. The dish is ready when enough stock has been absorbed to make the rice tender but still a bit firm in the center.

Bulgur with roasted tomatoes, onions and garbanzo beans

BULGUR IS A POPULAR MIDDLE EASTERN GRAIN. THIS MAIN-COURSE PILAF RECIPE (PICTURED OPPOSITE) WILL ALSO SERVE EIGHT AS A SIDE DISH.

2	pounds tomatoes, quartered
1	large onion, cut into ½-inch-thick wedges
2	tablespoons olive oil
1	15-ounce can garbanzo beans (chickpeas), drained
4	garlic cloves, crushed
2½	cups water
2	cups bulgur*
4	tablespoons chopped fresh parsley
2	tablespoons chopped fresh dill
1	tablespoon fresh lemon juice

4 SERVINGS

Preheat oven to 400°F. Arrange tomatoes and onion in single layer in large roasting pan. Drizzle with oil. Sprinkle with salt and pepper. Roast 30 minutes, stirring occasionally. Stir in garbanzo beans and garlic. Roast until onion is golden, stirring occasionally, about 25 minutes longer. Remove pan from oven. Add 2½ cups water to pan and stir, scraping up any browned bits.

Transfer roasted vegetable mixture to large saucepan. Bring to boil. Stir in bulgur. Reduce heat to low, cover and simmer until bulgur is tender and liquid is absorbed, about 10 minutes.

Stir 3 tablespoons parsley, 1½ tablespoons dill and lemon juice into pilaf. Season to taste with salt and pepper. Transfer to bowl. Sprinkle pilaf with remaining 1 tablespoon parsley and ½ tablespoon dill.

*Also called cracked wheat, bulgur is available at natural foods stores and many supermarkets nationwide.

What are some of the more unusual grains that can be found in supermarkets and health foods stores?

Aside from the typical wheat, oats, corn and cornmeal products, look for these other grains to add some variety to your cooking.

BARLEY Pearl barley, with a flavor and texture similar to the rice-shaped pasta called orzo, is the most popular barley that is available.

BULGUR These steamed, dried and crushed wheat kernels have a ten-der, chewy texture and closely resemble cracked wheat (they're often referred to as such).

MILLET These tiny grains, which are white, have a delicate, nutty flavor that pairs well with many kinds of fruits and vegetables.

QUINOA These bean-shaped seeds, which are ivory in color, have a mild flavor and a light, chewy texture.

Couscous with leeks, corn and olives

ALTHOUGH COUSCOUS IS ACTUALLY A FORM OF PASTA, WE EAT IT LIKE A GRAIN. IT COOKS QUICKLY, MAKING THIS SIDE DISH A GREAT ADDITION TO WEEKDAY MEALS.

3 tablespoons olive oil

2 medium leeks (white and pale green parts only), chopped

1 cup fresh corn kernels (from about 2 ears of corn)

1 cup water

1 cup dry white wine

1 cup Basic Chicken Stock (see recipe on page 22) or canned low-salt chicken broth

2 teaspoons chopped fresh thyme

1 10-ounce package couscous

1 cup pitted Kalamata olives or other brine-cured black olives (about 4 ounces), coarsely chopped

3 tablespoons fresh lemon juice

6 SERVINGS

Heat oil in heavy medium saucepan over medium heat. Add leeks and corn and sauté until vegetables are soft, about 3 minutes. Add 1 cup water, wine, stock and thyme; bring mixture to boil. Remove pan from heat and mix in couscous. Cover and let stand 5 minutes. Using fork, fluff couscous. Mix in olives and lemon juice. Season to taste with salt and pepper. Serve warm or at room temperature.

Equipment

The only truly essential pieces of equipment for cooking beans and grains are pots, both small and large, for simmering, and a strainer for draining. And a fork—the better to eat them with.

Also useful: Electric rice cookers make fluffy rice every time, turn off automatically when the rice is cooked, and keep it warm for several hours. Look for a rice cooker with a three-, five-, or ten-cup yield and a nonstick interior pan for easy cleaning. You might also want to consider a pressure cooker, which can cut risotto and dry-bean cooking times in half. Look for a four- to eight-quart cooker with an aluminum core and with safety features that ensure the cooker is securely locked when closed.

Basic polenta

TRADITIONAL POLENTA CALLS FOR THE COARSE (NOT REGULAR) TYPE OF CORNMEAL. THIS QUICK-COOKING VERSION, WHICH USES YELLOW CORNMEAL, TAKES ABOUT HALF THE TIME TO COOK.

2½ **cups Basic Chicken Stock (page 22) or canned low-salt chicken broth**

⅔ **cup yellow cornmeal**

¾ **cup grated Gruyère cheese**

1½ **tablespoons butter**

4 SERVINGS

Bring stock to boil in heavy medium saucepan over medium-high heat. Gradually whisk in cornmeal. Reduce heat to medium and whisk constantly until mixture thickens, about 6 minutes. Remove from heat. Add cheese and butter; stir until cheese melts. Season polenta to taste with salt and pepper and serve.

There are lots of flavored prepared polenta varieties on the market. What's the best way to flavor homemade polenta?

While salt, butter and cheese will bring out the natural corn flavor of polenta, there are many other add-ins to try.

A SMALL amount of lemon zest or fresh herbs like marjoram, basil, oregano or rosemary can be stirred into the polenta just before serving.

ADD ¼ cup chopped sun-dried tomatoes to the boiling liquid before adding the dry polenta.

MIX some pitted sliced brine-cured black olives (such as Kalamata) with a couple teaspoons of fresh herbs. Stir them into the polenta when you're adding the cheese.

Polenta triangles with rosemary and walnuts

FOLLOW THE TECHNIQUE OUTLINED IN THE POLENTA RECIPE ABOVE TO CREATE THIS FIRM, OVEN-BAKED ROSEMARY- AND WALNUT-FLAVORED VARIATION.

⅓ **cup walnuts, toasted, finely chopped**

1½ **teaspoons chopped fresh rosemary**

Basic Polenta (see recipe above)

1½ **tablespoons butter**

8 **walnut halves**

8 SERVINGS

Butter 9-inch-diameter glass pie dish. Stir walnuts and rosemary into polenta. Transfer polenta to prepared dish; using buttered knife, spread evenly. Cool until polenta is firm, at least 1 hour.

Line baking sheet with foil. Cut polenta into 8 wedges. Transfer wedges, bottom side up, to sheet. Dot with butter. Place 1 walnut half on each wedge. *(Can be prepared 1 day ahead. Cover; chill.)*

Preheat oven to 350°F. Bake polenta until heated through, 12 minutes.

White beans with bacon and endive

FOR THIS DISH (PICTURED ON PAGE 59) GREAT NORTHERN BEANS ARE PREPARED USING THE QUICK-SOAK METHOD. IT TAKES ABOUT TWO HOURS, BUT IF TIME IS SHORT, USE CANNED WHITE KIDNEY BEANS (CANNELLINI) INSTEAD.

½ pound dried Great Northern beans, picked over

3½ cups water

1 small bay leaf

¼ teaspoon salt

¼ teaspoon ground black pepper

8 slices bacon, coarsely chopped

1 medium onion, chopped

1 1¼- to 1½-pound head of curly endive, rinsed, leaves torn coarsely

2 large garlic cloves, chopped

⅓ cup Basic Beef Stock (see recipe on page 24) or canned beef broth

8 SERVINGS

Place dried beans in large pot. Pour enough cold water over beans to cover by 3 inches. Bring to boil. Boil 2 minutes. Remove from heat. Cover beans and let stand 1 hour. Drain. Return beans to same pot. Add 3½ cups water and bay leaf; bring to boil. Reduce heat to medium-low; simmer 30 minutes. Add salt and pepper to beans; continue to simmer until beans are tender, about 30 minutes longer. Drain well. Transfer beans to large bowl. Discard bay leaf.

Cook bacon in heavy large pot over medium-high heat until brown and crisp. Using slotted spoon, transfer bacon to paper towels to drain. Set bacon aside. Add onion to drippings in pot and sauté until beginning to soften, about 4 minutes. Add half of endive with water still clinging to leaves. Cover pot and cook until endive is wilted, stirring once, about 4 minutes. Add remaining half of endive and chopped garlic. Cover and cook until endive is wilted but still bright green, stirring once, about 4 minutes. Add beans, beef stock and bacon. Cook bean mixture until heated through, stirring often, about 5 minutes. Season to taste with salt and pepper.

Tips

BEANS provide plenty of protein and complex carbohydrates, and they have been shown to lower cholesterol. When served together, beans and grains yield complete, high-quality protein.

DRIED BEANS can be kept sealed in airtight containers in your pantry almost indefinitely.

COOKED beans can be frozen still in their cooking liquid in an airtight container for as long as several months. To reuse, first defrost them in the refrigerator or microwave, then drain them and use in recipes as you would any canned beans.

Two-bean chili

DRIED BEANS CAN ALSO BE PREPARED USING THE LONG-SOAK METHOD, WHICH INVOLVES SOAKING THEM OVERNIGHT. BOTH TYPES OF BEANS IN THIS CHILI ARE READIED IN THIS MANNER. THIS RECIPE SERVES A CROWD: IT'S PRESENTED IN BREAD BOWLS, BUT YOU CAN SERVE IT STRAIGHT FROM THE POT, IF YOU LIKE.

2¼   pounds dried Great Northern beans

2¼   pounds dried pinto beans

½   cup olive oil

7   large yellow onions, chopped (about 14 cups)

½   cup chili powder

5   tablespoons tomato paste

3   tablespoons minced garlic

3   tablespoons ground cumin

1½   tablespoons dried oregano

1½   tablespoons dried basil

¾   teaspoon cayenne pepper

14   cups (or more) Basic Chicken Stock (see recipe on page 22) or canned chicken broth or vegetable broth

3   15-ounce cans corn (undrained)

5   6-ounce jars roasted red peppers, drained

3   8-ounce cans tomato sauce

20   8-ounce round loaves sourdough bread or ten 1-pound round loaves sourdough bread

1   cup (2 sticks) butter, melted

3   pounds Italian sausages

2½   cups chopped fresh cilantro

4   cups grated cheddar cheese

2½   cups chopped red onions

2   cups sour cream

20 SERVINGS

Place all beans in large pot with enough cold water to cover by at least 3 inches. Let stand overnight.

Drain beans. Divide beans between 2 large pots. Add enough cold water to each pot to cover beans by about 3 inches. Simmer until beans are almost tender, stirring occasionally, about 1 hour. Drain well. Transfer beans to large bowl. Set aside.

Heat ¼ cup oil in each pot over medium-high heat. Add half of yellow onions to each pot; sauté until tender, about 15 minutes. Add half of chili powder, tomato paste, minced garlic, cumin, oregano, basil and cayenne to each pot; stir 1 minute. Divide beans, 14 cups stock, corn with liquid, roasted red peppers and tomato sauce between pots. Bring to boil. Reduce heat to medium and simmer until beans are tender and chili thickens, stirring occasionally, about 1½ hours. Season chili to taste with salt and pepper.

If using twenty 8-ounce bread loaves, cut off tops. Using small knife, cut out centers, leaving 1-inch shell. If using ten 1-pound loaves, cut each horizontally in half. Cut off thin slice from top half of each loaf. Turn top of loaf trimmed side down. Cut out center of top and bottom halves, leaving 1-inch shell. Reserve trimmings for another use. *(Chili and bread bowls can be made 1 day ahead. Cover bread bowls and let stand at room temperature. Cover and chill chili. Bring to simmer before serving, thinning with more stock if necessary.)*

Preheat oven to 400°F. Brush insides of bread bowls with melted butter. Place bread bowls on oven racks. Bake until crusty and brown, about 15 minutes. Transfer bread bowls to plates.

Meanwhile, working in batches, cook sausages in heavy large skillet over medium-high heat until cooked through, turning occasionally, about 15 minutes. Cut into rounds. Transfer to bowl.

Mix cilantro into chili. Ladle chili into bread bowls. Serve, passing sausages, cheese, red onions and sour cream separately.

6

Meats

Not so long ago, meat was the centerpiece of every meal, and the friendly local butcher was happy to give advice on how to roast, stew or fry any cut. These days, meat isn't always front and center on the plate, and most cooks are perfectly happy to get their chops and steaks at the supermarket.

As convenient as that may be, there's seldom anyone knowledgeable around who can tell you what to buy and how to prepare it once you get it home. And that's where this chapter comes in. By following the recipes here, you'll learn foolproof ways to prepare satisfying roasts, stews and more. You'll also learn which cuts result in the tenderest grilled steaks, how to shop for lamb, and how to defrost meat safely in the microwave. And whether you eat meat several nights a week or just occasionally, you may well learn how to make it the star of the meal—every time.

Steak with Roquefort, Green Onions and Walnuts (page 70)

Basic sautéed steak

SAUTÉING, OR PAN-FRYING, IS AN IDEAL METHOD FOR PREPARING SMALL STEAKS. SEARING THE MEAT GIVES IT A FLAVORFUL BROWN CRUST THAT SEALS IN MOST OF THE JUICES. USING A SKILLET JUST LARGE ENOUGH TO ACCOMMODATE THE STEAKS WILL KEEP THE MEAT FROM STEAMING WITHOUT BROWNING.

4 New York sirloin, rib-eye, tenderloin or top sirloin steaks (¾ to 1 inch thick)

1 tablespoon butter

1 tablespoon vegetable oil

4 SERVINGS

Pat steaks dry. Melt butter with oil in heavy large skillet over medium-high heat. Add steaks (do not crowd) and cook 3 to 4 minutes, adjusting heat if necessary to prevent burning. Using tongs or spatula, turn steaks and cook about 3 to 4 minutes more for medium-rare. Transfer steaks to platter. Season lightly with salt and pepper.

What are the different types of steaks, and how should I cook them?

Some of the best steaks come from either the rib section or the short loin section. Rib-eye steak, from the rib section, is among the most tender and flavorful. Porterhouse, top loin and New York steak (also known as New York strip steak or shell steak) all come from the large piece of meat known as the short loin—as does the most tender cut of all: filet mignon. Any of these is delicious sautéed, broiled or grilled.

Steak with Roquefort, green onions and walnuts

AS THE STEAKS IN THIS VARIATION (PICTURED ON PAGE 69) ARE SAUTÉED, SOME OF THE JUICES COLLECT IN THE PAN. THESE PROVIDE THE BASE FOR A QUICK SAUCE, CALLED A DEGLAZING OR PAN SAUCE.

Basic Sautéed Steak (see recipe above)

1 tablespoon butter

2 tablespoons minced shallots

⅓ cup dry white wine

1 cup whipping cream

½ cup Roquefort cheese, crumbled

2 to 3 tablespoons minced green onions

3 tablespoons chopped toasted walnuts

4 SERVINGS

Preheat oven to 180°F. Prepare sautéed steak. Transfer steaks to ovenproof platter and keep warm in oven. Do not wash skillet.

Pour off drippings from skillet. Add 1 tablespoon butter and melt over low heat. Add shallots and stir 1 minute. Increase heat to high. Stir in wine and bring to boil, scraping up any browned bits. Cook until reduced to 2 tablespoons, stirring constantly, about 2 minutes. Add cream and boil until sauce thickens and lightly coats spoon, stirring constantly, about 3 minutes. Reduce heat to low. Whisk in cheese. Stir in green onions. Season with salt and pepper. Transfer steaks to plates. Spoon some of sauce down center of each. Sprinkle walnuts over sauce and serve immediately.

Grilled rib-eye steaks with six-spice rub

GRILLING IS ANOTHER QUICK AND TASTY WAY TO PREPARE STEAKS. HERE, RIB-EYE STEAKS ARE COVERED WITH A FLAVORFUL SPICE RUB BEFORE BEING COOKED.

2	tablespoons ground cumin
1	tablespoon ground paprika
1½	teaspoons ground ginger
1½	teaspoons ground coriander
1	teaspoon ground black pepper
¼	teaspoon cayenne pepper
2	tablespoons olive oil
4	1-pound boneless rib-eye steaks (each about 1¼ inches thick), trimmed
8	lemon wedges

8 SERVINGS

Blend first 6 ingredients in small bowl. Mix in oil to form smooth paste. Rub mixture over steaks. Transfer to baking pan. Cover with plastic wrap and refrigerate at least 3 hours or overnight.

Prepare barbecue (medium-high heat). Sprinkle steaks with salt. Grill to desired doneness, about 5 minutes per side for medium-rare. Place on cutting board; let stand 4 minutes. Cut steaks into ½-inch-thick diagonal slices. Transfer to platter. Sprinkle with salt. Serve with lemon.

Beef ribs with sweet-and-sticky barbecue sauce

SIMMERING THE RIBS IN ADVANCE RIDS THEM OF EXCESS FAT, WHICH CAN CAUSE FLARE-UPS ON THE GRILL. BOTH THE RIBS AND THE SAUCE CAN BE MADE AHEAD, LEAVING JUST THE GRILLING FOR THE LAST MINUTE.

3½	cups ketchup
1	cup honey
1	8-ounce can crushed pineapple in juice
2¼	teaspoons garlic powder
1	teaspoon dried oregano
1	teaspoon dried thyme
½	teaspoon dried crushed red pepper
3	racks beef back ribs (about 9 pounds total), each rack cut in half
2½	cups coarsely chopped celery
1	onion, halved lengthwise
1½	cups coarsely chopped carrots
2	whole bay leaves
10	whole black peppercorns
1	tablespoon salt

6 SERVINGS

Combine first 7 ingredients in large deep saucepan. Bring to boil. Reduce heat to low and simmer until very thick, stirring occasionally, about 1 hour. Cool sauce. *(Can be prepared 1 week ahead. Cover; chill.)*

Place ribs in heavy large pot. Add celery, onion, carrots, bay leaves, peppercorns and 1 tablespoon salt. Add enough water to cover ribs and bring to boil. Reduce heat to medium and simmer until meat is tender, about 1 hour. Using tongs, remove rib racks from pot. Cool slightly. Cut between bones into individual ribs. *(Can be prepared 1 day ahead. Cover; refrigerate.)*

Prepare barbecue (medium heat). Brush ribs with some of sauce. Grill ribs until brown and thickly glazed, occasionally turning and basting with more sauce, about 10 minutes.

Beef and broccoli stir-fry

STIR-FRYING IS A GOOD METHOD FOR A LEAN CUT OF MEAT. HERE, A SOY-SAUCE-BASED MARINADE ADDS FLAVOR AND HELPS TENDERIZE FLANK STEAK. SERVE THIS OVER RICE.

¼ cup soy sauce

¼ cup dry Sherry

1 tablespoon honey

1 tablespoon chopped garlic

2 teaspoons grated orange peel

1 pound flank steak, cut diagonally across grain into thin strips

1 large head broccoli, cut into florets

2 tablespoons vegetable oil

1 tablespoon cornstarch

4 SERVINGS

Whisk first 5 ingredients in large bowl to blend. Add meat; toss to coat. Cover and refrigerate at least 1 hour and up to 4 hours.

Cook broccoli in large pot of boiling salted water 2 minutes. Drain. Rinse under cold water; drain well.

Heat oil in wok or heavy large skillet over high heat. Drain meat well, reserving marinade. Add cornstarch to reserved marinade and mix until smooth; set aside. Add meat to wok and stir-fry until almost cooked through, about 2 minutes. Add broccoli and stir-fry until crisp-tender, about 2 minutes. Add reserved marinade mixture and boil until sauce thickens and coats meat and broccoli, stirring constantly, about 2 minutes. Season to taste with salt and pepper.

Roast beef with root vegetables

ROASTING RESULTS IN A WELL-BROWNED, MOIST AND JUICY SERVING OF BEEF. CHOOSE A TENDER CUT, SAVING THE TOUGHER ONES FOR BRAISING OR STEWING. THE SPICE RUB USED HERE GIVES THIS RECIPE A REAL KICK, BUT IT CAN BE ELIMINATED FOR A MORE TRADITIONAL TAKE ON ROAST BEEF.

1 teaspoon cumin seeds

1 teaspoon coriander seeds

½ teaspoon whole black peppercorns

¾ teaspoon salt

½ teaspoon ground ginger

⅛ teaspoon cayenne pepper

2½ pounds russet potatoes, peeled, cut into 1-inch chunks

8 medium carrots, peeled, cut diagonally into 2-inch lengths

4 tablespoons extra-virgin olive oil

Preheat oven to 350°F. Place first 3 ingredients in heavy small plastic bag. Using meat mallet or rolling pin, crush spices. Transfer crushed spices to small bowl; mix in salt, ginger and cayenne.

Toss potatoes, carrots and 3 tablespoons olive oil in large bowl. Sprinkle with salt and pepper. Arrange vegetables in single layer in large roasting pan. Roast about 30 minutes.

Meanwhile, using tip of knife, make several slits in roast; insert garlic slices into slits. Brush roast with remaining 1 tablespoon olive oil. Rub spice mixture over roast.

1 **3- to 3¼-pound beef eye of round roast**

1 **garlic clove, thinly sliced**

2 **tablespoons chopped fresh cilantro**

6 TO 8 SERVINGS

Push vegetables to sides of pan, leaving space in center. Place roast in center of pan. Cook until meat thermometer inserted into center of roast registers 125°F for medium-rare, about 1 hour. Transfer roast to platter. Tent with foil to keep warm. Increase oven temperature to 450°F. Spread vegetables in pan; continue roasting until vegetables are tender and brown, about 10 minutes. Sprinkle with cilantro.

Surround roast with vegetables. Cut roast into thin slices and serve.

Basic beef stew

A GOOD STEW NEEDS TO COOK FOR A COUPLE OF HOURS, BUT IT NEEDS ONLY MINIMAL ATTENTION AND CAN MORE OR LESS BE LEFT ALONE WHILE IT SIMMERS. ALSO, A STEW IS OFTEN BETTER WHEN PREPARED A DAY OR TWO AHEAD, SINCE THE FLAVORS MELD OVER TIME.

¼ **cup vegetable oil**

1¼ **pounds stew beef, cut into 1-inch pieces**

6 **large garlic cloves, minced**

8 **cups Basic Beef Stock (see recipe on page 24) or canned beef broth**

2 **tablespoons tomato paste**

1 **tablespoon sugar**

1 **tablespoon dried thyme**

1 **tablespoon Worcestershire sauce**

2 **bay leaves**

2 **tablespoons (¼ stick) butter**

3 **pounds russet potatoes, peeled, cut into ½-inch pieces (about 7 cups)**

1 **large onion, chopped**

2 **cups ½-inch pieces peeled carrots**

2 **tablespoons chopped fresh parsley**

4 TO 6 SERVINGS

Heat oil in heavy large pot over medium-high heat. Add beef and sauté until brown on all sides, about 5 minutes. Add garlic and sauté 1 minute. Add beef stock, tomato paste, sugar, thyme, Worcestershire sauce and bay leaves. Stir to combine. Bring mixture to boil. Reduce heat to medium-low, cover and simmer 1 hour, stirring occasionally.

Meanwhile, melt butter in another large pot over medium heat. Add potatoes, onion and carrots; sauté until golden, about 20 minutes.

Add vegetables to beef stew. Simmer uncovered until vegetables and beef are very tender, about 40 minutes. Discard bay leaves. Tilt pan and spoon off fat. *(Can be prepared up to 2 days ahead. Cool slightly. Refrigerate uncovered until cold, then cover and keep refrigerated. Bring to simmer before serving.)* Transfer stew to serving bowl. Sprinkle with parsley and serve.

Pan-fried veal chops

BECAUSE VEAL HAS VERY LITTLE NATURAL FAT, IT IS EASY TO OVERCOOK. THIS QUICK PAN-FRYING TECHNIQUE FOR VEAL CHOPS IS AN EXCELLENT WAY TO ENSURE THAT DOESN'T HAPPEN.

4	12-ounce veal chops
¾	cup all purpose flour
¾	cup dry breadcrumbs
2	large eggs
1	tablespoon milk
8	tablespoons olive oil

4 SERVINGS

Preheat oven to 375°F. Sprinkle veal with salt and pepper. Place flour and breadcrumbs in separate shallow bowls. Whisk eggs and milk in another shallow bowl to blend. Working with 1 veal chop at a time, dredge in flour, then egg mixture, allowing excess to drip off. Dredge in breadcrumbs, coating completely. Place on baking sheet.

Heat 2 tablespoons oil in heavy large skillet over medium-high heat. Add 1 chop; cook until golden, about 2 minutes per side. Return chop to baking sheet. Repeat with remaining oil and chops in 3 more batches, wiping skillet clean between batches. Transfer chops to oven; bake about 5 minutes for medium.

Pan-fried veal chops with green peppercorn sauce

PAN-FRIED VEAL CHOPS TASTE GREAT ON THEIR OWN, BUT THEY ARE EVEN BETTER WITH THIS DELICIOUS GREEN PEPPERCORN SAUCE FLAVORED WITH SHALLOTS (PICTURED OPPOSITE). GREEN PEPPERCORNS ARE THE SOFT UNDERRIPE BERRIES OF THE PEPPER PLANT THAT HAVE BEEN PRESERVED IN BRINE.

½	cup white wine vinegar
3	tablespoons minced shallots
3	tablespoons green peppercorns in brine, drained
1	cup Basic Beef Stock (see recipe on page 24) or canned beef broth
1	cup Basic Chicken Stock (see recipe on page 22) or canned low-salt chicken broth
1	tablespoon honey
2	tablespoons water
1	teaspoon cornstarch
¼	cup diced red bell pepper
	Pan-fried Veal Chops (see recipe above)
1	tablespoon chopped green onion

4 SERVINGS

Boil vinegar, shallots and peppercorns in heavy medium saucepan over medium heat until almost all liquid evaporates, about 6 minutes. Add beef and chicken stocks and honey; bring to boil. Reduce heat and simmer until sauce is reduced to 1 cup, about 20 minutes. Mix 2 tablespoons water and cornstarch in bowl. Add to sauce and bring to boil, stirring constantly. Add diced bell pepper. Season sauce to taste with salt and pepper. Set aside.

Prepare veal chops. Meanwhile, bring sauce to simmer. Place 1 veal chop on each of 4 plates. Spoon sauce over chops. Garnish with chopped green onion and serve immediately.

Traditional osso buco

HERE'S A CLASSIC ITALIAN VEAL DISH. *OSSO BUCO* MEANS "BONE WITH A HOLE," A REFERENCE TO THE ROUND MARROW BONE IN THE CENTER OF EACH VEAL SHANK. THE SHANKS ARE BRAISED IN THE OVEN UNTIL TENDER, THEN SERVED WITH A *GREMOLATA*—A MINCED LEMON PEEL AND PARSLEY GARNISH.

3 tablespoons minced fresh parsley

1 small garlic clove, finely minced

½ teaspoon finely grated lemon peel

4 2-inch-thick veal shank pieces, preferably from meaty part of hind shanks (about 3 pounds total), tied around center

¼ cup all purpose flour

2 tablespoons (¼ stick) unsalted butter

2 tablespoons vegetable oil or olive oil

1 medium onion, minced

1 medium carrot, finely chopped

1 medium celery stalk, finely chopped

3 fresh thyme sprigs

2 parsley sprigs

1 bay leaf

½ cup dry white wine

3 medium garlic cloves, minced

1½ cups Basic Chicken Stock (see recipe on page 22) or canned low-salt chicken broth

1½ pounds ripe tomatoes, peeled, seeded, chopped

1 tablespoon tomato paste

4 SERVINGS

Mix 3 tablespoons minced parsley, 1 minced small garlic clove and lemon peel in small bowl. Set gremolata aside. *(Can be prepared up to 1 day ahead. Cover and refrigerate.)*

Preheat oven to 350°F. Pat veal dry. Sprinkle both sides with salt and pepper. Dredge in flour, patting off excess. Melt butter with oil in large ovenproof pot over medium-high heat. Add veal and brown on all sides. Transfer veal to plate.

Reduce heat to low. Add onion, carrot and celery to pot. Stir until vegetables are tender, scraping up any browned bits, about 5 minutes. Tie thyme sprigs, parsley sprigs and bay leaf in cheesecloth. Add to pot. Mix in wine and 3 minced medium garlic cloves. Boil until almost all liquid evaporates, stirring constantly. Return veal to pot. Add stock and tomatoes. Bring to boil. Cover pot, transfer to oven and bake until veal is very tender when pierced with sharp knife, about 1½ hours.

Discard herb bag. Transfer veal to serving platter. Stir tomato paste into sauce. Boil until reduced to about 2 cups, stirring frequently, about 10 minutes. Season with salt and pepper. Return veal to pot with sauce. Cover and bring sauce to simmer.

Sprinkle gremolata evenly over veal and sauce. Cover and simmer 2 minutes longer. Serve immediately.

Lamb chops with lemon and thyme

THIS RECIPE FOR LAMB CHOPS IS HIGHLY VERSATILE. YOU CAN USE RIB OR LOIN CHOPS, AND GRILL THEM OR BROIL THEM, WHICHEVER YOU PREFER. EITHER WAY, YOU'LL END UP WITH AN EASY, DELICIOUS ENTRÉE.

½ cup Dijon mustard

½ cup fresh lemon juice

6 tablespoons balsamic vinegar

3 tablespoons chopped fresh thyme

1 teaspoon ground black pepper

⅔ cup extra-virgin olive oil

24 lamb rib chops or loin chops

1 lemon, halved

Fresh thyme sprigs (optional)

Lemon wedges (optional)

8 SERVINGS

Mix mustard, lemon juice, vinegar, chopped thyme and pepper in medium bowl. Gradually whisk in oil. Divide marinade between 2 large shallow glass baking dishes. Add 12 chops to each dish; turn to coat in marinade. Cover; chill at least 2 hours and up to 4 hours.

Prepare barbecue (medium-high heat) or preheat broiler. Grill or broil lamb to desired doneness, about 7 minutes per side for medium-rare. Transfer to platter. Season with salt. Squeeze juice from lemon halves over chops. Garnish with thyme sprigs and lemon wedges, if desired.

Equipment

An accurate instant-read thermometer, either digital or analog, is essential for cooking meat—and a good carving set can make simple work of serving it. Look for a ten-inch-long knife blade with a cutting edge that either is smooth or, if serrated, has shallow scallops that won't shred the meat. A fork with two six- to eight-inch tines is best. A curved or straight shape is a matter of personal preference. Both the knife and the fork should have strong and comfortable handles.

Also useful: a roasting pan and rack; for slow-cooking, a five-quart or larger dome-lidded Dutch oven or enameled casserole (choose one that can be used for both stove-top and oven cooking); a slow cooker (yes, they're back) for simmering chili and stews; a wooden carving board; and tongs (try the spring-loaded variety, which opens and closes with a minimum of effort).

Roast leg of lamb with mustard

WHEN YOU WANT A CENTERPIECE DISH FOR A SPECIAL DINNER, THIS MUSTARD-COATED LEG OF LAMB WILL FILL THE BILL. ASK YOUR BUTCHER TO REMOVE THE LARGE HIP BONE, LEAVING JUST THE SHANK BONE ON THE LEG OF LAMB. THIS WILL MAKE THE LAMB MUCH EASIER TO CARVE. WHEN SLICING, HOLD THE CARVING KNIFE ALMOST PARALLEL TO THE MEAT AND CUT IT INTO THIN SLICES.

1   6- to 6¼-pound leg of lamb, large bone removed, shank bone left intact

2   tablespoons Dijon mustard

2   tablespoons olive oil

5   garlic cloves, pressed

1   teaspoon dried thyme

2   cups Basic Beef Stock (see recipe on page 24) or canned beef broth

¾   cup dry white wine

3   shallots, minced

6 SERVINGS

Preheat oven to 375°F. Place rack in heavy roasting pan. Trim all fat and connective tissue from lamb. Place lamb on rack in pan. Mix mustard, oil, garlic and thyme in small bowl. Spread mustard mixture over lamb; season with salt and pepper. Roast until meat thermometer inserted into thickest part of lamb registers 125°F for medium-rare, about 1½ hours. Transfer lamb to platter. Add stock, wine and shallots to roasting pan; boil over medium-high heat until sauce is reduced to 1 cup, scraping up any browned bits, about 10 minutes. Slice lamb and serve, passing sauce separately.

Tips

TO ACHIEVE the perfect roast, the most important thing is to start with the right cut of meat. Select a tender and flavorful cut from the butcher (such as a lean round roast, or something from the tenderloin or rib sections) and use an instant-read meat thermometer to test for doneness. Beef is very rare when it has an internal temperature of 120°F, and rare at 125°F; it's medium at 145°F to 150°F, and well done at 160°F.

SEALED in an airtight container, ground beef and lamb will keep in the freezer at 0°F for three to four months—but will last only one to two days in the refrigerator at 40°F, according to the United States Department of Agriculture.

DEFROSTING meat in the microwave is quick and convenient—just be sure to cook the meat immediately afterward. During microwave defrosting, portions of the meat are sometimes partially cooked, and can harbor bacteria as a result. The only way to ensure that the meat is safe is to cook it fully.

A SPICE RUB adds flavor to roasts, steaks and chops. Mix dried herbs and spices, such as paprika, cumin, pepper, oregano and salt, in a small bowl. Rub the dry spice mixture over the meat and refrigerate several hours before cooking to allow the flavors to penetrate.

Butterflied leg of lamb with rosemary

ASK THE BUTCHER TO BONE AND BUTTERFLY THE LEG OF LAMB FOR YOU. THE MEAT NEEDS TO MARINATE OVERNIGHT; AFTER THAT, IT REQUIRES ONLY A QUICK TURN ON THE GRILL.

¾ cup dry red wine

½ cup extra-virgin olive oil

⅓ cup coarse-grained mustard

¼ cup red wine vinegar

4 tablespoons fresh rosemary leaves (6 sprigs)

2 tablespoons drained green peppercorns in brine

1 tablespoon dried oregano

2 large garlic cloves

1 4- to 5-pound leg of lamb, boned, butterflied, trimmed of excess fat

6 SERVINGS

Combine first 8 ingredients in blender. Puree until rosemary is completely ground, about 3 minutes.

Place lamb in large glass baking dish with 2-inch-high sides. Pour marinade over lamb, making certain all parts of lamb are covered with marinade. Cover; chill at least 8 hours or overnight. Let stand 2 hours at room temperature before cooking.

Prepare barbecue (medium-high heat). Remove lamb from marinade. Sprinkle both sides of lamb generously with salt and pepper. Grill until lamb is brown and crusty on outside and meat thermometer inserted into thickest part registers 130°F for medium-rare, turning occasionally, about 20 minutes. Transfer to platter and tent with foil. Let stand 10 minutes. Cut on diagonal into thin slices and serve.

What do I need to know about buying and cooking lamb?

The most common cuts of lamb are loin (great for roasting and excellent as chops or medallions); leg (excellent for roasting, or cubed for kebabs); rib, known as rack of lamb (best quickly roasted); shank (wonderful braised); and shoulder (good cut up for stews).

Look for meat that is pinkish-red. A darker color can mean the animal is older, with meat that is strongly flavored. Make sure that the thin layer of fat, called the fell, has already been removed, or cut it away yourself with a sharp knife.

Roast lamb racks with olive crust

IF THE LAMB RACKS HAVE NOT ALREADY BEEN TRIMMED, CUT OFF THE OUTER LAYER OF FAT AND TWO INCHES OF FAT BETWEEN THE BONES; THIS TECHNIQUE IS CALLED FRENCHING.

3   1¼- to 1½-pound racks of lamb, trimmed, frenched

1¼   cups purchased tapenade or olive paste

3   cups fresh breadcrumbs made from French bread

6 SERVINGS

Preheat oven to 400°F. Sprinkle lamb with salt and pepper. Spread tapenade over both sides of lamb. Press breadcrumbs gently onto tapenade to adhere, coating lamb completely.

Arrange lamb racks, meat side up, on rimmed baking sheet. Roast until meat thermometer inserted into center of lamb registers 130°F for medium-rare, about 35 minutes.

Roast lamb with olive crust, red bell pepper sauce and basil oil

THIS IS AN ELEGANT VARIATION ON THE ROAST LAMB RACK RECIPE ABOVE. IT HAS AN EASY BELL PEPPER SAUCE AND BASIL OIL ADDED FOR INTEREST.

½   cup (lightly packed) fresh basil leaves

⅓   cup plus 6 tablespoons olive oil

Roast Lamb Racks with Olive Crust (see recipe above)

3   large red bell peppers

3   tablespoons Sherry wine vinegar

6 SERVINGS

Cook basil in medium saucepan of boiling water 20 seconds. Drain. Pat basil dry with paper towels. Transfer basil to processor and blend well. With machine running, add ⅓ cup oil through feed tube and blend until smooth. Season basil oil to taste with salt and pepper. Set aside.

Prepare lamb racks with olive crust. Transfer lamb to work surface. Tent with foil; let stand 5 minutes.

Meanwhile, char peppers over gas flame or in broiler until blackened on all sides. Enclose in paper bag; let stand 10 minutes. Peel and seed. Combine peppers and vinegar in processor; puree. With machine running, add remaining 6 tablespoons oil through feed tube; blend until smooth. Pour into small saucepan. Stir over medium heat just until warm (do not boil). Season with salt and pepper.

Cut lamb racks between bones into chops. Spoon sauce onto plates. Arrange chops atop sauce. Drizzle some basil oil over and serve.

Roast pork tenderloins

PORK TENDERLOIN MAKES A QUICK AND SATISFYING ROAST. HERE, IT'S COATED WITH A MIXTURE OF THYME, SALT AND PEPPER, THEN BROWNED IN A SKILLET BEFORE BEING TRANSFERRED TO THE OVEN AND ROASTED.

4½ teaspoons dried thyme

1½ teaspoons salt

1½ teaspoons ground black pepper

3 1-pound pork tenderloins, excess fat trimmed

3 tablespoons vegetable oil

8 SERVINGS

Mix thyme, salt and pepper in small bowl. Place pork in large baking dish. Pat dry with paper towel. Brush with 2 tablespoons oil. Rub thyme mixture over pork. (Can be prepared 1 day ahead. Cover; chill.)

Preheat oven to 400°F. Heat remaining 1 tablespoon oil in heavy large ovenproof skillet over high heat. Add pork and cook until brown, turning frequently, about 5 minutes. Transfer skillet to oven and roast pork until meat thermometer inserted into thickest part of pork registers 160°F, about 20 minutes. Transfer pork to platter.

Roast pork tenderloins with cranberry-Port sauce

THE ROAST PORK TENDERLOINS ABOVE ARE GREAT PAIRED WITH A SWEET-TART CRANBERRY-PORT SAUCE. (MAKE THE SAUCE A DAY AHEAD, IF YOU LIKE, AND BRING IT TO A SIMMER BEFORE SERVING.)

3 tablespoons butter

2 cups chopped onions

4 garlic cloves, minced

3 teaspoons grated orange peel

1½ teaspoons dried sage leaves

1 teaspoon dried thyme

2 cups Basic Chicken Stock (see recipe on page 22) or canned low-salt chicken broth

1½ cups cranberry juice cocktail

2 cups fresh or frozen (unthawed) cranberries

½ cup sugar

¼ cup tawny Port

1 tablespoon cornstarch

Roast Pork Tenderloins (see recipe above)

8 SERVINGS

Melt butter in heavy large skillet over medium-high heat. Add onions; sauté until golden, about 8 minutes. Add garlic, 1½ teaspoons orange peel, sage and thyme; stir 1 minute. Add stock and cranberry juice; simmer until mixture is reduced to 2½ cups, about 8 minutes. Strain sauce into heavy medium saucepan, pressing on solids with back of spoon. Add cranberries and sugar; boil just until berries pop, about 5 minutes. Mix Port and cornstarch in small bowl to blend. Add to sauce; boil until sauce thickens, about 1 minute. Season to taste with salt and pepper. (Can be prepared 1 day ahead. Cover and refrigerate.)

Prepare pork tenderloins; cover to keep warm. Do not wash skillet. Add cranberry-Port sauce and remaining 1½ teaspoons orange peel to skillet and bring to simmer, stirring frequently.

Cut pork into ½-inch-thick diagonal slices. Divide slices among 8 plates. Drizzle sauce over pork and serve.

Pork roast with mushroom sauce

A CARDAMOM SPICE RUB FLAVORS THIS PORK ROAST, WHICH IS SERVED WITH A CREAMY MUSHROOM SAUCE.

1½ cups chopped onion

5 tablespoons olive oil

2¼ teaspoons ground cardamom

1 large garlic clove

1 4-pound boneless pork rib roast

1½ pounds mushrooms, halved

2 cups Basic Chicken Stock (see recipe on page 22) or canned low-salt chicken broth

½ cup whipping cream

1 tablespoon all purpose flour

1 tablespoon butter, room temperature

8 SERVINGS

Preheat oven to 350°F. Puree ½ cup chopped onion, 2 tablespoons oil, 2 teaspoons cardamom and garlic in processor. Spread ½ cup chopped onion in center of large roasting pan; top with pork. Sprinkle pork generously with salt and pepper; coat with onion puree. Toss mushrooms, remaining ½ cup onion and 3 tablespoons oil in bowl; sprinkle with salt and pepper; arrange around pork.

Roast pork 1 hour. Spoon mushrooms into heavy large saucepan. Add 1½ cups stock to roasting pan. Roast pork until meat thermometer inserted into thickest part registers 160°F, about 20 minutes longer. Transfer pork to platter; tent loosely with aluminum foil (temperature will rise 5 to 10 degrees as pork roast stands).

Scrape juices from roasting pan into saucepan with mushrooms. Add cream, remaining ½ cup stock and ¼ teaspoon cardamom to pan; bring to boil. Blend flour and butter in small cup; mix into mushroom sauce. Cook sauce, stirring often, until reduced enough to coat spoon, about 5 minutes. Season sauce with salt and pepper; serve with pork.

Do I need to take any special precautions when preparing pork to ensure that the meat is safely cooked through?

According to the USDA, pork is safely cooked when it has reached a temperature of 160°F. At this temperature, all organisms that can cause food-related illness have been destroyed. It is important to check the temperature of pork by using a thermometer designed for meat and poultry (not for candy).

It's easy to check a meat thermometer to see if it's precise: Just place it in boiling water, and it should read 212°F. (For those who live at high altitude, the temperature at which water boils decreases by about 2°F for every one thousand feet above sea level.) Insert the thermometer into the thickest part of the pork and make sure it does not touch bone, fat or gristle. If the thermometer reads 160°F, the pork is safe to eat and will be medium. If you like it well done, cook it to about 170°F.

Cider-brined pork chops with leeks and apples

BRINING THE PORK OVERNIGHT IN A MIXTURE OF APPLE CIDER AND SALT MAKES IT ESPECIALLY JUICY. THE CHOPS ARE SERVED WITH CREAMED LEEKS AND SAUTÉED APPLES.

4¼ cups apple cider

3 tablespoons coarse salt

6 allspice berries

1 bay leaf

4 10-ounce bone-in center-cut pork rib chops

4 tablespoons (½ stick) butter

5 large leeks (white and pale green parts only), thinly sliced

1 cup whipping cream

1½ pounds Granny Smith apples, peeled, cored, halved, each half cut into 4 wedges

2 tablespoons sugar

½ cup Basic Chicken Stock (see recipe on page 22) or canned low-salt chicken broth

⅓ cup Calvados

Olive oil

4 SERVINGS

Bring 4 cups cider, salt, allspice and bay leaf to boil in large saucepan, stirring to dissolve salt. Cool completely. Place pork in 13x9x2-inch glass baking dish. Pour brine over. Cover; refrigerate overnight.

Melt 2 tablespoons butter in heavy large skillet over medium-low heat. Add leeks; sauté until tender, about 7 minutes. Add cream and simmer until slightly thickened, about 3 minutes. Season to taste with salt and pepper. (Creamed leeks can be made 1 day ahead. Cover and chill.)

Melt remaining 2 tablespoons butter in large nonstick skillet over medium heat. Add apples and sauté 10 minutes. Add sugar and sauté until apples are golden, about 6 minutes longer. Add stock, then Calvados and remaining ¼ cup cider. Simmer until liquid thickens slightly and apples are tender, stirring occasionally, about 5 minutes. Remove from heat and set aside.

Prepare barbecue (medium heat) or preheat broiler. Drain pork. Rinse under cold water; pat dry. Brush pork with oil. Grill or broil to desired doneness, about 5 minutes per side for medium.

Meanwhile, rewarm leeks, thinning with 1 to 3 tablespoons water if necessary. Bring apples to simmer. Spoon leeks onto plates. Top with pork chops, then apples, and serve.

Glazed ham

THIS IS A CLASSIC RECIPE FOR BAKED HAM, A DELICIOUS CENTERPIECE DISH PERFECT FOR ANY FESTIVE
OCCASION. AN APRICOT AND MANGO GLAZE ADDS APPEALING SWEETNESS.

1 **16-pound bone-in fully cooked whole ham with rind**

¼ **cup (about) whole cloves**

2 **cups mango nectar**

¼ **cup apricot preserves**

4 **teaspoons minced peeled fresh ginger**

1 **tablespoon grated lemon peel**

1 **tablespoon grated lime peel**

2 **teaspoons ground coriander**

½ **teaspoon fresh lime juice**

20 SERVINGS

Position rack in bottom third of oven and preheat to 350°F. Using sharp knife, cut parallel lines 1 inch apart in fat layer and rind on ham. Cut more lines in crosswise direction, making diamond pattern. Stick 1 whole clove into center of each diamond. Place rack in roasting pan. Place ham on rack. Roast ham 2 hours. Reduce oven temperature to 300°F. Continue to roast ham until golden, about 1 hour longer.

Meanwhile, combine mango nectar and next 6 ingredients in heavy medium saucepan. Bring to simmer over medium heat. Simmer until glaze thickens and coats spoon, stirring frequently, about 14 minutes; remove from heat and set glaze aside.

Remove ham from oven. Maintain oven temperature. Using pastry brush, dab all of glaze over ham, being careful not to dislodge crisp diamonds of fat and rind. Return ham to oven. Roast until ham is heated through and glaze is brown, about 35 minutes.

Transfer ham to platter; let stand 15 minutes. Slice ham and serve.

Is the iridescent shine that sometimes appears on ham a sign of spoilage?

An iridescent shine on ham is the result of oxidation, which takes place when ham is exposed to the air. However, if the ham has been taken care of properly, it is still safe to eat. A fully cooked ham should be kept refrigerated and served cold, or heated through to a temperature of 140°F. (Remember, meat should never stand at room temperature for more than two hours.)

Tropical glazed ham with curried pineapple chutney

A CURRIED PINEAPPLE CHUTNEY PROVIDES A SPICY, EXOTIC TWIST TO THE GLAZED HAM (OPPOSITE). THE CHUTNEY CAN BE MADE A FEW DAYS IN ADVANCE TO STREAMLINE THE RECIPE.

6 tablespoons vegetable oil

1 large red onion, chopped

2 medium-size red bell peppers, chopped

5 tablespoons minced seeded jalapeño chilies

3 tablespoons curry powder

9 cups ½-inch cubes peeled quartered cored pineapple (from 2 large)

1½ cups orange juice

1½ cups apple cider vinegar

1½ cups (packed) golden brown sugar

Glazed Ham (see recipe opposite)

20 SERVINGS

Heat oil in heavy large pot over medium-high heat. Add red onion and bell peppers; sauté until onion begins to soften, about 8 minutes. Add jalapeño chilies and curry powder; stir 2 minutes. Add pineapple cubes, orange juice, vinegar and brown sugar. Bring to boil. Reduce heat to medium and simmer mixture until thickened and reduced to about 7½ cups, stirring often, about 1 hour 10 minutes. Season chutney to taste with salt and pepper. *(Can be prepared 4 days ahead. Cool completely, then cover and refrigerate.)*

Prepare ham. Spoon chutney into bowl and serve alongside.

 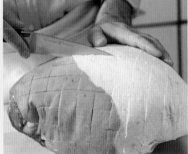 

GLAZED HAM WITH CHUTNEY:

STEP 1. To prepare each pineapple for the chutney, cut off the top and bottom. Stand the pineapple upright, and cut it into quarters. Use a knife to remove the skin and the core portion from each quarter. Then the pineapple can easily be cut into half-inch cubes.

STEP 2. The ham will come with the rind partially trimmed, exposing the white layer of fat. Create a diamond pattern by cutting parallel lines, about 1 inch apart and ⅓ inch deep, across the ham into the rind and fat; then repeat the process, cutting at an angle to the existing lines.

STEP 3. Check whether the ham is heated through by inserting a long metal skewer or thin knife into the center of the ham (do not touch the bone). Leave it in about 30 seconds. If the skewer or knife is hot when you pull it out, so is the center of the ham.

Chicken is universally loved (even picky kids will gnaw on a chicken leg), inexpensive, healthful, and supremely versatile—not to mention delicious. Learn how to roast a chicken and sauté chicken breasts (we'll show you how here), and you'll have a world of great meals to choose from. Then, keep it simple *and* keep experimenting, with fried chicken, stir-fries, pot pies and more.

And there's no reason to stop there. Duck, Cornish game hens and even turkey are all as easily prepared as chicken and great to add to your list of dinnertime favorites. Read on to find out how to make a good thing even better.

Poultry

Chicken and Vegetable Pot Pie with Cream Cheese Crust (page 97)

Basic roast chicken with lemon and thyme

LEARN HOW TO MAKE A ROAST CHICKEN, AND YOU'LL ALWAYS KNOW "WHAT'S FOR DINNER?" BEGINNING THE ROASTING PROCESS AT A HIGH HEAT GIVES THE SKIN AN APPEALING CRISPNESS THAT ALSO SEALS IN FLAVOR.

3   tablespoons minced fresh thyme

2   tablespoons extra-virgin olive oil

5   garlic cloves, chopped

2   teaspoons grated lemon peel

1   7-pound roasting chicken

1   lemon, quartered

¼   cup dry white wine

1   cup (about) Basic Chicken Stock (see recipe on page 22) or canned low-salt chicken broth

2   teaspoons all purpose flour

4 TO 6 SERVINGS

Preheat oven to 450°F. Mix first 4 ingredients in bowl. Rinse chicken; pat dry. Place chicken on rack in roasting pan. Reserve 1 tablespoon garlic-thyme oil; rub remainder over chicken. Sprinkle with salt and pepper. Place lemon in cavity of chicken. Tie legs together with string.

Roast chicken 20 minutes. Reduce oven temperature to 375°F. Continue roasting chicken until meat thermometer inserted into thickest part of thigh registers 180°F, about 1 hour 15 minutes. Lift chicken and tilt slightly, emptying juices from cavity into pan. Transfer chicken to serving platter. Tent chicken with aluminum foil to keep warm.

Pour pan juices into large glass measuring cup. Spoon fat off top. Add wine to pan; place over high heat. Bring to boil, scraping up any browned bits. Pour wine mixture into measuring cup with pan juices (do not clean roasting pan). Add enough chicken stock to cup to measure 1½ cups. Return stock mixture to roasting pan. Mix flour into reserved 1 tablespoon garlic-thyme oil. Whisk into stock mixture. Boil in roasting pan set over 2 burners until slightly thickened, about 2 minutes. Season pan sauce with salt and pepper. Pour into sauceboat. Serve chicken, passing pan sauce separately.

What is the easiest way to carve roast fowl?

STEP 1: Position the bird breast side up with drumsticks pointing toward you. Begin by slicing through the meat between leg and breast.

STEP 2: Use a carving knife to pry the leg away from the body, exposing the hip joint. Slice through the joint to separate leg from bird.

STEP 3: Hold the drumsticks in place with a fork, and cut between thigh and drumstick.

STEP 4 (this step plus steps 5 and 7 are only for turkey and other large birds): Carve the drumstick by cutting a thick slice from one side of the bone. Turn the drumstick onto the flat side created by the cut, and slice off another thick piece. Continue, cutting all the meat off both drumsticks.

STEP 5: Use the knife to find the thigh bone; then, cutting parallel to the bone, slice off the meat.

STEP 6: Cut off the wings by slicing through their joints.

STEP 7: Thinly slice off breast meat from both sides of the center bone.

Roast chicken with wild mushroom stuffing

STUFFING THE CHICKEN ADDS A LITTLE TO THE COOKING TIME, BUT IT PROVIDES A RICH, READY-MADE SIDE DISH. THIS ONE FEATURES AN ASSORTMENT OF WILD MUSHROOMS, WHICH ARE ALSO IN THE PAN SAUCE. TO ENSURE FOOD SAFETY, REMEMBER TO STUFF THE BIRD RIGHT BEFORE PLACING IT IN THE OVEN.

1   ½-ounce package dried porcini mushrooms*

2   cups 1-inch cubes baguette

1   pound assorted fresh wild mushrooms (such as oyster and portobello)

¼   cup (½ stick) butter

2   large shallots, chopped

¾   teaspoon dried thyme

4   juniper berries (optional), crushed

1   6- to 7-pound roasting chicken; liver, heart and gizzard reserved, finely chopped

1   cup (or more) Basic Chicken Stock (see recipe on page 22) or canned low-salt chicken broth

2   tablespoons chopped fresh parsley

¾   teaspoon salt

½   teaspoon ground black pepper

1   tablespoon brandy

4 SERVINGS

Preheat oven to 400°F. Place porcini in small bowl. Pour enough hot water over to cover; let stand 20 minutes. Drain.

Arrange baguette cubes in single layer on small rimmed baking sheet. Bake until cubes are golden, about 10 minutes. Transfer toasted bread cubes to large bowl. Maintain oven temperature.

Slice half of fresh mushrooms; set aside for sauce. Coarsely chop remaining fresh mushrooms. Melt butter in large skillet over medium-high heat. Add chopped mushrooms and shallots; sauté until tender, about 5 minutes. Add porcini, thyme, and juniper berries if desired; stir 1 minute. Add to bowl with bread. Mix in chopped liver, heart and gizzard, then ⅓ cup chicken stock, parsley, salt and pepper.

Rinse chicken inside and out; pat dry with paper towels. Sprinkle chicken cavity with salt and pepper. Fill with stuffing. Tie legs together. Sprinkle outside of chicken with salt and pepper. Place on rack in roasting pan. Roast until thermometer inserted into thickest part of thigh registers 180°F and juices run clear when thickest part of thigh is pierced with fork, 1 hour 45 minutes. Transfer to platter; cover with foil.

Pour pan drippings into measuring cup. Transfer 3 tablespoons fat from top of drippings to heavy large skillet. Spoon off remaining fat from pan drippings and discard. Heat fat in skillet over medium-high heat. Add reserved sliced mushrooms and sauté until tender, about 5 minutes. Add ⅔ cup chicken stock, pan drippings and brandy; cook 3 minutes, thinning with more stock if desired. Season sauce with salt and pepper. Serve chicken with stuffing and sauce.

*Dried porcini mushrooms are available at Italian markets, specialty foods stores and many supermarkets nationwide.

Peppery fried chicken

HERE'S A CLASSIC METHOD FOR FRIED CHICKEN. THE BATTER IS SIMPLY SEASONED FLOUR COMBINED WITH MILK AND EGGS, BUT THE CRISP COATING THAT RESULTS IS DELICIOUS. WHITE MEAT DOES NOT TAKE AS LONG TO COOK AS DARK, SO REMOVE THE BREASTS FROM THE FRYING PAN SOONER THAN THE DRUMSTICKS AND THIGHS.

4 cups all purpose flour

1 tablespoon paprika

1 tablespoon freshly ground black pepper

1 tablespoon salt

2 cups milk

2 large eggs

2 frying chickens, cut into 8 pieces each, patted dry

Vegetable oil (for deep-frying)

6 SERVINGS

Mix flour, paprika, pepper and salt in large bowl. Whisk milk and eggs in another bowl. Coat chicken on all sides in flour mixture, shaking off excess. Dip in milk mixture, allowing excess to drip into bowl. Dredge chicken in flour mixture again.

Add enough oil to heavy large skillet to reach depth of 2 inches; heat to 360°F. Fry chicken in batches (do not crowd) until cooked through and coating is golden brown, about 20 minutes for white meat and 25 minutes for dark. Using tongs, transfer chicken to paper towels. Serve warm or at room temperature.

Oven-fried chicken

"OVEN-FRYING" CHICKEN RESULTS IN A CRISP COATING SIMILAR TO THAT OF FRIED CHICKEN, BUT IT REQUIRES LESS ATTENTION. START PREPARING THIS RECIPE (PICTURED OPPOSITE) SEVERAL HOURS IN ADVANCE, SO THAT THE CHICKEN HAS TIME TO "MARINATE" IN THE FLAVORINGS BEFORE BEING BREADED.

3 eggs, beaten to blend

5 to 6 large garlic cloves, minced

2 tablespoons finely chopped parsley

1 3½-pound chicken, cut into 8 pieces, patted dry

2 cups seasoned dry breadcrumbs

1 cup freshly grated Parmesan cheese

½ cup (1 stick) butter

4 SERVINGS

Combine eggs, garlic and parsley in medium bowl. Season with salt and pepper. Add chicken, turning to coat. Cover and refrigerate 3 hours, turning occasionally.

Preheat oven to 350°F. Combine breadcrumbs and cheese in medium bowl. Melt butter in 10x15-inch jelly-roll pan in oven. Drain chicken. Pat dry. Coat chicken on all sides in breadcrumb mixture. Add chicken, skin side down, to pan with butter. Bake until chicken is golden brown, turning occasionally, about 45 minutes.

Basic sautéed chicken breasts

ANOTHER BASIC COOKING TECHNIQUE FOR CHICKEN. ONCE MASTERED, THE RECIPE HAS ALMOST LIMITLESS VARIATIONS. USING DIFFERENT HERBS WILL LEND INTEREST, AS WILL ADDING LEMON PEEL WITH THE HERBS.

2 chicken breast halves with skin and bones

2 tablespoons olive oil

½ cup finely chopped onion

½ cup dry white wine

1½ tablespoons chopped fresh herbs (such as sage or thyme) or 1½ teaspoons dried

2 SERVINGS

Sprinkle chicken with salt and pepper. Heat oil in heavy medium skillet over medium-high heat. Add chicken and sauté until browned, about 3 minutes per side. Transfer chicken to plate. Add onion to skillet; sauté until onion begins to brown, about 5 minutes. Return chicken and any accumulated juices to skillet. Add wine and herbs to skillet. Bring to boil. Reduce heat to medium-low, cover and simmer until chicken is cooked through, turning occasionally, about 12 minutes. Serve chicken with pan sauce.

What's an easy way to remove the fat from pan drippings?

Several tools are available to help remove fat from gravy. The most useful item is a degreasing cup (or fat separator), which looks like a measuring cup with a spout that begins at the base. When hot pan juices are poured into the cup, the fat rises to the top. The juices can be poured out through the spout while the fat stays in the cup. There are also fat-separating basters and ladles, which give the same result.

Quick chicken sauté with tomato-basil sauce

USING SKINLESS BONELESS CHICKEN BREASTS INSTEAD OF THE BONE-IN KIND FOR A SAUTÉ CUTS THE COOKING TIME ALMOST IN HALF. THIS RECIPE INCLUDES AN EASY FRESH TOMATO SAUCE.

1 tablespoon olive oil

2 skinless boneless chicken breast halves

1 shallot, chopped

1½ cups chopped seeded tomatoes

¼ cup dry white wine

1 tablespoon drained capers, 1 teaspoon brine reserved

2 tablespoons chopped fresh basil

2 SERVINGS

Heat olive oil in heavy medium skillet over medium-high heat. Sprinkle chicken breast halves with salt and pepper. Add chicken to skillet and cook until golden and cooked through, about 5 minutes per side. Transfer to plate. Add chopped shallot to same skillet; sauté 30 seconds. Stir in tomatoes, white wine, capers and caper brine. Boil until tomatoes release juices, about 4 minutes. Stir in chopped basil. Season sauce with salt and pepper. Return chicken to skillet. Cook until warmed through, spooning sauce over chicken, about 1 minute. Transfer chicken with sauce to 2 plates and serve.

Stir-fried chicken with onion and hoisin sauce

THE TECHNIQUE OF COATING THE CHICKEN IN AN EGG WHITE AND CORNSTARCH MIXTURE BEFORE STIR-FRYING IS CALLED VELVETING. IT GIVES THE CHICKEN A SUPERBLY MOIST TEXTURE. SERVE THIS OVER STEAMED RICE.

1 large egg white

1 tablespoon plus 2 teaspoons dry Sherry

½ teaspoon salt

1 pound skinless boneless chicken breasts, all fat and sinew trimmed, cut into 1x2-inch pieces

1 tablespoon cornstarch

5 tablespoons vegetable oil

1 tablespoon minced peeled fresh ginger

1 large garlic clove, minced

¼ teaspoon dried crushed red pepper

6 tablespoons hoisin sauce*

1 tablespoon soy sauce

6 cups water

1 large onion, cut into 1-inch pieces

1 large bell pepper, cut into 1-inch pieces

¾ cup toasted unsalted cashews

4 SERVINGS

Beat egg white, 1 tablespoon Sherry and salt in medium bowl to blend. Add chicken and stir to coat. Mix in cornstarch, then 1 tablespoon vegetable oil. Refrigerate at least 30 minutes. *(Can be prepared 1 day ahead. Keep refrigerated.)*

Combine minced ginger, garlic and dried crushed red pepper in small bowl. Combine hoisin sauce, soy sauce and remaining 2 teaspoons Sherry in another small bowl.

Bring 6 cups water to boil in large saucepan. Add 1 tablespoon oil, then chicken; stir gently to separate. Cook until coating is white, about 45 seconds. Drain in colander.

Heat 1 tablespoon oil in wok or heavy large skillet over medium-high heat. Add onion and stir-fry 2 minutes. Add bell pepper. Sprinkle with salt. Stir-fry until vegetables begin to soften, about 2 minutes longer. Transfer to plate. Add remaining 2 tablespoons oil to wok. Add ginger mixture and stir until aromatic, about 20 seconds. Add hoisin mixture and bring to simmer. Return chicken and vegetables to wok. Stir until chicken is cooked through, about 2 minutes. Mix in cashews; serve.

*Available at Asian markets and in the Asian foods section of some supermarkets.

Chili-rubbed chicken with barbecue table mop

CHICKEN TAKES WELL TO THE BARBECUE. IN THIS RECIPE, CHICKEN PIECES ARE COVERED WITH A DRY RUB BEFORE BEING GRILLED. A TANGY BARBECUE SAUCE, SOMETIMES CALLED A "TABLE MOP," IS PASSED SEPARATELY.

¾ cup chili powder (about 3½ ounces)

3 tablespoons brown sugar

2 teaspoons cayenne pepper

1 cup hickory barbecue sauce

¾ cup ketchup

⅓ cup orange juice

1 tablespoon soy sauce

1 teaspoon hot pepper sauce

2 3½-pound chickens, quartered, backbones discarded

3 cups mesquite wood chips, soaked in cold water (optional)

6 SERVINGS

Mix chili powder, brown sugar and cayenne in small bowl.

Mix barbecue sauce and next 4 ingredients in medium bowl. Arrange chicken in single layer on large baking sheet. Season with salt and pepper. Sprinkle chili rub generously on both sides of chicken; press to adhere. Let stand at room temperature 1 hour.

Prepare barbecue (medium-high heat). When coals are white, drain chips, if using, and scatter over coals. Place chicken, skin side down, on grill rack away from direct heat. Cover grill and cook chicken until cooked through, turning every 5 minutes and covering grill, about 35 to 40 minutes (chili rub may look slightly burned). Serve chicken hot or warm, passing table mop separately.

Rosemary chicken and pattypan squash kebabs

HERE'S ANOTHER WAY TO COOK CHICKEN. CHUNKS OF BONELESS CHICKEN ARE MARINATED, THEN THREADED ON SKEWERS FOR GRILLING. TO VARY THIS RECIPE, ADD BELL PEPPER, ZUCCHINI OR RED ONION.

2 tablespoons olive oil

1 tablespoon fresh lemon juice

1 tablespoon chopped fresh rosemary or 1½ teaspoons dried

2 garlic cloves, minced

1 teaspoon grated lemon peel

2 skinless boneless chicken breast halves, each cut into 6 pieces

3 large pattypan squash, each quartered

4 metal skewers

2 SERVINGS

Prepare barbecue (medium-high heat). Whisk first 5 ingredients in medium bowl. Add chicken and squash; toss to coat. Let stand 10 minutes; toss chicken mixture occasionally.

Alternate 3 chicken pieces with 3 squash pieces on each of 4 skewers. Sprinkle with salt and pepper. Grill until chicken is cooked through and squash is just tender, turning often, about 10 minutes.

Classic coq au vin

THIS TRADITIONAL FRENCH STEW HAS STOOD THE TEST OF TIME. CHICKEN PIECES ARE COOKED WITH BACON, MUSHROOMS, ONIONS AND HERBS IN RED WINE (OR *VIN*).

1   cup plus 2 tablespoons all purpose flour

6   slices bacon, chopped

1   tablespoon olive oil

12   chicken thighs (with skin and bones), excess fat trimmed

¾   cup chopped shallots

3   garlic cloves, minced

1   pound boiling onions, peeled

12   ounces crimini mushrooms, quartered (about 5 cups)

2   tablespoons chopped fresh marjoram

1   750-ml bottle dry red wine

2   cups Basic Chicken Stock (see recipe on page 22) or canned low-salt chicken broth

2   tablespoons (¼ stick) butter, room temperature

¼   cup chopped fresh chives

6 SERVINGS

Preheat oven to 350°F. Place 1 cup flour in shallow dish. Cook chopped bacon in heavy large pot over medium-high heat until crisp, about 4 minutes. Using slotted spoon, transfer bacon to paper-towel-lined plate to drain. Add 1 tablespoon olive oil to bacon drippings in pot. Sprinkle chicken thighs with salt and pepper. Working in batches, coat chicken with flour and add to pot; cook until brown, about 4 minutes per side. Arrange chicken in 15x10x2-inch glass baking dish.

Pour off all but 3 tablespoons fat from pot. Add shallots and garlic to pot; sauté 1 minute. Add onions, mushrooms and marjoram; sauté until onions begin to brown, about 10 minutes. Add wine and bring to boil, scraping up browned bits. Add stock and bacon; boil 5 minutes. Pour wine mixture over chicken in baking dish. Cover tightly with foil; bake until chicken is cooked through, about 1 hour.

Using tongs, transfer chicken thighs to platter. Strain wine mixture from baking dish into heavy medium saucepan. Transfer onion mixture to platter with chicken; tent with foil to keep warm. Mix remaining 2 tablespoons flour and butter in small bowl to blend. Bring wine mixture to boil. Whisk in flour mixture; boil until sauce thickens and is reduced to 2¾ cups, about 8 minutes. Season with salt and pepper. Ladle sauce over chicken and vegetables; sprinkle with chives.

Equipment

For roasting poultry, you'll need a roasting pan made of nonreactive metal, so that you can make sauces and gravies from the pan drippings using wine, tomatoes or vinegar without ruining the pan or the food. Look for stainless steel, anodized aluminum or enameled steel. Select a pan with riveted-to-the-body, upright handles. A roaster that is 16 inches long and 13 inches wide will accommodate most turkeys and all chickens—but measure your oven first to make sure the pan will fit.

Also useful: an instant-read meat thermometer; a gravy separator (specialized bulb, cup and ladle versions are all fine); a mallet for pounding poultry to uniform thickness; a bulb baster; a heavy, large nonstick skillet; string for tying; and poultry shears.

Curried chicken

HERE'S AN EASY TAKE ON A TRADITIONAL EAST INDIAN DISH—CURRY. THE SAUCE CAN BE MADE A DAY AHEAD.

3 tablespoons vegetable oil

3 cups chopped onions

¼ cup minced peeled fresh ginger

3 garlic cloves, minced

3 tablespoons curry powder

1 teaspoon ground cumin

¼ teaspoon ground cinnamon

2 tablespoons all purpose flour

1 cup plain yogurt

3 tablespoons tomato paste

3 cups Basic Chicken Stock (see recipe on page 22) or canned low-salt chicken broth

1 cup unsweetened applesauce

4 pounds skinless boneless chicken breasts, cut crosswise into ½-inch-thick slices

1 10-ounce package frozen peas

½ cup sour cream

½ cup canned unsweetened coconut milk*

Fresh cilantro sprigs

Steamed white rice

Major Grey mango chutney

Sliced peeled bananas

Chopped pitted peeled mangoes

Shredded unsweetened coconut

Chopped toasted peanuts

8 TO 10 SERVINGS

Heat oil in heavy large pot over medium heat. Add onions and sauté until golden, about 15 minutes. Add ginger and garlic; sauté 1 minute. Add curry, cumin and cinnamon; sauté until fragrant, about 1 minute. Add flour, then yogurt and tomato paste, whisking until sauce is smooth, about 1 minute. Add stock and applesauce. Bring to boil. Reduce heat; simmer until sauce thickens slightly, stirring occasionally, about 30 minutes. *(Can be made 1 day ahead. Cool slightly. Cover and chill. Bring to simmer before continuing.)*

Add chicken and peas to sauce. Simmer until chicken is almost cooked through, about 3 minutes. Add sour cream and coconut milk. Reduce heat to medium-low. Stir until chicken is cooked through and sauce thickens enough to coat spoon, about 3 minutes (do not boil). Season with salt and pepper. Transfer to bowl. Garnish with cilantro.

Place rice, chutney, bananas, mangoes, coconut and peanuts in separate bowls. Serve alongside curry.

*Available at Indian, Southeast Asian and Latin American markets and at many supermarkets nationwide.

Chicken and vegetable pot pies with cream cheese crust

A HOME-STYLE CLASSIC, THESE POT PIES (PICTURED ON PAGE 87) COMBINE CHUNKS OF CHICKEN MEAT WITH VEGETABLES AND A RICH CREAMY SAUCE, TOPPED WITH A PASTRY CRUST.

CRUST

2½ cups all purpose flour

½ teaspoon salt

1 cup (2 sticks) unsalted butter, cut into pieces, room temperature

1 8-ounce package cream cheese, cut into pieces, room temperature

CHICKEN

1 3½-pound whole chicken

12 cups water

2 large onions, quartered

2 large carrots, coarsely chopped

1 large leek, sliced

12 small fresh thyme sprigs

1 bay leaf

FILLING

3 tablespoons olive oil

2 red bell peppers, cut into strips

1 large onion, chopped

8 ounces shiitake mushrooms, stemmed, caps sliced

4 ounces green beans, trimmed, cut into 1-inch pieces

¾ cup chopped green onions

½ cup drained oil-packed sun-dried tomatoes, chopped

1 tablespoon chopped fresh rosemary

½ cup (1 stick) unsalted butter

½ cup plus 2 tablespoons all purpose flour

1 cup whole milk

¼ cup whipping cream

4½ teaspoons beef base*

1 egg, beaten to blend (for glaze)

MAKES 6

FOR CRUST: Mix flour and salt in processor. Add butter and cream cheese; blend until moist clumps form. Shape dough into 6-inch-long log. Wrap in plastic; chill while making chicken and filling.

FOR CHICKEN: Place all ingredients in large pot; bring to boil. Reduce heat and simmer until chicken is cooked through, about 45 minutes. Transfer chicken to large bowl; cool. Discard skin and bones. Cut meat into 1-inch pieces; return to bowl.

Strain chicken cooking liquid into large saucepan. Boil until reduced to 3 cups stock, about 1 hour.

MEANWHILE, PREPARE FILLING: Heat 1 tablespoon oil in large skillet over medium heat. Add peppers and onion; cook until soft, about 6 minutes. Transfer to bowl with chicken. Heat 2 tablespoons oil in same skillet over medium-high heat. Add mushrooms; sauté until just brown, about 4 minutes. Add to bowl with chicken. Bring large saucepan of salted water to boil. Add beans; boil 1 minute. Drain; place beans in bowl of cold water and drain again. Mix beans, green onions, sun-dried tomatoes and rosemary into bowl with chicken.

Melt butter in large saucepan over medium heat. Add flour; whisk 2 minutes. Gradually whisk in 3 cups stock, then milk, cream and beef base; bring to boil. Season sauce with salt and pepper. Stir 3 cups sauce into chicken mixture (reserve remaining sauce for another use).

Cut prepared dough crosswise into 6 equal pieces. Roll out pieces to 7-inch rounds on lightly floured surface. Divide filling among six 2-cup soufflé dishes. Cover each dish with 1 dough round. Press overhang to sides of dish to adhere. *(Can be prepared 1 day ahead. Cover; chill.)*

Preheat oven to 350°F. Brush top of each dough round with egg glaze; cut 3 slits in each to allow steam to escape. Bake pies until crust is golden brown and filling is heated through, about 45 minutes.

*Available at specialty foods stores and many supermarkets.

Spiced game hens

ROASTING CORNISH GAME HENS ISN'T MUCH DIFFERENT FROM ROASTING A CHICKEN—IT JUST TAKES LESS TIME. FOR ADDED FLAVOR, THE HENS ARE COATED WITH A MIX OF SPICES.

1   tablespoon cumin seeds

1   tablespoon coriander seeds

2   teaspoons cardamom seeds

2   teaspoons fennel seeds

1   teaspoon whole cloves

½   cinnamon stick, broken into pieces

1   bay leaf

¼   cup orange juice

2   tablespoons olive oil

2   garlic cloves, minced

4   Cornish game hens (about 1½ pounds each), rinsed

1   pound carrots, peeled, cut diagonally into ½-inch-thick slices

½   cup Basic Chicken Stock (see recipe on page 22) or canned low-salt chicken broth

4 SERVINGS

Preheat oven to 400°F. Finely grind first 7 ingredients in spice grinder or coffee grinder. Transfer to small bowl. Whisk in orange juice, oil and garlic. *(Spice mixture can be prepared 1 day ahead. Cover and chill.)*

Pat hens dry with paper towels. Rub spice mixture all over hens. Sprinkle hens inside and out with salt and pepper. Tie legs together to hold shape. Place hens in large roasting pan. Arrange carrots in pan around hens. Sprinkle carrots with salt and pepper. Roast 30 minutes. Add stock to roasting pan. Roast hens until juices run clear when thickest part of thigh is pierced and carrots are tender, basting hens occasionally with pan juices, about 35 minutes longer. Place 1 hen on each of 4 plates. Arrange carrots alongside.

Spiced game hens with orange-honey sauce

AN EXOTIC ORANGE-HONEY SAUCE ADDS INTEREST TO THE GAME HEN RECIPE ABOVE.

Spiced Game Hens (see recipe above)

1   cup Essencia (orange Muscat wine) or late-harvest Riesling

⅔   cup chopped shallots (about 4 large)

½   cup orange juice

1   tablespoon honey

2½ cups Basic Chicken Stock (see recipe on page 22) or canned low-salt chicken broth

3   tablespoons chilled butter, cut into 3 pieces

4 SERVINGS

Prepare game hens. Meanwhile, whisk wine, shallots, orange juice and honey in heavy medium saucepan. Simmer over medium heat until mixture is reduced to ½ cup, about 12 minutes. Add stock and simmer until sauce is reduced to 1¼ cups, about 20 minutes. Whisk in butter 1 piece at a time, allowing each piece to melt before adding next. Season sauce to taste with salt and pepper. Keep warm.

Spoon warm orange-honey sauce over hens and serve.

Basic roast turkey with pan gravy

ROASTING A TURKEY IS SIMPLER THAN YOU MIGHT THINK. HERE'S A STEP-BY-STEP RECIPE (COMPLETE WITH THE GRAVY) THAT GUARANTEES A DELICIOUS, MOIST AND BROWN BIRD.

GIBLET BROTH

Neck, gizzard and heart from one 16- to 18-pound turkey

4 cups water

1 onion, chopped

2 celery stalks with leaves, chopped

3 fresh parsley sprigs

1 bay leaf

TURKEY

1 16- to 18-pound turkey

1 tablespoon dried rosemary

2 teaspoons ground sage

2 teaspoons dried thyme

1½ teaspoons salt

1½ teaspoons ground black pepper

½ cup (1 stick) butter, melted

GRAVY

6 tablespoons all purpose flour

¾ cup whipping cream

3 tablespoons medium-dry Sherry, dry Marsala or Port (optional)

16 SERVINGS

FOR GIBLET BROTH: Combine all ingredients in medium saucepan. Bring to boil, skimming surface. Reduce heat to low, cover partially and simmer 2 hours. Strain broth, reserving giblets. Chop giblets finely. Cover broth and giblets separately and refrigerate. *(Can be prepared 1 day ahead; keep chilled.)*

FOR TURKEY: Preheat oven to 375°F. Pat turkey dry inside and out. Combine rosemary, sage, thyme, salt and pepper in small bowl. Rub some herb mixture in each cavity. Close with skewer. Tuck in wings. Tie legs together. Place turkey, breast side up, on rack in roasting pan. Brush with melted butter. Sprinkle with remaining herbs.

Roast turkey 1 hour, basting every 30 minutes with butter. Cover turkey breast with foil. Continue roasting 1 hour, basting occasionally with pan drippings. Uncover turkey breast and continue roasting until thermometer inserted into thickest part of thigh registers 175°F, basting occasionally, 30 minutes to 1¼ hours longer, depending on size of turkey. Transfer turkey to platter, reserving juices in roasting pan for gravy. Tent turkey with foil and let rest 20 minutes. (Internal temperature will rise 5 to 10 degrees.)

FOR GRAVY: Pour turkey pan juices into large measuring cup and skim off fat, reserving ¼ cup fat (do not wash roasting pan). Add enough giblet broth to juices to measure 3⅓ cups. Pour about ½ cup juices into turkey roasting pan. Set atop 2 burners and bring to boil over medium-high heat, scraping up any browned bits.

Transfer reserved fat to heavy medium saucepan. Add flour and stir roux over medium-low heat 2 minutes. Gradually whisk in juices from pan and measuring cup. Bring to boil, stirring frequently. Cook until thickened, about 2 minutes. Add cream and simmer until slightly thickened, about 2 minutes. Add Sherry, if desired, and reserved giblets. Season to taste with salt and pepper. Serve turkey with gravy.

Roast turkey with pan gravy and sausage-apple stuffing

THIS SLIGHTLY MORE ELABORATE ROAST TURKEY INCLUDES A SWEET-AND-SAVORY STUFFING THAT CAN BE BAKED INSIDE THE TURKEY OR IN A DISH ALONGSIDE THE BIRD.

GIBLET BROTH

    Neck, gizzard and heart from one 16- to 18-pound turkey

4 cups water

1 onion, chopped

2 celery stalks with leaves, chopped

3 fresh parsley sprigs

1 bay leaf

STUFFING

11 cups ½-inch cubes firm-textured white bread (about 1¼ pounds)

½ cup (1 stick) butter

1 large onion, chopped

¾ pound mushrooms, sliced

2 teaspoons dried rosemary

1¼ cups chopped celery

1 tart apple, peeled, cored, chopped

¾ cup chopped fresh parsley

1 teaspoon ground sage

1 teaspoon dried thyme

¾ pound Italian sausage (hot or sweet), casings removed

¾ to 1¾ cups Basic Chicken Stock (see recipe on page 22) or canned low-salt chicken broth

TURKEY

1 16- to 18-pound turkey

1 tablespoon dried rosemary

2 teaspoons ground sage

2 teaspoons dried thyme

1½ teaspoons salt

1½ teaspoons ground black pepper

FOR GIBLET BROTH: Combine all ingredients in medium saucepan. Bring to boil, skimming surface. Reduce heat to low, cover partially and simmer 2 hours. Strain broth, reserving giblets. Chop giblets finely. Cover broth and giblets separately; chill. *(Can be made 1 day ahead.)*

FOR STUFFING: Preheat oven to 250°F. Spread bread cubes on baking sheet. Bake bread cubes until dry to touch, stirring occasionally, about 20 minutes. Transfer to large bowl.

Melt butter in heavy large skillet over medium-low heat. Add onion and cook until tender, stirring occasionally, about 8 minutes. Add mushrooms, rosemary and generous amount of ground black pepper; cook until mushrooms are tender, stirring occasionally, about 6 minutes. Add celery and apple; stir 1½ minutes. Mix in parsley, sage and thyme. Add mushroom mixture to bread and toss to blend.

Increase heat to medium-high. Place sausage in same skillet and cook until beginning to brown, breaking up with fork. Using slotted spoon, transfer to bowl with bread. Add ½ cup chicken stock to stuffing and mix to blend well. Season with salt.

FOR TURKEY: Preheat oven to 375°F. Pat turkey dry inside and out. Combine rosemary, sage, thyme, salt and pepper in small bowl. Rub some herb mixture in each cavity. *To bake stuffing in turkey:* Fill neck-end cavity loosely with some stuffing. Close with skewer. Tuck in wings. Fill main cavity loosely with some stuffing. Fold in tail over stuffing. Skewer opening; lace closed with string. Tie legs together. Place turkey, breast side up, on rack in roasting pan. Brush with melted butter. Sprinkle with remaining herbs. Add enough stock to remaining stuffing to moisten slightly (¼ to ¾ cup, depending on amount of remaining stuffing). Generously butter baking dish. Spoon remaining stuffing into prepared dish. Cover with buttered foil, buttered side down.

To bake all of stuffing in baking dish: Generously butter 15x10x2-inch glass baking dish. Add enough chicken stock to stuffing to moisten (¾ cup to 1¼ cups). Transfer stuffing to prepared dish. Cover with buttered foil, buttered side down.

¼ to 1¼ cups (about) Basic
Chicken Stock (see recipe on
page 22) or canned low-salt
chicken broth

½ cup (1 stick) butter, melted

GRAVY

6 tablespoons all purpose flour

¾ cup whipping cream

3 tablespoons medium-dry
Sherry, dry Marsala or
Port (optional)

16 SERVINGS

Roast turkey 1 hour, basting every 30 minutes with butter. Cover breast with foil. Continue roasting 1 hour, basting occasionally with pan drippings. Uncover breast and continue roasting until thermometer inserted into thickest part of thigh registers 175°F, basting occasionally, 1 to 1¾ hours longer, depending on size of turkey. Place covered baking dish of stuffing in oven during last 40 minutes. Transfer turkey to platter, reserving juices in roasting pan for gravy. Tent turkey with foil; let rest 20 minutes. (Internal temperature will rise 5 to 10 degrees.) Uncover stuffing in dish and bake 20 minutes longer.

FOR GRAVY: Pour turkey pan juices into large measuring cup and skim off fat, reserving ¼ cup fat (do not clean roasting pan). Add enough giblet broth to juices to measure 3⅓ cups. Pour about ½ cup juices into turkey roasting pan. Set atop 2 burners and bring to boil over medium-high heat, scraping up any browned bits.

Transfer reserved fat to heavy medium saucepan. Add flour and stir roux over medium-low heat 2 minutes. Gradually whisk in juices from pan and measuring cup. Bring to boil, stirring frequently. Cook until thickened, about 2 minutes. Add cream and simmer until thickened slightly, about 2 minutes. Add Sherry, if desired, and reserved giblets. Season with salt and pepper. Serve turkey with stuffing and gravy.

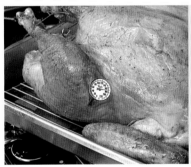

ROASTING A TURKEY:

STEP 1: Inserting the thermometer into the thickest part of the thigh, without touching any bone, ensures an accurate reading. The turkey is ready to remove from the oven at 175°F. The temperature will rise five to ten degrees as the turkey rests.

STEP 2: Deglaze the roasting pan by bringing a combination of the pan juices and the giblet broth to boil over medium-high heat. A wooden spatula is used to scrape up the browned bits, which add flavor to the pan gravy.

STEP 3: Pan juices are gradually whisked into the roux, the lightly cooked blend of reserved fat and flour traditionally used to thicken gravy. It will be cooked until thickened, then enhanced with Sherry and giblets. The result is an ideal sauce for the roast turkey and stuffing.

Roast turkey breast with Madeira sauce

WHEN A LARGE TURKEY IS TOO MUCH FOOD FOR THE OCCASION, THIS BASIC ROAST TURKEY BREAST IS
THE PERFECT ALTERNATIVE. A QUICK PAN GRAVY IS A NICE FINISHING TOUCH.

1   whole turkey breast with
    bone (4 pounds)

3   tablespoons butter,
    room temperature

1   tablespoon plus ½ teaspoon
    poultry seasoning

1   cup Basic Chicken Stock (see
    recipe on page 22) or canned
    low-salt chicken broth

¼   cup dry Madeira

1   tablespoon all purpose flour

6 TO 8 SERVINGS

Preheat oven to 325°F. Rinse turkey; pat dry with paper towels. Rub 2 tablespoons butter and 1 tablespoon poultry seasoning over turkey. Transfer turkey to roasting pan; sprinkle with salt and pepper. Roast in oven until meat thermometer inserted into center registers 175°F, about 1¾ hours. Transfer turkey to platter; tent with foil to keep warm.

Pour stock and Madeira into roasting pan. Stir with spatula, scraping up browned bits from roasting pan. Melt 1 tablespoon butter in heavy medium saucepan over medium heat. Add flour and stir 1 minute. Add stock mixture from pan and remaining ½ teaspoon poultry seasoning. Boil until mixture thickens to thin gravy consistency, about 4 minutes. Season gravy with salt and pepper. Slice turkey; serve with gravy.

Tips

DON'T BOTHER removing the skin from chicken before cooking, unless the recipe specifies doing so. The fat in chicken skin is not absorbed by the meat during cooking, and the skin actually forms a protective layer, sealing in the moisture and keeping the chicken from drying out.

OIL TEMPERATURE is key when frying chicken. If the oil isn't hot enough, the food will absorb it and become greasy. If the oil is too hot, the food

will burn. So use a deep-fry thermometer and immerse the thermometer's bulb in the oil, without letting it touch the bottom of the pan. A temperature between 350°F and 375°F is good for frying.

GRAVY recipes usually get their start with a roux, a combination of fat and flour. The roux is cooked for a couple of minutes to eliminate the raw flour flavor before the liquid (pan juices, broth, wine or cream, or a mixture) is added.

MANY EXPERTS recommend placing a turkey on a rack inside the roasting pan. That way, the bottom of the turkey is not directly exposed to the heat of the pan, and the hot air from the oven can get under the bird to cook it evenly. A flat rack, which simply elevates the bird, works fine; the V-shaped rack, which cradles the bird while keeping it suspended above the pan, holds oddly shaped roasts (like turkeys) more securely.

Roast duck with potatoes, turnips and olives

ROAST A DUCK MUCH AS YOU WOULD A CHICKEN, EXCEPT PIERCE THE DUCK SKIN WITH A FORK FIRST. THIS ALLOWS THE EXCESS FAT TO DRAIN OUT DURING COOKING. THE VEGETABLES AND OLIVES COMPLEMENT THE FLAVOR OF THE DUCK. AN ADDED BONUS: THE ROOT VEGETABLES BECOME AN INSTANT SIDE DISH.

2   5-pound ducks

Chopped fresh thyme or dried thyme

2   large onions, sliced

4   russet potatoes, quartered lengthwise, cut crosswise into ½-inch-thick pieces

5   turnips, peeled, quartered lengthwise, cut crosswise into ½-inch-thick pieces

1   cup Niçois olives*

Fresh thyme sprigs (optional)

1½   cups Basic Beef Stock (see recipe on page 24) or canned beef broth

½   cup dry white wine

6 SERVINGS

Preheat oven to 450°F. Pat ducks dry. Remove fat pieces from cavities. Sprinkle cavities with thyme, salt and pepper. Place a few onion slices in cavity of each duck. Tie legs together to hold shape. Place each duck in separate large roasting pan. Pierce all over with fork. Rub outside of ducks with generous amounts of thyme, salt and pepper. Surround with remaining onion slices. Roast 15 minutes.

Remove roasting pans from oven and add potatoes and turnips. Sprinkle vegetables with salt, pepper and chopped thyme. Stir vegetables to coat with duck drippings. Return pans to oven and roast 15 minutes longer. Reduce oven temperature to 375°F. Continue roasting until juices run slightly rosy when ducks are pierced in thickest part of thigh or drumstick, turning vegetables occasionally, about 55 minutes longer. Transfer ducks to serving platter. Mix olives into vegetables. Using slotted spoon, transfer vegetable mixture to platter with ducks. Garnish with thyme sprigs, if desired.

Pour drippings from pans into large glass measuring cup. Skim fat off drippings, reserving 2 tablespoons fat. Add stock and white wine to 1 roasting pan. Bring to boil, scraping up browned bits. Pour mixture into second pan. Add reserved 2 tablespoons fat to wine mixture in second roasting pan. Add drippings to same pan. Boil until syrupy, scraping up browned bits, about 5 minutes. Season sauce with chopped thyme, salt and pepper. Serve with duck and vegetables.

*Small brine-cured black olives, available at Italian markets, specialty foods stores and some supermarkets.

Whenever you think there's nothing new to serve for dinner, consider seafood. There's a wonderful variety of fish and shellfish available: salmon, tuna, shrimp, trout, crab, lobster, scallops, snapper. The trick is in knowing the best way to prepare each kind.

Well, it's easy. Just like meat and poultry, seafood can be baked, sautéed, oven-poached or grilled—we'll tell you which technique works best with each type of fish. And since seafood preparation is fast, fish makes a speedy midweek meal—or an elegant, no-fuss dinner party favorite, for that matter. Could you ask for anything more?

Seafood

Individual Scallop Gratin (page 114)

Basic fish sauté

SAUTÉING FISH IS ONE OF THE EASIEST METHODS OF PREPARATION. ALL YOU NEED IS A LITTLE BUTTER OR OIL FOR THE PAN AND SALT, PEPPER AND LEMON FOR THE FISH. SEA BASS IS USED HERE, WITH A TOUCH OF SUGAR AND NUTMEG FOR ADDED FLAVOR. YOU CAN ALSO TRY THIS WITH SOLE, SNAPPER OR HALIBUT.

2 tablespoons olive oil

4 6-ounce sea bass fillets (about 1 inch thick)

1 teaspoon sugar

Ground nutmeg

2 teaspoons fresh lemon juice

4 SERVINGS

Heat 2 tablespoons oil in heavy large skillet over medium-high heat. Sprinkle fish with salt and pepper. Add to skillet; sauté until golden on bottom, about 5 minutes. Sprinkle ¼ teaspoon sugar and pinch of nutmeg over top of each fish fillet. Turn fish over; cook until golden on second side and opaque in center, about 4 minutes longer.

Transfer 1 sea bass fillet to each of 4 plates. Drizzle 1 teaspoon pan drippings over each. Drizzle ½ teaspoon lemon juice around each fillet.

Sautéed sea bass with parsley puree

ADD A COLORFUL PARSLEY PUREE TO THE FISH SAUTÉ RECIPE ABOVE AND YOU HAVE AN EASY YET ELEGANT MAIN COURSE THAT IS PERFECT FOR ENTERTAINING.

1 bunch Italian parsley, large stems trimmed (about 2 cups packed)

2 tablespoons olive oil

½ teaspoon chopped fresh marjoram

½ teaspoon minced lemon peel

Pinch of ground nutmeg

Basic Fish Sauté (see recipe above)

Additional minced lemon peel (optional)

4 SERVINGS

Fill medium bowl with ice water. Cook parsley in pot of lightly salted boiling water just until bright green, about 5 seconds. Drain, reserving ½ cup cooking liquid. Transfer parsley to ice water. Drain well. Coarsely chop parsley. Combine parsley, reserved ½ cup cooking liquid, oil, marjoram, ½ teaspoon lemon peel and pinch of nutmeg in blender; puree until smooth. Season with salt and pepper. *(Parsley puree can be prepared 1 day ahead. Cover; chill. Stir over medium heat until heated through before continuing.)* Cover to keep warm.

Prepare fish sauté. Spoon warm parsley puree around each fillet. Garnish with additional lemon peel, if desired.

Spiced pan-fried trout

THIS BASIC PAN-FRIED TROUT IS ENHANCED WITH CHILI POWDER AND GROUND CUMIN. A QUICK PAN SAUCE FINISHES THE DISH. IF YOU LIKE, SUBSTITUTE MACKEREL, POMPANO OR SMALL SALMON FOR THE TROUT.

2   8- to 10-ounce trout, boned, butterflied

1   cup milk

⅓ cup yellow cornmeal

2   tablespoons all purpose flour

1   teaspoon chili powder

1   teaspoon ground cumin

4   tablespoons (½ stick) butter

2   tablespoons vegetable oil

½   teaspoon salt

1   tablespoon fresh lemon juice
    Minced fresh parsley

    2 SERVINGS

Open butterflied trout and arrange in shallow pan. Add milk and soak 20 minutes, turning trout occasionally.

Combine cornmeal, flour, ½ teaspoon chili powder and ½ teaspoon cumin in another shallow pan. Season generously with salt and pepper. Melt 2 tablespoons butter with oil in heavy large skillet over medium-high heat. Remove trout from milk and dip into cornmeal mixture, coating both sides completely. Add to skillet, skin side down. Cook until just opaque in center, about 1½ minutes per side. Transfer trout to plates; tent with foil to keep warm.

Pour off pan drippings and wipe out skillet. Melt remaining 2 tablespoons butter in same skillet over medium-high heat. Add remaining ½ teaspoon chili powder, ½ teaspoon cumin and ½ teaspoon salt; stir 30 seconds. Stir in lemon juice (mixture will foam). Pour over trout. Sprinkle with parsley and serve.

Equipment

First of all, you should have a good sauté pan—preferably one featuring stainless steel on the outside and on the cooking surface, but with an internal core layer of copper or aluminum. With this combination you get stainless steel's terrific searing and browning capabilities, its neutrality (it won't react with acidic foods), its easy-care advantages and its near-indestructibility, plus copper or aluminum's super heat-conducting ability. Also useful: a nonstick grill basket (helpful in handling fish over the coals); a medium (four- to eight-quart) stock pot for simmering lobster; fish servers (long-handled spoon/spatulas); and a long fish knife.

Poached snapper with tomato and herb broth

HERE, THE POACHING LIQUID BECOMES A DELICATELY FLAVORED BROTH. RED SNAPPER IS USED, BUT ANY OTHER FIRM-FLESHED FISH WOULD WORK JUST AS WELL.

2 cups dry white wine

2 cups water

2 onion slices

2 garlic cloves, halved

2 ¼-inch-thick slices fresh ginger

2 bay leaves

2 fresh thyme sprigs or ¼ teaspoon dried

2 2x½-inch strips orange peel (orange part only)

4 6-ounce red snapper fillets

⅔ cup drained diced canned tomatoes

2 tablespoons minced fresh chives

2 teaspoons fresh thyme leaves (optional)

4 SERVINGS

Bring first 8 ingredients to boil in large deep skillet. Reduce heat to medium-low and simmer 5 minutes. Season snapper with salt and pepper. Add to liquid in skillet. Cover and simmer until fish is opaque in center, about 8 minutes. Transfer fish to shallow soup bowls. Cover bowls with foil and keep warm.

Strain cooking liquid into saucepan. Reserve orange peel. Boil liquid until reduced to 1½ cups, about 8 minutes. Slice orange peel into small strips; return to broth. Stir in tomatoes and chives. Divide hot broth among bowls with fish. Garnish with thyme leaves, if desired.

Chinese-style steamed fish

THE CLASSIC CHINESE METHOD OF STEAMING FISH IS TO PLACE IT IN A BAMBOO STEAMER SET OVER A WOK FILLED WITH BOILING WATER. THIS RECIPE HAS BEEN ADAPTED TO INCLUDE A PIE DISH THAT IS SET ATOP A CAKE RACK INSIDE A SKILLET OF BOILING WATER.

2 6-ounce red snapper fillets

2 tablespoons dry white wine

1½ teaspoons minced peeled fresh ginger

2 small garlic cloves, minced

4 teaspoons soy sauce

1½ teaspoons oriental sesame oil

2 tablespoons chopped fresh cilantro

2 SERVINGS

Place small cake rack in large (12-inch-diameter) skillet; place 9-inch-diameter glass pie dish on rack. Put fish in dish; sprinkle lightly with salt and pepper. Sprinkle wine, ginger and garlic in dish around fish. Top fish with soy sauce, sesame oil and 1 tablespoon cilantro. Pour enough water into skillet to reach depth of 1 inch. Bring water to boil. Cover skillet; steam fish until just opaque in center, about 10 minutes. Transfer fish to plates; top with juices from dish and remaining cilantro.

Basic baked salmon

MOST TYPES OF SEAFOOD TAKE WELL TO BAKING. IT'S A VERSATILE COOKING METHOD THAT ALLOWS YOU TO SERVE THE FISH SIMPLY, AS HERE, OR ADD A SAUCE (SEE THE VARIATION BELOW).

2   1½-pound center-cut salmon fillets

¼   cup (½ stick) unsalted butter, melted

3   tablespoons golden brown sugar

3   tablespoons soy sauce

2   tablespoons fresh lemon juice

2   tablespoons dry white wine

8 SERVINGS

Line large baking pan with foil. Arrange fish, skin side down, in single layer on foil. Mix butter, brown sugar, soy sauce, lemon juice and wine in bowl. Pour over fish. Cover; chill at least 1 hour and up to 6 hours.

Preheat oven to 400°F. Uncover fish and bake until just cooked through, basting occasionally with pan drippings, about 18 minutes. Arrange salmon on platter; serve.

Baked salmon with mustard sauce

MUSTARD, WORCESTERSHIRE SAUCE AND A PINCH OF CAYENNE GIVE THE BAKED SALMON SOME ZIP. YOU CAN PREPARE THE SAUCE AFTER THE FISH HAS GONE INTO THE OVEN, OR MIX UP THE MUSTARD BASE BEFOREHAND AND REWARM IT WHILE THE FISH IS BAKING, ADDING THE SOUR CREAM JUST BEFORE THE FISH IS DONE.

1   cup whipping cream

¾   cup Creole mustard or other coarse-grained mustard

1   tablespoon Dijon mustard

4   teaspoons Worcestershire sauce

¾   teaspoon ground black pepper

½   teaspoon dried basil

¼   teaspoon ground white pepper

¼   teaspoon cayenne pepper

1   cup sour cream

Basic Baked Salmon (see recipe above)

8 SERVINGS

Combine first 8 ingredients in heavy medium saucepan. Simmer until very thick, stirring frequently, about 5 minutes. *(Mustard mixture can be prepared 1 day ahead. Cover and refrigerate. Before continuing, rewarm mustard mixture over low heat, stirring constantly.)*

Add sour cream to mustard mixture. Whisk over low heat just until heated through; do not boil. Season sauce with salt. Serve with salmon.

Halibut with roasted potatoes, orange and rosemary

OVEN-ROASTING IS A SIMPLE WAY TO PREPARE FISH. A HIGH OVEN TEMPERATURE IS USED SO THAT THE FISH WILL TURN OUT MOIST AND FLAVORFUL. THIS RECIPE INCLUDES A TANGY ORANGE SAUCE.

½   cup chopped fresh Italian parsley

1   tablespoon minced orange peel

2   teaspoons chopped fresh rosemary

3   garlic cloves, minced

1½   pounds white potatoes, peeled, cut into ½-inch pieces

1½   tablespoons olive oil

4   6-ounce halibut fillets (each about 1¼ inches thick)

½   cup fresh orange juice

1   tablespoon balsamic vinegar

4 SERVINGS

Mix parsley, orange peel, rosemary and 2 minced garlic cloves in bowl.

Preheat oven to 450°F. Spread potatoes in 13x9x2-inch metal baking pan. Drizzle with oil and toss to coat. Sprinkle with salt and pepper. Roast potatoes until almost tender and golden brown, stirring occasionally, about 25 minutes.

Place halibut fillets atop potatoes. Sprinkle fish with salt and pepper. Roast until fish are opaque in center and potatoes are tender, about 15 minutes. Divide potatoes and fish among 4 plates.

Combine orange juice, vinegar, 2 tablespoons parsley mixture and remaining 1 minced garlic clove in same baking pan. Set pan over 2 burners and boil until liquid is reduced to ⅓ cup, scraping up any browned bits, about 2 minutes. Season sauce with salt and pepper. Pour over fish on each plate; sprinkle with remaining parsley mixture.

Tips

MAKE a variety of flavorful mayonnaises for seafood. Experiment by adding any of these to prepared mayonnaise: chopped roasted peppers from a jar, garlic, lemon juice and lemon peel, herbs, tapenade, mustard, olives, capers, chopped sun-dried tomatoes or purchased pesto.

WHEN cooking with scallops, consider the types available.

Among the most common are sea scallops, the largest at about 1½ to 2 inches in diameter. Next in size are bay scallops, about ½ inch in diameter; these are tender with a sweet, delicate flavor. Then come calico scallops, about the size of pencil erasers and easily overcooked. When purchasing, ask for "dry" scallops that have not been soaked in a preservation solution to keep them from spoiling.

TO REMOVE the shell and dark "vein" (the lower part of the digestive tract) on the back of shrimp, use a sharp pair of scissors or cut a slit lengthwise down the back, then peel off the shell and remove the exposed vein. Or peel by hand with a knife or a special tool called a shrimper or deveiner, available at cookware stores.

Grilled tuna steaks with cantaloupe salsa

GRILLING FISH IS A QUICK WAY TO GET DINNER ON THE TABLE. TUNA TAKES ESPECIALLY WELL TO THE TECHNIQUE. IN THIS RECIPE, IT'S GRILLED AND SERVED WITH A SWEET-AND-SPICY MELON SALSA.

¾ cup coarsely chopped cantaloupe

¼ cup chopped onion

2 tablespoons chopped fresh cilantro

4 teaspoons olive oil

1 tablespoon fresh lime juice

1 teaspoon minced seeded jalapeño chili

2 5- to 6-ounce fresh tuna steaks (about ½ inch thick)

2 SERVINGS

Prepare barbecue (medium-high heat). Mix cantaloupe, onion, cilantro, 2 teaspoons oil, lime juice and jalapeño chili in small bowl. Season salsa to taste with salt and pepper. Let stand 15 minutes.

Brush tuna steaks on both sides with remaining 2 teaspoons oil; sprinkle with salt and pepper. Grill tuna until just opaque in center, about 3 minutes per side. Transfer tuna to plates. Spoon salsa alongside.

Are there any tricks to grilling fish?

The key to excellent grilled seafood is to avoid overcooking—which means starting with a clean grill that is hot enough to cook the fish quickly. This will result in a nice, crispy exterior while sealing in the flavors. Uncooked large shrimp in the shell require only two minutes or so per side; thicker fish fillets like sea bass will take about three to four minutes per side.

Grilled trout with lemon-sage butter

ANOTHER SIMPLE PREPARATION FOR GRILLED FISH. THE TROUT USED IN THIS RECIPE ARE BRUSHED WITH A LEMON- AND SAGE-INFUSED BUTTER BEFORE GRILLING.

¾ cup (1½ sticks) butter

2½ tablespoons grated lemon peel

1½ tablespoons chopped fresh sage

12 trout fillets, butterflied
Fresh lemon wedges

12 SERVINGS

Melt butter in heavy small saucepan over medium-low heat. Remove from heat. Add lemon peel and sage. Season with salt and pepper.

Prepare barbecue (medium-high heat). Brush flesh and skin sides of fish with butter mixture. Sprinkle with salt and pepper. Close fish; secure with toothpicks. Grill until just opaque in center, about 4 minutes per side. Remove toothpicks. Serve, passing lemon wedges separately.

New Orleans-style shrimp

SIMMERING SHELLFISH IN A FLAVORFUL LIQUID UNTIL JUST COOKED IS A FAST AND EASY METHOD OF PREPARATION. THE SHRIMP FOR THIS RECIPE (PICTURED OPPOSITE) MAY BE PEELED OR LEFT IN THE SHELL FOR COOKING. LEAVING THE SHELLS ON DOES IMPART EXTRA FLAVOR, BUT MAKES THE DISH MESSIER TO EAT—SO PROVIDE PLENTY OF EXTRA NAPKINS.

3 tablespoons butter

2 garlic cloves, minced

1 teaspoon dried rosemary

¼ teaspoon cayenne pepper

¾ cup dry white wine

2 tablespoons Worcestershire sauce

¾ pound uncooked large shrimp; peeled, deveined, if desired

French bread

2 SERVINGS

Melt butter in heavy medium skillet over high heat. Add garlic, rosemary and cayenne; stir 30 seconds. Add wine and Worcestershire sauce; boil until liquid is reduced by half, about 5 minutes. Add shrimp to sauce. Simmer until shrimp are just opaque in center, about 3 minutes for peeled or 5 minutes for unpeeled. Serve with bread.

Broiled shrimp with spicy ginger-lime butter

BROILING SHRIMP IS AN EFFICIENT, ALL-WEATHER COOKING TECHNIQUE. THE SHRIMP CAN ALSO BE SKEWERED AND GRILLED, IF YOU LIKE.

5 tablespoons butter

2 tablespoons minced peeled fresh ginger

⅛ to ¼ teaspoon cayenne pepper

2 tablespoons fresh lime juice

2 teaspoons grated lime peel

1 pound uncooked large shrimp, peeled, deveined

½ cup chopped green onions

Lemon wedges

4 SERVINGS

Preheat broiler. Melt butter in heavy medium skillet over medium heat. Stir in ginger and cayenne. Remove from heat. Stir in lime juice and peel. Season ginger-lime butter to taste with salt and pepper.

Place shrimp in bowl. Add ginger-lime butter; toss to coat. Transfer shrimp to rimmed baking sheet. Broil until pink and just cooked through, about 2 minutes per side. Transfer shrimp to plate; drizzle with pan juices. Sprinkle with onions. Serve with lemon wedges.

Pan-seared scallops with mint and chives

SEARING PLUMP AND MEATY SCALLOPS IN A SKILLET OVER MEDIUM-HIGH HEAT SEALS IN THE JUICES WHILE MAKING THE OUTSIDES CRISP AND GOLDEN.

3 tablespoons butter

12 sea scallops, patted dry

⅓ cup bottled clam juice

1 tablespoon fresh lemon juice

1 tablespoon chopped fresh mint

1 tablespoon chopped fresh chives

2 SERVINGS

Melt butter in heavy medium skillet over medium-high heat. Sprinkle scallops with salt and pepper. Add scallops to skillet and sauté until golden and just opaque in center, about 3 minutes per side. Using tongs, transfer scallops to plates. Add clam juice, lemon juice, mint and chives to same skillet. Boil until sauce thickens enough to coat spoon, about 3 minutes. Pour sauce over scallops and serve.

Individual scallop gratins

SCALLOPS CAN ALSO BE BAKED, AS IN THIS RECIPE (PICTURED ON PAGE 105). THEY'RE SPOONED INTO INDIVIDUAL GRATIN DISHES AND TOPPED WITH SEASONED BREADCRUMBS BEFORE BAKING.

5 tablespoons chopped fresh parsley

3 tablespoons unsalted butter, room temperature

1 tablespoon chopped shallot

2 garlic cloves, minced

1½ teaspoons grated lemon peel

1½ tablespoons olive oil

1½ cups fresh breadcrumbs made from French bread

1½ pounds sea scallops, side muscles trimmed

4 SERVINGS

Mix 4 tablespoons chopped parsley, butter, shallot, garlic and lemon peel in medium bowl to blend. Season to taste with salt and pepper. *(Seasoned butter can be prepared 1 day ahead. Cover and refrigerate. Bring to room temperature before using.)*

Preheat oven to 400°F. Heat olive oil in heavy large skillet over medium heat. Add breadcrumbs and sauté until crisp and golden, about 6 minutes. Transfer to plate.

Rub some of seasoned butter on bottom and sides of four 1¼-cup ramekins or custard cups. Divide scallops among prepared dishes. Spread 1 teaspoon remaining seasoned butter atop scallops in each dish. Top with breadcrumbs, dividing equally. Dot breadcrumbs with remaining seasoned butter.

Place scallop gratins on large baking sheet. Bake until scallops are cooked through, about 25 minutes. Sprinkle with remaining 1 tablespoon chopped parsley and serve.

Basic crab cakes

THIS IS A DELICIOUS CLASSIC RECIPE FOR CRAB CAKES. TO KEEP THEM FROM FALLING APART WHEN FRIED, REFRIGERATE FOR AT LEAST AN HOUR BEFORE COOKING.

¾ cup plain dry breadcrumbs

1 pound fresh crabmeat, drained well, picked over

¼ cup mayonnaise

3 tablespoons chopped fresh chives

1 tablespoon Worcestershire sauce

1 tablespoon Dijon mustard

¼ teaspoon hot pepper sauce

1 large egg, beaten to blend

¼ cup vegetable oil

MAKES 20

Line baking sheet with waxed paper. Place ½ cup breadcrumbs in shallow dish. Mix crabmeat, mayonnaise, chives, Worcestershire sauce, mustard, hot pepper sauce and remaining ¼ cup breadcrumbs in medium bowl to blend. Season to taste with salt and pepper. Mix in egg. Using 2 tablespoonfuls for each, form crab mixture into twenty 1½-inch-diameter cakes. Coat crab cakes with breadcrumbs in dish, pressing to adhere. Transfer crab cakes to prepared baking sheet. Cover and refrigerate at least 1 hour and up to 6 hours.

Heat oil in heavy large skillet over medium heat. Working in batches, add crab cakes to skillet and cook until golden and heated through, about 2 minutes per side. Transfer crab cakes to paper-towel-lined plate to drain. Transfer to platter and serve.

Crab cakes and baby greens with lemon vinaigrette

TO ENHANCE THE SIMPLE PREPARATION ABOVE, THE CRAB CAKES ARE SERVED ALONGSIDE GREENS DRIZZLED WITH A LEMON VINAIGRETTE. FOR A MAIN COURSE, SERVE THREE TO FOUR CRAB CAKES PER PERSON ALONG WITH CRUSTY SOURDOUGH ROLLS.

½ cup olive oil

3 tablespoons fresh lemon juice

1 tablespoon minced shallot

1½ teaspoons Dijon mustard

½ teaspoon grated lemon peel

½ teaspoon sugar

Basic Crab Cakes (see recipe above)

12 cups mixed baby greens

Chopped fresh chives

10 FIRST-COURSE SERVINGS

Whisk first 6 ingredients in bowl to blend. Season vinaigrette to taste with salt and pepper. (Can be made 6 hours ahead. Chill. Bring to room temperature and rewhisk before using.)

Prepare crab cakes. Place mixed greens in large bowl. Toss with enough vinaigrette to coat. Divide greens among 10 plates. Place 2 crab cakes alongside greens on each plate. Drizzle 1 teaspoon vinaigrette over each crab cake. Sprinkle with chives and serve.

Basic boiled lobster

WHEN BOILING FRESH LOBSTERS, IT IS IMPORTANT NOT TO OVERCROWD THE POT. A TALL, NARROW POT THAT
HOLDS FOUR TO SIX GALLONS OF WATER IS IDEAL. BE SURE TO BRING THE WATER TO A ROLLING BOIL.

8 live lobsters
(1½ pounds each)

Lemon wedges

1½ cups (3 sticks) butter, melted

8 SERVINGS

Drop 2 lobsters headfirst into large pot of boiling water. Cover and cook until shells are bright red and centers are opaque, about 9 minutes. Using tongs, remove lobsters from pot. Repeat with remaining lobsters, boiling 2 at a time. Arrange lobsters, shell side down, on work surface. Place tip of large knife in center of 1 lobster. Cut lobster lengthwise in half from center to end of head (knife may not cut through shell), then cut lobster in half from center to end of tail. If necessary, use kitchen shears to cut through shell. Remove green tomalley (liver), if desired. Transfer 1 lobster to each of 8 plates. Garnish with lemon wedges. Serve with melted butter.

Roasted lobster with basil oil

BEFORE LOBSTERS ARE ROASTED, THEY MUST FIRST BE BRIEFLY BOILED. A SIMPLE, VIBRANTLY COLORED
BASIL OIL ADDS INTEREST TO THIS DISH.

1 cup fresh basil leaves

1½ cups olive oil

8 live lobsters
(1½ pounds each)

8 SERVINGS

Bring medium saucepan of water to boil. Add basil and boil 20 seconds. Drain. Transfer basil to processor and blend well. With machine running, add 1 cup oil through feed tube and blend until smooth. Season with salt and pepper. *(Basil oil can be prepared 1 day ahead. Cover and chill. Bring to room temperature before using.)*

Preheat oven to 400°F. Bring large pot of water to rolling boil. Add 2 lobsters headfirst; boil 2 minutes. Using tongs, remove from pot. Repeat with remaining lobsters, boiling 2 at a time. Arrange lobsters, shell side down, on work surface. Using heavy large knife, cut lobsters lengthwise in half. If necessary, use kitchen shears to cut through shells. Remove green tomalley (liver), if desired. Place lobsters cut side up on baking sheets. Brush with remaining ½ cup olive oil. Season with salt and pepper. Roast lobsters until cooked through, about 20 minutes. Brush some basil oil over. Serve, passing remaining basil oil separately.

Steamed clams with spicy sausage and tomatoes

STEAMING CLAMS IS AN ESPECIALLY GENTLE COOKING METHOD. FRESH CLAMS SHOULD CLOSE WHEN YOU HANDLE THEM. IF AN UNCOOKED CLAM DOES NOT CLOSE AFTER HANDLING, IT IS PROBABLY DEAD AND COULD BE CONTAMINATED. THE SAME IS TRUE FOR CLAMS THAT DO NOT OPEN DURING COOKING.

- 2 tablespoons olive oil
- 1 pound Italian hot sausages, casings removed
- ½ cup chopped shallots
- 4 garlic cloves, chopped
- ¼ teaspoon dried crushed red pepper
- 1 14½-ounce can diced tomatoes in juice
- 1 cup Basic Chicken Stock (see recipe on page 22) or canned low-salt chicken broth
- 2 tablespoons balsamic vinegar
- 4 pounds littleneck clams (about 3 dozen), scrubbed
- ½ cup chopped fresh basil
  French bread

6 FIRST-COURSE OR
4 MAIN-COURSE SERVINGS

Heat oil in heavy large pot over medium-high heat. Add sausages; sauté until almost cooked through, breaking up with fork, about 10 minutes. Add shallots, garlic and dried red pepper. Sauté until sausages are cooked through, about 5 minutes. Mix in tomatoes with juices, stock and vinegar. Add clams; cover and boil until clams open, about 8 minutes (discard any that do not open). Mix in basil. Serve in bowls with bread on the side.

Mussels in cream sauce

MUSSELS TAKE WELL TO A NUMBER OF COOKING METHODS. THEY MAY BE FRIED, SAUTÉED, BROILED OR SIMMERED, AS IN THIS SIMPLE RECIPE WITH CREAM AND WHITE WINE.

- 1 tablespoon butter
- 1 small leek (white and pale green parts only), halved, thinly sliced
- 2 pounds mussels, scrubbed, debearded
- 1 cup dry white wine
- ½ cup whipping cream
- 4 tablespoons chopped fresh parsley

2 SERVINGS

Melt butter in heavy large pot over medium heat. Add leek; sauté 3 minutes. Add mussels and wine. Cover and simmer until mussels open, about 4 minutes (discard any that do not open). Using slotted spoon, transfer mussels to 2 bowls.

Stir cream and 2 tablespoons parsley into liquid in pot. Simmer uncovered 3 minutes. Season sauce with salt and pepper. Pour sauce over mussels. Sprinkle with remaining 2 tablespoons parsley.

Shellfish cioppino

A HEARTY SEAFOOD STEW, CIOPPINO WAS CREATED IN SAN FRANCISCO IN THE MID 1800S. IT HAS SINCE BECOME A CLASSIC. A FOOD MILL IS RECOMMENDED TO HELP PRODUCE A THICK STEW BASE FROM THE SIMMERED VEGETABLES AND FISH. IF YOU DON'T HAVE ONE, USE A LARGE, HEAVY-DUTY MESH SIEVE TO STRAIN THE BROTH, PUSHING THROUGH ENOUGH FISH AND VEGETABLES TO MAKE 13 CUPS OF STEW BASE.

STEW BASE

- 2 1⅓- to 1½-pound live lobsters
- 2 pounds uncooked large shrimp with shells
- 1¼ cups olive oil
- 2 medium onions, chopped
- 1 cup chopped celery
- 1 cup chopped fresh fennel bulb
- 12 garlic cloves, peeled, flattened
- ¼ cup tomato paste
- 1 28-ounce can plus 2 cups diced tomatoes in juice
- 1 bunch fresh basil
- 4 large fresh thyme sprigs
- 4 large fresh parsley sprigs
- 2 large fresh oregano sprigs
- 2 bay leaves
- 1 teaspoon dried crushed red pepper
- 4 8-ounce bottles clam juice
- 2 cups dry white wine
- 2 pounds red snapper fillets

TO FINISH STEW

- 16 large sea scallops
- 1 pound large lump crabmeat (optional)
- ½ cup all purpose flour
- 6 tablespoons olive oil
- 3 tablespoons unsalted butter

Bring large pot of water to rolling boil. Add 1 lobster headfirst. Cover pot; cook lobster 5 minutes. Transfer lobster to large bowl of ice. Cook remaining lobster; cool. Working over rimmed baking sheet, twist tail and large claws off lobsters. Using lobster cracker or nutcracker, crack claws; remove meat in 1 piece. Remove tail meat from shell; slice each tail crosswise into 6 medallions. Place lobster meat in small bowl; cover and chill. Place lobster shells and juices in heavy resealable plastic bag; using mallet, smash shells into smaller pieces; reserve.

Peel and devein shrimp, leaving tails intact; reserve shells. Place shrimp in medium bowl; cover and chill.

Heat oil in large pot (at least 8-quart capacity) over medium-high heat. Add onions, celery, fennel and garlic; sauté 5 minutes. Mix in tomato paste and sauté 5 minutes. Add tomatoes with juices, herbs and dried red pepper; cook 5 minutes. Add clam juice, wine, snapper fillets, lobster shells and juices, and shrimp shells; bring to boil. Reduce heat and simmer stew uncovered 1 hour.

Working in batches, strain stew through large sieve into second large pot, reserving solids. Set food mill over second pot. Working with 2 cups reserved stew-base solids at a time, press through food mill to extract remaining broth and some fish and vegetables to make 13 cups stew base. Discard remaining solids.

Boil stew base until reduced to 10 cups, stirring occasionally, about 15 minutes. (Can be made 1 day ahead. Chill stew base uncovered until cold, then cover and keep chilled. Keep lobster and shrimp chilled.)

TO FINISH STEW: Bring stew base to simmer; keep warm. Combine scallops, crabmeat if desired, shrimp and lobster meat in large bowl. Add flour; toss gently to coat. Place seafood in sieve; shake off excess flour. Heat 3 tablespoons oil in heavy large skillet over medium-high

6 tablespoons chopped fresh parsley

2 large garlic cloves, minced

1 large shallot, minced

½ cup dry white wine

8 SERVINGS

heat. Add half of seafood. Sauté 1 minute. Add half of butter, then 2 tablespoons parsley, half of garlic and half of shallot. Sauté until scallops and shrimp are just opaque in center and all seafood is beginning to brown, about 4 minutes. Transfer to large bowl. Repeat with remaining oil, butter, seafood, 2 tablespoons parsley, garlic and shallot; transfer to same bowl. Add wine to skillet; boil until reduced to glaze, scraping up browned bits, 3 minutes. Mix glaze into seafood.

Ladle stew base into shallow bowls. Arrange seafood in center. Sprinkle with 2 tablespoons parsley.

MAKING CIOPPINO:

STEP 1: Break the tough lobster claws with a lobster cracker or heavy-duty nutcracker. Then gently pull out the claw meat in one piece.

STEP 2: Lobster shells and juices add flavor to the stew base. Collect them in a resealable plastic bag. Hammer the shells into small pieces with a kitchen mallet.

STEP 3: Peel the shrimp, leaving the tails intact and reserving the shells for the stew base. Then devein the shrimp by cutting a shallow slit down the back of each and pulling out the black "vein."

6

When it comes to comfort food, pasta and pizza can't be beat. Whether you're feeding a crowd or just the family, these are the dishes you know everyone will love. But as simple as they are, they still require knowing a few techniques.

We'll answer those questions that always seem to strike just as you start cooking: How much pasta is enough? Should oil be added to simmering pasta? What's the best substitute for fresh tomatoes in a sauce? Is there a quick way to make a pizza crust?

We'll also share recipes for a delicious lasagna; that spaghetti classic, *alla carbonara*; and homemade pepperoni pizza, among many others. The result? A new repertoire of comfort favorites.

Pasta & Pizza

Lamb and Zucchini Fusilli with Basil Butter (page 125)

Tomato sauce with Italian sausage

TRY THIS FLAVORFUL AND WONDERFULLY CHUNKY TOMATO SAUCE WITH SOME OF THE LARGER PASTA SHAPES, SUCH AS RIGATONI OR TAGLIATELLE. IT ALSO WORKS GREAT OVER FETTUCCINE—OR EVEN PLAIN OLD SPAGHETTI.

2 tablespoons olive oil

1 pound Italian hot sausages, casings removed

1 cup chopped onion

3 large garlic cloves, chopped

2 teaspoons dried oregano

¼ teaspoon dried crushed red pepper

1 28-ounce can crushed tomatoes with added puree

1 14½-ounce can diced tomatoes with green pepper and onion (do not drain)

MAKES ABOUT 5 CUPS

Heat oil in heavy large pot over medium-high heat. Add sausages, onion, garlic, oregano and dried red pepper; sauté until sausages are cooked through, breaking up with back of fork, about 10 minutes. Add crushed tomatoes and diced tomatoes with juices. Bring sauce to boil. Reduce heat to medium and simmer 5 minutes to blend flavors. Season with salt and pepper. (Can be prepared 1 day ahead. Chill until cold, then cover and keep chilled.)

Fettuccine with porcini mushroom sauce

HERE'S A DELICIOUS CREAM SAUCE TO TOSS WITH PASTA. DRIED PORCINI ADD AN INTENSE, EARTHY FLAVOR. MOST RECIPES INSTRUCT YOU TO RECONSTITUTE THE MUSHROOMS; THIS ONE, HOWEVER, HAS ENOUGH LIQUID THAT YOU MAY SIMPLY ADD THEM WITHOUT PRE-SOAKING.

¼ cup (½ stick) butter

4 large shallots, chopped

1 ounce dried porcini mushrooms, rinsed if sandy

2 cups Basic Chicken Stock (page 22) or canned low-salt chicken broth

1 cup whipping cream

12 ounces fettuccine

Grated Parmesan cheese

4 TO 6 SERVINGS

Melt butter in heavy large skillet over medium-high heat. Add shallots and sauté until beginning to brown, about 4 minutes. Add mushrooms and stir to coat. Add stock and cream; bring sauce to boil. Reduce heat to medium-low, cover and simmer until mushrooms are tender, about 20 minutes. Uncover and boil until sauce thickens slightly, stirring occasionally, about 5 minutes. Season sauce with salt and pepper.

Meanwhile, cook pasta in pot of boiling salted water until tender but still firm to bite, stirring occasionally. Drain, reserving ½ cup cooking liquid. Return pasta to pot. Add sauce; toss over medium-low heat until heated through, adding reserved liquid by tablespoonfuls if pasta is dry. Season with salt and pepper. Serve, passing cheese separately.

Farfalle with Gorgonzola sauce

THIS DISH IS THE ITALIAN EQUIVALENT OF MACARONI AND CHEESE, WITH A CREAMY BLUE CHEESE SAUCE. IT SERVES FOUR AS A FIRST COURSE BUT COULD SERVE TWO AS A (RICH) MAIN COURSE.

1¼ cups crumbled Gorgonzola cheese (about 5 ounces)

1 cup whipping cream

8 ounces farfalle (bow-tie) pasta

⅓ cup walnuts, toasted, chopped

3 tablespoons chopped fresh Italian parsley

4 SERVINGS

Combine 1 cup cheese and cream in heavy small saucepan. Cover and bring to boil over medium heat. Uncover; whisk until cheese melts and sauce is smooth, about 2 minutes. (Can be prepared 1 day ahead and refrigerated. Rewarm before tossing with pasta.)

Cook pasta in pot of boiling salted water until tender but still firm to bite. Drain pasta; return to pot. Add Gorgonzola sauce. Toss over medium heat until pasta is heated through and sauce coats pasta thickly, about 3 minutes. Season with salt and pepper. Transfer to serving bowl. Sprinkle with remaining ¼ cup cheese, walnuts and parsley.

Spaghetti alla carbonara

A CLASSIC DISH, *SPAGHETTI ALLA CARBONARA* IS A CROSS BETWEEN A CREAM-BASED PASTA SAUCE AND A CHEESE-BASED SAUCE, SINCE IT HAS BOTH (ALONG WITH EGGS AND BACON).

1¼ cups grated Parmesan cheese

3 large eggs

¾ cup whipping cream

12 ounces spaghetti or other thin-strand pasta

6 bacon slices, chopped

1 large onion, chopped

2 teaspoons minced garlic

¾ to 1 teaspoon dried crushed red pepper

¾ cup dry vermouth or white wine

4 SERVINGS

Whisk ¾ cup cheese, eggs and cream in medium bowl; set aside.

Cook pasta in large pot of boiling salted water until tender but still firm to bite, stirring occasionally. Drain pasta, reserving ½ cup cooking liquid. Return pasta to same pot.

Meanwhile, sauté bacon in heavy large skillet over medium heat until crisp. Add onion, garlic and dried red pepper. Sauté until onion is translucent, about 8 minutes. Add vermouth. Simmer until almost all vermouth has evaporated, about 8 minutes.

Add onion mixture and egg mixture to pasta. Toss over low heat until egg mixture thickens and coats pasta, adding reserved cooking liquid by tablespoonfuls if sauce is too thick, about 4 minutes (do not boil). Season with salt and pepper.

Transfer pasta to large bowl. Pass remaining Parmesan separately.

Linguine primavera

PRIMAVERA, ITALIAN FOR "SPRING," ALWAYS REFERS TO A DISH WITH FRESH VEGETABLES. IN THIS RECIPE, LINGUINE IS TOSSED WITH A MIX OF MUSHROOMS, ZUCCHINI AND BROCCOLI *RABE*.

1 **cup Basic Chicken Stock (see recipe on page 22) or canned low-salt chicken broth**

16 **sun-dried tomato halves (not packed in oil)**

1 **pound linguine**

5 **tablespoons olive oil**

8 **garlic cloves, minced**

8 **ounces shiitake mushrooms, stemmed, sliced**

1 **medium zucchini, chopped**

12 **broccoli rabe florets or 12 small broccoli florets**

½ **cup chopped fresh basil**

1 **cup freshly grated Parmesan cheese**

4 TO 6 SERVINGS

Bring chicken stock to simmer in small saucepan. Remove from heat. Add tomatoes; let stand until soft, about 20 minutes. Drain, reserving stock. Thinly slice tomatoes.

Cook linguine in large pot of boiling salted water until tender but still firm to bite, stirring occasionally.

Meanwhile, heat oil in heavy large skillet over medium-high heat. Add garlic; sauté until golden, about 1 minute. Add reserved stock, sun-dried tomatoes, mushrooms, zucchini, broccoli rabe and basil. Simmer until vegetables are tender, about 3 minutes.

Drain linguine; return to pot. Add vegetables and toss to combine. Season to taste with salt and pepper. Transfer pasta mixture to bowl; sprinkle with cheese and serve.

Equipment

These down-to-earth foods don't require much equipment. For pasta, choose a large pot and a big colander-drainer; a sharp cheese grater (box, rotary crank or rasp style); and a heavy, deep skillet for cooking sauces (allowing you to add the pasta to the sauce in the skillet before serving). For pizza? A pizza pan will do the trick.

Also useful: a food processor for pureeing sauces; a spaghetti rake for scooping up long strands of thin pasta; a garlic press for making quick work of garlic cloves that are used in a variety of pasta sauces; and a pizza or bread stone, which will conduct steady heat and absorb water from the dough, producing a crisp bottom crust.

Lamb and zucchini fusilli with basil butter

THIS PASTA (PICTURED ON PAGE 121) FEATURES A HEARTY MEAT-AND-VEGETABLE SAUCE. FOR A LIGHTER VARIATION, SUBSTITUTE GROUND TURKEY FOR THE LAMB.

¼ cup (½ stick) butter

½ cup chopped fresh basil

2 tablespoons olive oil

1 onion, chopped

3 large shallots, chopped

8 ounces ground lamb

1 pound zucchini, trimmed, grated (about 3½ cups)

½ cup dry white wine or 2 tablespoons fresh lemon juice

1 pound fusilli or other corkscrew pasta

¾ cup grated Parmesan cheese (about 2½ ounces)

6 SERVINGS

Melt butter in small saucepan over medium heat. Stir in basil.

Heat oil in heavy large skillet over medium heat. Add onion and shallots; sauté until soft, about 5 minutes. Add lamb; sauté until cooked through, stirring occasionally, about 8 minutes. Increase heat to medium-high. Add zucchini; sauté until soft, about 7 minutes. Add wine; reduce heat and simmer until reduced by half, about 5 minutes.

Meanwhile, cook pasta in large pot of boiling salted water until tender but still firm to bite, stirring occasionally. Drain. Return to pot. Add zucchini-lamb mixture and basil butter; toss to coat. Season with salt and pepper. Transfer pasta to large bowl. Sprinkle with Parmesan.

Pasta with pesto, green beans and potatoes

HERE'S AN EASY PESTO MADE FROM SCRATCH. USE IT IN THIS RECIPE WITH FETTUCCINE AND GREEN BEANS, OR TOSS IT WITH OTHER PASTAS LIKE LINGUINE, *ORECCHIETTE* OR EVEN PURCHASED GNOCCHI.

⅓ cup freshly grated Parmesan cheese

2 tablespoons pine nuts

2 garlic cloves

6½ ounces fresh basil, stemmed

¼ cup extra-virgin olive oil

3 medium red-skinned potatoes, peeled, cut crosswise into ¼-inch-thick slices

6 ounces thin green beans, trimmed

14 ounces fettuccine

1 tablespoon butter

4 TO 6 SERVINGS

Finely grind cheese, nuts and garlic in processor. Add basil and puree. Add oil in thin steady stream, processing until well blended. Season pesto with salt and pepper. *(Can be prepared 2 days ahead. Press plastic wrap onto surface and refrigerate.)*

Cook potatoes in large pot of boiling salted water until just tender, about 5 minutes. Using slotted spoon, transfer potatoes to large bowl. Add green beans to same pot and boil until tender, about 3 minutes. Using slotted spoon, transfer beans to bowl with potatoes. Cook pasta in same pot until tender but still firm to bite. Drain, reserving ⅓ cup liquid. Add pasta to potatoes and beans.

Whisk enough reserved liquid into pesto to moisten. Add pesto and butter to pasta. Toss to coat and serve.

Shrimp and leek linguine in white wine sauce

THIS DISH (PICTURED OPPOSITE) COMBINES SHRIMP, LEEKS, *PEPERONCINI* PEPPERS AND A TOUCH OF LEMON WITH LINGUINE. IT'S FINISHED WITH A WHITE WINE SAUCE.

1	pound small uncooked shrimp, peeled, deveined, shells reserved
1¾	cups water
6	tablespoons olive oil
2	large garlic cloves, minced
2½	cups thinly sliced leeks (white and pale green parts only; from about 2 large)
¼	cup thinly sliced stemmed drained peperoncini (about 4 whole)
3	tablespoons chopped fresh oregano
2	teaspoons minced lemon peel
¼	cup dry white wine
2	tablespoons fresh lemon juice
1	pound linguine
	Chopped fresh parsley

4 TO 6 SERVINGS

Place shrimp shells in medium saucepan. Add 1¾ cups water and generous pinch of salt. Bring to boil over medium-high heat. Cover, reduce heat to medium-low and simmer until reduced to 1 cup liquid, about 15 minutes. Strain into measuring cup, pressing on shells to extract as much liquid as possible.

Meanwhile, heat 3 tablespoons oil in heavy large skillet over medium-high heat. Add shrimp and sauté until opaque, about 2 minutes. Using slotted spoon, transfer to medium bowl. Reduce heat to low. Add remaining 3 tablespoons oil to same skillet. Add garlic and sauté until soft, about 1 minute. Stir in leeks, peperoncini, oregano and lemon peel. Cover and cook until leeks are soft, about 3 minutes. Uncover; add wine, lemon juice and shrimp-shell liquid. Increase heat to high and boil until reduced by half, about 2 minutes. Remove from heat.

Cook pasta in large pot of boiling salted water until tender but still firm to bite, stirring occasionally. Drain, reserving 1 cup cooking liquid. Add pasta and shrimp to skillet with sauce and toss to coat. Add enough reserved cooking liquid to moisten, if necessary. Season to taste with salt and pepper. Transfer to large bowl. Garnish with parsley.

Pasta shells filled with feta and herbs

HERE'S AN OLD-FASHIONED FAVORITE WITH A NEW-FASHIONED FILLING. BASIL AND CHIVES ACCENT THE RICOTTA (A CLASSIC INGREDIENT USED FOR FILLED PASTAS) AND FETA CHEESE FILLING.

SAUCE

¼ cup olive oil

1 onion, chopped

2 garlic cloves, minced

¼ teaspoon dried crushed red pepper

2 28-ounce cans Italian plum tomatoes, pureed in processor with juices

1 cup chopped fresh basil

FILLING

2 15-ounce containers ricotta cheese

3½ cups crumbled feta cheese

½ cup chopped fresh basil

2 bunches fresh chives, chopped

2 large eggs

1 12-ounce package jumbo pasta shells

Fresh basil sprigs

6 SERVINGS

FOR SAUCE: Heat oil in heavy large saucepan over medium heat. Add onion and sauté 5 minutes. Add garlic and sauté until onion is tender, about 5 minutes. Add dried red pepper and sauté 30 seconds. Add tomatoes. Simmer until sauce is reduced to 5 cups, stirring occasionally, about 1 hour. Season to taste with salt and pepper. Remove from heat and mix in basil. *(Can be prepared 1 day ahead. Cover and chill.)*

FOR FILLING: Combine ricotta, 1⅓ cups feta, ½ cup chopped basil and chives. Season to taste with salt and pepper. Mix in eggs.

Cook shells in large pot of boiling salted water until tender but still firm to bite. Drain. Rinse with cold water until cool. Drain thoroughly.

Preheat oven to 350°F. Spread ¾ cup sauce over bottom of each of two 13x9x2-inch glass baking dishes. Fill 30 shells and divide between dishes. Top with remaining sauce. Sprinkle with remaining feta. *(Can be prepared 1 day ahead. Cover and refrigerate.)* Bake shells until heated through, about 30 minutes. Garnish with basil sprigs.

Ricotta and spinach tortelloni in tomato sauce

A LARGER VERSION OF THE "LITTLE TWISTS" KNOWN AS TORTELLINI, *TORTELLONI* ARE MADE SIMPLE BY USING WONTON WRAPPERS. ONCE YOU'VE MASTERED THE EASY FOLDING TECHNIQUE, FILL THEM ANY WAY YOU LIKE.

5 tablespoons olive oil

1 cup chopped onion

12 garlic cloves, sliced

6 large tomatoes, chopped (about 5 cups)

1 cup chopped fresh basil

Heat 3 tablespoons oil in large skillet over medium-high heat. Add onion and half of garlic; sauté 5 minutes. Add tomatoes and ¾ cup basil. Cook 15 minutes to blend flavors, stirring often and adding water if dry. Season with salt and pepper. *(Can be made 1 day ahead. Chill.)*

Heat remaining 2 tablespoons oil in heavy large saucepan over medium heat. Add remaining garlic; sauté 1 minute. Add spinach;

1   10-ounce package spinach
    leaves, stems trimmed

1   cup ricotta cheese

½   cup freshly grated Parmesan
    cheese

    Ground nutmeg

24 square wonton wrappers

    4 SERVINGS

cook until almost all liquid evaporates, stirring often, about 5 minutes. Drain and cool spinach mixture. Squeeze out liquid. Place spinach mixture in processor. Add ricotta and blend well. Blend in ½ cup Parmesan. Season filling to taste with nutmeg, salt and pepper.

Place 1 wonton wrapper on work surface. Brush edges with water. Place 1 scant tablespoon filling on 1 half. Fold wrapper diagonally in half, forming triangle. Press edges to seal. Overlap 2 ends together; press to adhere. Repeat with remaining wrappers, water and filling. Place in single layer on floured baking sheet. (Can be prepared 4 hours ahead. Cover with plastic wrap and refrigerate.)

Working in batches, cook tortelloni in pot of boiling salted water until tender but still firm to bite, stirring occasionally, about 3 minutes. Using slotted spoon, transfer to 4 bowls.

Meanwhile, bring sauce to simmer. Spoon over tortelloni. Sprinkle with remaining ¼ cup basil and serve.

Ravioli with herbed walnut sauce

IT USED TO BE THAT MAKING RAVIOLI WAS A LABOR-INTENSIVE PROCESS INVOLVING A PASTA MACHINE AND HOMEMADE PASTA DOUGH. LUCKILY, THERE IS NOW A WIDE SELECTION OF FROZEN AND FRESH PURCHASED RAVIOLI VARIETIES AVAILABLE AT THE SUPERMARKET. THIS DELICIOUS RECIPE USES PREPARED RAVIOLI AND A QUICK SAUCE THAT TAKES ONLY TEN MINUTES TO MAKE. WHAT COULD BE SIMPLER?

1   pound purchased cheese
    ravioli

½   cup (½ stick) butter

¾   cup coarsely chopped walnuts

3   garlic cloves, minced

1   cup dry white wine

¼   cup chopped fresh parsley

1   tablespoon chopped fresh
    rosemary

    4 SERVINGS

Cook pasta in large pot of boiling salted water until tender but still firm to bite, or according to directions on package. Drain.

Melt butter in heavy large skillet over medium-high heat. Add walnuts; sauté until golden, about 2 minutes. Add garlic; sauté 30 seconds. Add wine. Simmer until slightly reduced, about 2 minutes. Add parsley and rosemary. Simmer 1 minute. Add ravioli and toss to coat with sauce. Season with salt and pepper; serve.

Macaroni and cheese with red peppers

OLD-FASHIONED COMFORT FOOD AT ITS BEST, THIS BAKED PASTA DISH GETS A LITTLE KICK FROM RED PEPPERS AND TWO CHEESES—PARMESAN AND BLUE CHEESE.

2 tablespoons (¼ stick) butter

2 large red bell peppers (about 1½ pounds), cut into ½-inch pieces

5 celery stalks, chopped

1½ cups whipping cream

1½ cups half and half

1 pound blue cheese, crumbled

1 teaspoon celery seeds

Cayenne pepper

3 large egg yolks

½ cup chopped celery leaves

1 pound penne

¾ cup freshly grated Parmesan cheese (about 2 ounces)

4 TO 6 SERVINGS

Melt butter in heavy large skillet over medium-high heat. Add bell peppers and celery and sauté until just beginning to soften, about 7 minutes. Remove from heat. Season with salt and pepper.

Combine cream, half and half and blue cheese in heavy medium saucepan. Stir over low heat until cheese melts. Remove from heat. Add celery seeds. Season sauce with cayenne, salt and pepper. Beat yolks in medium bowl to blend. Gradually whisk in half of cheese sauce. Return mixture to saucepan and whisk to blend. Add celery leaves.

Butter 13¾x10½x2¾-inch (4-quart-capacity) oval baking dish. Cook pasta in pot of boiling salted water until tender but still firm to bite, stirring occasionally. Drain. Return to same pot. Add sauce and vegetables; stir to blend. Transfer to baking dish. *(Can be made 1 day ahead. Cover; chill. Let stand at room temperature 1 hour before continuing.)*

Preheat oven to 400°F. Sprinkle Parmesan over surface of pasta. Bake until pasta is heated through, sauce is bubbling and top is beginning to brown, about 25 minutes.

Sausage, cheese and basil lasagna

LASAGNA DOESN'T HAVE TO BE A LABOR-INTENSIVE DISH. THE NO-BOIL NOODLES USED HERE ARE A GREAT TIME-SAVER. BE SURE TO LEAVE SPACE BETWEEN THE INDIVIDUAL NOODLES TO ALLOW FOR EXPANSION AS THEY COOK.

FILLING

1½ cups (packed) fresh basil leaves

1 15-ounce container plus 1 cup part-skim ricotta cheese

1½ cups (packed) grated mozzarella cheese (about 6 ounces)

¾ cup grated Parmesan cheese (about 2 ounces)

1 large egg

FOR FILLING: Using on/off turns, chop fresh basil leaves finely in processor. Add ricotta, mozzarella, Parmesan, egg, ½ teaspoon salt and ¼ teaspoon pepper. Using on/off turns, process until filling is just blended and texture is still chunky.

FOR ASSEMBLY: Preheat oven to 375°F. Spread 1¼ cups tomato-sausage sauce in 13x9x2-inch glass baking dish. Arrange 3 noodles atop sauce. Drop 1½ cups filling over noodles, then spread evenly to cover. Sprinkle with ¾ cup mozzarella cheese and ¼ cup Parmesan cheese. Repeat layering of sauce, noodles, filling and cheeses 2 more times. Top with

½ teaspoon salt

¼ teaspoon ground black pepper

ASSEMBLY

Tomato Sauce with Italian Sausage (see recipe on page 122)

12 no-boil lasagna noodles from one 8-ounce package

3 cups (packed) grated mozzarella cheese (about 12 ounces)

1 cup grated Parmesan cheese (about 3 ounces)

Nonstick olive oil spray

6 TO 8 SERVINGS

remaining 3 noodles. Spoon remaining sauce atop noodles. Sprinkle with remaining cheeses. *(Can be prepared up to 1 day ahead. Cover tightly with plastic wrap and refrigerate. Let stand at room temperature 1 hour before baking.)* Spray large piece of aluminum foil with nonstick spray. Cover lasagna with foil, sprayed side down.

Bake lasagna 40 minutes. Carefully uncover. Increase oven temperature to 400°F. Bake until noodles are tender, sauce is bubbling thickly and edges of lasagna are golden and puffed, about 20 minutes longer. Transfer to work surface; let stand 15 minutes before serving.

PREPARING SAUSAGE, CHEESE AND BASIL LASAGNA:

STEP 1: Combine the ingredients for the filling in the processor using on/off turns instead of continuous blending. That way, the texture will be chunky rather than smooth.

STEP 2: To layer the noodles properly, place three crosswise in a 13x9x2-inch baking dish, leaving space between them.

STEP 3: After sprinkling grated mozzarella and Parmesan over the filling, top with another layer of tomato-sausage sauce.

Sicilian sauce

THIS ROBUST SAUCE FLAVORED WITH FRESH MINCED GARLIC MAKES A GOOD ALL-PURPOSE PIZZA SAUCE. IT CAN BE PREPARED UP TO A MONTH AHEAD OF TIME AND FROZEN.

3 tablespoons olive oil

1 medium onion, finely chopped

2 teaspoons dried basil

1 teaspoon dried oregano

3 large garlic cloves, minced

2 tablespoons tomato paste

1 28-ounce can crushed tomatoes with added puree

MAKES ABOUT 2½ CUPS

Heat oil in heavy medium saucepan over medium heat. Add onion, basil and oregano. Cook until onion is slightly softened, stirring occasionally, about 6 minutes. Mix in garlic and cook 2 minutes. Add tomato paste; cook 3 minutes, stirring often. Add crushed tomatoes; simmer until sauce is very thick, about 45 minutes. Season with salt and pepper. *(Sauce can be made ahead. Cover and refrigerate up to 1 week or freeze up to 1 month. Bring to simmer before using.)*

Basic pizza crust

PURCHASED PIZZA SHELLS CAN BE LIFESAVERS DURING THE WEEK, BUT WHEN TIME PERMITS THERE'S NO COMPETING WITH A PIZZA MADE ENTIRELY FROM SCRATCH—INCLUDING THE CRUST.

¾ cup warm water (105°F to 115°F)

1 teaspoon honey

1 envelope dry yeast

2 cups bread flour

1½ teaspoons plus 1 tablespoon olive oil

¾ teaspoon salt

Cornmeal

MAKES TWO 9- TO 10-INCH CRUSTS

Place ¾ cup warm water and honey in processor. Sprinkle yeast over; let stand until mixture is foamy, about 5 minutes. Add flour, 1½ teaspoons oil and salt. Process until dough forms. Turn dough out onto lightly floured surface. Knead until smooth, about 5 minutes. Transfer dough to large oiled bowl; turn to coat. Cover with plastic wrap, then kitchen towel. Let rise in warm draft-free area until doubled in volume, about 1½ hours. Punch down dough. Divide into 2 balls.

Roll and stretch each dough ball on lightly floured surface to 9- to 10-inch circle. *(Can be prepared 2 weeks ahead. Wrap pizza crusts individually and freeze. Bring to room temperature before continuing.)* Dust 2 large baking sheets with cornmeal; place crusts on sheets. Brush edges of crusts with remaining 1 tablespoon oil.

Tomato, roasted pepper and pepperoni pizza

USE THE SAUCE AND CRUST RECIPES OPPOSITE TO MAKE THIS DELICIOUS PIZZA.

¾ cup Sicilian Sauce (see recipe opposite)

1 Basic Pizza Crust (see recipe opposite)

2 cups grated mozzarella cheese (about 7 ounces)

4 ounces pepperoni, sliced

1 7-ounce jar roasted red peppers, drained, cut into strips

1 cup Italian olives, halved, pitted

¼ cup grated Parmesan cheese

2 TO 4 SERVINGS

Position rack in bottom third of oven and preheat to 500°F. Spread sauce over pizza crust. Sprinkle with mozzarella. Top with pepperoni, peppers and olives. Sprinkle with Parmesan. Bake pizza until crust is golden brown, about 20 minutes, and serve.

Tips

WHEN USING fresh tomatoes for pasta or pizza sauce, select only ripe and flavorful ones. Otherwise, substitute canned crushed tomatoes or peeled plum tomatoes in tomato juice or puree. If you're short on time, use purchased marinara sauce and embellish it with your choice of any of the following: Kalamata olives, capers, dried red pepper, cooked sausage, sun-dried tomatoes, fresh basil, roasted red peppers, or grilled or sautéed vegetables.

HOW MUCH pasta is enough? The rule of thumb: one pound of pasta for four to six entrée servings (though parents of teenagers will tell you that two to four servings is a more realistic estimate) or six to eight first-course servings.

COOK pasta in plenty of rapidly boiling, generously salted water. Never add oil. Remove pasta from the water when it is tender but still firm, or al dente (which means "to the tooth" in Italian). Pasta will continue cooking once removed from the water. Drain and serve immediately. Never rinse—that decreases its ability to absorb flavor from the sauce.

10

Homemade bread is wonderful on so many different levels. It makes your house smell good, it tastes great, and last but certainly not least, it's so much fun to make. Setting aside a lazy week-end afternoon to bake yeast bread or whip up a batch of scones for a special breakfast treat is one of the most satis-fying kitchen tasks we know.

If the thought of working with yeast gives you pause, don't worry. We have plenty of recipes—for French bread, rolls, focaccia and breadsticks—that will show you how straightforward a process it is. And homey quick breads are even simpler to make, once you learn the tips here. Just gather your ingredients and begin the steps that will take you to truly wonderful bread.

Breads

Whole Wheat Bread with Crystallized Ginger (page 138)

Classic French bread

SHAPE THIS VERSATILE DOUGH ANY WAY YOU LIKE. THE RECIPE SHOWS YOU HOW TO FORM BAGUETTES, *FICELLES* (SMALLER TAPERED LOAVES) AND A COUNTRY FRENCH BREAD ROUND.

1 **cup warm water (105°F to 115°F)**

1 **envelope dry yeast**

1 **tablespoon sugar**

½ **teaspoon balsamic vinegar**

1¼ **teaspoons salt**

2 **cups bread flour**

¾ **cup (about) all purpose flour**

2 **tablespoons (about) vegetable oil**

¼ **cup (½ stick) unsalted butter**

Baking tiles*

4 **cups boiling water**

MAKES 2 BAGUETTES, 3 FICELLES OR 1 COUNTRY FRENCH LOAF

HAND METHOD: Measure 1 cup warm water into large bowl. Sprinkle yeast and sugar over; stir to dissolve. Let stand until foamy, about 5 minutes. Mix vinegar and 1 teaspoon salt into yeast mixture. Add 1½ cups bread flour and mix 4 minutes. Stir in remaining ½ cup bread flour. Knead on floured surface until smooth, elastic and slightly sticky dough forms, using dough scraper as aid and adding all purpose flour to dough as necessary to prevent sticking, about 10 minutes.

MIXER METHOD: Measure 1 cup warm water into bowl of heavy-duty electric mixer. Sprinkle yeast and sugar over; stir. Let stand until foamy, about 5 minutes. Mix vinegar and 1 teaspoon salt into yeast mixture. Add bread flour and mix 5 minutes, using paddle attachment. Replace paddle with dough hook. Add ½ cup all purpose flour and knead until soft and slightly sticky dough forms, adding more all purpose flour if dough is very sticky, about 7 minutes.

PROCESSOR METHOD: Measure 1 cup warm water into glass measuring cup. Sprinkle yeast and sugar over; stir. Let stand until foamy, about 5 minutes. Add vinegar to yeast mixture. Combine 1 teaspoon salt, bread flour and ½ cup all purpose flour in work bowl of processor fitted with Steel Knife. Add yeast mixture and process until sticky ball forms. If dough does not form ball, add more all purpose flour 1 tablespoon at a time, incorporating each addition before adding next. If dough is dry, add water 1 teaspoon at a time, incorporating each addition before adding next. Process until smooth, elastic and slightly sticky, about 45 seconds.

Oil hands; transfer dough to floured surface. Knead until elastic, using dough scraper as aid, 2 minutes.

FOR ALL LOAVES: Grease large bowl with 2 tablespoons oil. Add dough, turning to coat entire surface. Cover bowl with plastic wrap. Let dough rise in warm draft-free area until tripled in volume, about 1½ hours. (To test, press 2 fingers into dough; if fully risen, indentations will remain. If indentations fill in, cover with plastic and let dough rise longer.)

FOR BAGUETTES OR FICELLES: Grease double baguette pan or triple ficelle pan. Punch down dough and knead until smooth, about 2 minutes. Divide dough in half for baguettes or in thirds for ficelles. Roll 1 piece out on unfloured work surface to 14-inch-long rectangle, oiling rolling pin if dough sticks. Roll up dough jelly-roll fashion, starting at 1 long side. Roll ends between palms and work surface to taper slightly. Transfer to prepared pan, seam side down. Repeat rolling and shaping with remaining dough.

FOR COUNTRY FRENCH LOAF: Grease baking sheet. Punch down dough. Form into round ball, smoothing top. Place on large baking sheet, flattening slightly.

FOR ALL LOAVES: Melt butter with remaining ¼ teaspoon salt. Brush over loaves. Let loaves rise in warm draft-free area 45 minutes. Brush with glaze again. Let rise until tripled in volume, about 35 minutes longer.

Position 1 rack in bottom third and 1 rack in center of oven. Place baking pan on bottom rack. Place baking tiles on center rack.

FOR BAGUETTES OR FICELLES: Preheat oven to 450°F. Brush loaves with glaze again. Using sharp knife, slash each with 3 long diagonal cuts about ⅓ inch deep. Pour 4 cups boiling water into baking pan in oven (water will steam). Close oven 2 minutes. Place bread in pans on tiles and bake until loaves are golden brown and crisp dry crust forms, about 20 minutes. Cool loaves on rack.

FOR COUNTRY FRENCH LOAF: Preheat oven to 400°F. Brush loaf with glaze again. Slash dough in ticktacktoe pattern or with swirled slashes radiating from center. Pour 4 cups boiling water into baking pan in oven (water will steam). Close oven 2 minutes. Bake bread on baking sheet on tiles until loaf is golden brown and sounds hollow when tapped on bottom, about 35 minutes. Cool on rack.

*Available at cookware stores. Unglazed quarry tiles, available at tile stores and some building supply stores, can also be used. Number of tiles needed will depend on oven size. If tiles are unavailable, heat baking sheet in oven 5 minutes.

Can quick-rising yeast be substituted for active dry yeast to speed things up?

Also called fast-rising yeast, quick-rising yeast rises 50 percent faster than active dry yeast, making it a handy time-saver. Such a rapid rising time, though, does not always allow for the full flavor and texture to develop, so it won't work well in every case. If you are making a recipe that does not specifically call for quick-rising yeast, use about a quarter less than the stated quantity of active dry yeast.

Whole wheat bread with crystallized ginger

BULGUR AND CRYSTALLIZED GINGER LEND APPEALING TEXTURE AND SWEETNESS TO THIS RECIPE FOR WHOLE WHEAT BREAD (PICTURED ON PAGE 135). WHEN KNEADING THE DOUGH, MAKE SURE THE WORK SURFACE IS EVENLY FLOURED, ADDING MORE FLOUR AS IT GETS KNEADED INTO THE DOUGH.

1½ **cups warm buttermilk (105°F to 115°F)**

¼ **cup (½ stick) unsalted butter, melted, cooled**

3 **tablespoons sugar**

1 **envelope dry yeast**

¾ **cup whole wheat flour**

1½ **teaspoons salt**

3 **cups (or more) unbleached all purpose flour**

¼ **cup chopped crystallized ginger**

3 **tablespoons bulgur***

MAKES 1 LOAF

Combine buttermilk, butter and sugar in large bowl. Sprinkle yeast over. Let stand until yeast dissolves, about 8 minutes. Mix in whole wheat flour and salt, then 2½ cups all purpose flour, ½ cup at a time. Stir until soft dough forms. Continue adding all purpose flour ¼ cup at a time if dough is very sticky. Mix in crystallized ginger and bulgur. Lightly flour work surface with ½ cup all purpose flour. Turn dough out onto work surface; knead until smooth and elastic, about 8 minutes.

Butter large bowl; add dough and turn to coat with butter. Cover bowl with plastic wrap. Let dough rise in warm draft-free area until almost doubled in volume, about 1½ hours.

Butter 9x5x3-inch loaf pan. Punch down dough; turn out onto work surface. Roll dough into cylinder; press into prepared pan. Cover with damp towel. Let rise in warm draft-free area until almost doubled in volume, about 40 minutes.

Preheat oven to 375°F. Bake bread until golden, about 35 minutes. Cool 10 minutes on rack. Remove from pan; cool completely.

*Also called cracked wheat; available at natural foods stores and supermarkets.

Equipment

A standing mixer with a dough hook is not a requirement—it will just make your life easier. If you're shopping for one, make sure the mixer has at least a 4½-quart capacity, a dough hook, a whisk and paddle, and a motor of 325 to 650 watts. These mixers are pricey, but for serious cooks the cost is worth it.

Also useful: a food processor for mixing dough and chopping flavorings; an instant-read thermometer—either digital or analog—to test water temperature for proofing yeast; a large cutting board for kneading; a large bowl with enough room for dough to rise; a serrated bread knife; various sizes of bread pans; a pizza or bread stone; and, of course, a rolling pin.

Butterhorn rolls

THESE FLAKY, CRESCENT-SHAPED ROLLS GET THEIR START WITH YEAST. THE BUTTER IN THE RECIPE MAKES THEM EXTRA-TENDER. THEY TAKE SOME TIME TO MAKE, BUT THE RESULTS ARE WORTH IT. AND THEY CAN BE PREPARED AND FROZEN UP TO TWO WEEKS AHEAD. SIMPLY REWARM THE ROLLS IN A 350°F OVEN FOR 15 MINUTES.

1 cup whole milk

¾ cup (1½ sticks) unsalted butter, cut into pieces

½ cup warm water (105°F to 115°F)

½ teaspoon plus ½ cup sugar

1 envelope plus ½ teaspoon dry yeast

3 large eggs, room temperature

5¼ cups (about) all purpose flour

1 tablespoon salt

½ cup (1 stick) butter, melted

MAKES 36

Stir milk and ¾ cup butter in heavy medium saucepan over low heat until butter melts. Cool to 120°F if necessary. Combine water and ½ teaspoon sugar in small bowl. Sprinkle yeast over; stir to blend. Let stand until foamy, about 5 minutes.

In large bowl of heavy-duty mixer fitted with whisk attachment, beat eggs and remaining ½ cup sugar at low speed until blended. Beat in milk mixture. Gradually add 2½ cups flour, beating until smooth. Replace whisk with dough hook. Add yeast mixture, salt and 2 cups flour; beat 8 minutes. Beat in enough flour by spoonfuls to form sticky dough that just begins to pull away from sides of bowl.

Pour 1 tablespoon melted butter into large bowl. Scrape in dough; let stand 5 minutes. Using spatula, turn dough over, coating with butter. Cover bowl with plastic wrap, then kitchen towel. Let rise in warm draft-free area until doubled, about 1½ hours.

Punch down dough. Cover with plastic and towel and let rise again in warm area until doubled, about 1 hour. Punch down dough.

Divide dough into 3 equal portions. Roll out 1 portion on floured surface to 12-inch round. Brush with some of melted butter. Cut into 12 triangles. Starting at wide end, roll up triangles toward point. Repeat rolling, cutting and shaping with remaining 2 dough portions and melted butter. Arrange rolls point side down on 2 ungreased heavy large baking sheets, spacing evenly. Cover rolls with clean kitchen towels; let rolls rise until almost doubled, about 45 minutes.

Position 1 rack in bottom third and 1 rack in top third of oven and preheat to 375°F. Brush rolls with melted butter. Bake 15 minutes. Switch top and bottom baking sheets and bake until rolls are golden, about 10 minutes longer. Cool rolls on racks. (Can be made ahead. Cool completely. Wrap in foil; store at room temperature 1 day or freeze up to 2 weeks. Rewarm wrapped rolls in 350°F oven about 15 minutes.)

Fennel seed focaccia with olives

THIS RUSTIC ITALIAN BREAD USES A YEAST STARTER, WHICH ENRICHES ITS FLAVOR AND TEXTURE. BE SURE TO PREPARE THE STARTER ONE DAY AHEAD. HUMIDITY MAKES THE CRUST CRISPER, SO THE RECIPE CALLS FOR SPRITZING THE OVEN WITH WATER; JUST USE A STANDARD SPRAY BOTTLE AND TAP WATER.

STARTER

1¼ cups unbleached all purpose flour

¼ teaspoon dry yeast

¾ cup lukewarm water (95°F to 100°F)

DOUGH

¼ cup warm water (105°F to 115°F)

½ teaspoon dry yeast

1 cup plus 2 tablespoons cool water (85°F to 90°F)

2 tablespoons olive oil

5 teaspoons coarse salt

1½ tablespoons whole milk

2 teaspoons fennel seeds, crushed

3⅔ cups (about) bread flour

1 cup pitted Kalamata olives; ⅔ cup chopped, ⅓ cup quartered

MAKES 1 LOAF

FOR STARTER: Mix flour and yeast in 8- to 10-cup bowl. Stir in ¾ cup water; beat until smooth dough forms, about 3 minutes. Scrape down sides of bowl. Cover with plastic; let stand 30 minutes. Chill overnight. Let stand at room temperature 30 minutes before continuing.

FOR DOUGH: Stir ¼ cup warm water and yeast in large bowl. Let stand 5 minutes. Add starter and 1 cup plus 2 tablespoons cool water. Using wooden spoon, mix 1 minute (mixture will look milky and foamy). Mix in 1½ tablespoons oil, 4 teaspoons salt, milk and fennel. Add 3⅓ cups bread flour, 1 cup at a time, mixing until very soft sticky dough forms.

Knead dough gently on floured surface until dough comes together but is still sticky, sprinkling with more flour and loosening dough with pastry scraper to prevent sticking, about 5 minutes. Return to same bowl. Cover with plastic; let rest until firmer and less sticky, about 20 minutes.

Knead dough gently on floured surface until supple and elastic, sprinkling with flour to prevent sticking, about 5 minutes. Push dough out to 12-inch square. Sprinkle with ⅔ cup chopped olives; fold dough over olives. Knead gently to distribute olives; shape into ball.

Oil large bowl with remaining ½ tablespoon oil. Add dough; turn to coat. Cover with plastic wrap. Let dough rise until almost doubled in volume, about 1 hour. Uncover; fold dough edges in toward center. Turn dough over, releasing some air but deflating as little as possible. Cover; let rise until almost doubled, about 1 hour.

Position rack in bottom third of oven; preheat to 425°F. Oil 17x11-inch baking sheet and line with parchment paper. Turn dough out onto sheet. Without deflating dough, gently stretch and push dough to cover sheet. If dough springs back, let rest 5 minutes, then stretch again. Repeat resting and stretching until dough stays in place. Press ⅓ cup quartered olives over surface. Indent dough with fingertips in several places. Let rise until puffy, about 20 minutes.

Sprinkle dough with remaining 1 teaspoon salt. Place sheet in oven. Spray oven with water 8 times. Close door 1 minute. Open and spray several times more. Close door; bake focaccia 15 minutes. Reduce oven temperature to 350°F. Bake focaccia until golden and crusty, about 12 minutes longer. Cool focaccia on rack 30 minutes.

MAKING FOCACCIA:

STEP 1: To make the dough, first blend the starter—a loose mixture of flour, yeast and water—with more water and yeast, creating a mixture that has a milky, foamy consistency.

STEP 2: Once bread flour is added to the dough, it will be firmer but still very soft. To keep the dough from sticking to the work surface while kneading, use a pastry scraper and sprinkle the dough with flour as needed.

STEP 3: Press parchment paper onto a large (17x11-inch) oiled baking sheet, then carefully pull and push the dough on the parchment to make a thin rectangle that covers the entire sheet.

Tips

STORE all purpose flour in an airtight container in a dry place for up to six months. Since whole wheat flour can go rancid, store it in an airtight container in the freezer for several months.

TO FIND out if fresh bread is properly baked, thump it and listen for a hollow sound. Or insert an instant-read thermometer into the center; it will register 195°F to 210°F when the bread is done.

HOMEMADE bread should be stored at room temperature in a paper bag. If you store your bread in plastic bags, the crust may become spongy and will develop mold quickly. But if you plan to freeze bread (most breads can be frozen from a couple of weeks to a couple of months), wrap it in a plastic bag before freezing.

TRY ADDING chopped fresh herbs such as chives to biscuits for added flavor. Cooked chopped bacon can be mixed in, too.

IF YOUR bread becomes stale, try using it to make French toast, breadcrumbs, croutons or *panzanella* (bread and tomato salad).

WHEN MAKING quick breads, like banana bread, experiment with add-ins: walnuts or almonds, chopped dried fruit like dates or apricots, or even chocolate chips.

Hazelnut breadsticks

BEGIN PREPARING THESE BREADSTICKS (PICTURED OPPOSITE) ONE DAY AHEAD, SINCE THE SOURDOUGH STARTER (YEAST AND FLOUR DISSOLVED IN WARM LIQUID) NEEDS TO PROOF OVERNIGHT.

½ cup plus 1 tablespoon warm water (105°F to 115°F)

2½ cups (or more) unbleached all purpose flour

1½ teaspoons dry yeast

¼ cup olive oil

¼ cup fresh sage leaves

½ cup hazelnuts, toasted, ground

¼ cup warm whole milk (105°F to 115°F)

1 teaspoon salt

MAKES 21

Mix ½ cup warm water, ½ cup flour and 1 teaspoon yeast in large bowl to blend. Cover; let starter stand at room temperature overnight.

Heat oil in heavy small saucepan over medium-low heat. Add sage and sauté until crisp, about 7 minutes. Cool.

Combine remaining 1 tablespoon warm water and ½ teaspoon yeast in small bowl; stir to blend. Let stand 10 minutes to dissolve yeast. Transfer yeast mixture to processor.

Add remaining 2 cups flour, hazelnuts, milk and salt to yeast mixture in processor. Using on/off turns, process until small moist clumps form. Add sage-oil mixture and starter. Process just until large moist clumps form. Transfer dough to clean work surface. Gather dough into ball. Knead dough until smooth and elastic, adding more flour if sticky, about 4 minutes. Form into ball.

Lightly oil another large bowl. Add dough; turn to coat. Cover bowl with plastic wrap, then towel. Let dough rise in warm draft-free area until doubled in volume, about 1 hour. Punch down dough. Cover and let dough rest 15 minutes.

Preheat oven to 400°F. Lightly oil 3 large baking sheets. Turn dough out onto floured work surface and knead briefly until smooth. Divide dough into thirds. Divide first third of dough into 7 equal pieces. Roll 1 dough piece between palms and work surface into 13-inch-long rope. Transfer rope to baking sheet. Repeat with remaining 6 dough pieces, spacing ropes evenly apart. If desired, shape 1 end of each rope decoratively. Let rise 10 minutes. Bake breadsticks until golden and very crisp, about 20 minutes. Transfer to racks to cool.

Meanwhile, shape second third of dough into 7 breadsticks and let rise 10 minutes. Bake as above. Repeat with final third of dough. (Breadsticks can be prepared ahead. Wrap tightly and store at room temperature 1 day or freeze up to 2 weeks.)

Cheddar and Stilton drop biscuits

THESE BISCUITS, WHICH REQUIRE NO KNEADING, ROLLING OR CUTTING, HAVE A CRISP CRUST AND A TENDER TEXTURE. ENGLISH STILTON AND SHARP CHEDDAR ADD FLAVOR.

2½ cups unbleached flour

2 tablespoons sugar

1 tablespoon baking powder

¾ teaspoon cream of tartar

½ teaspoon salt

7 tablespoons chilled unsalted butter, cut into ½-inch cubes

1 cup (packed) coarsely grated sharp cheddar cheese, chilled

½ cup crumbled Stilton cheese (about 2 ounces), chilled

1¼ cups chilled buttermilk

1 large egg

MAKES 12

Position 1 rack in bottom third and 1 rack in top third of oven and preheat to 400°F. Butter and flour 2 large baking sheets. Whisk first 5 ingredients in large bowl to blend well. Add butter and rub in with fingertips until mixture resembles coarse meal. Add both cheeses; rub in with fingertips until cheeses are reduced to small pieces. Whisk buttermilk and egg in small bowl. Add to flour mixture, stirring just until dough is evenly moistened.

Using ⅓ cup dough for each biscuit, drop 6 mounds onto each prepared sheet, spacing 2 to 3 inches apart. Bake biscuits 10 minutes. Reverse positions of sheets. Bake until biscuits are golden brown and tester inserted into center comes out clean, about 10 minutes longer.

What are the differences among the various kinds of flour?

For many breads, **all purpose flour**—a blend of low-gluten (protein) cake flour and high-gluten bread flour—is the flour of choice. But other flours are also used when making yeast and quick breads. Among them: **bread flour,** an enriched high-gluten blend, more commonly used by professional bakers; **self-rising flour**, all purpose flour to which baking powder and salt have been added; **whole wheat flour**, unrefined, unbleached flour containing the iron- and vitamin B-rich wheat bran and germ; **rye flour**, often used along with a higher-protein flour, since rye has less gluten than all purpose or whole wheat flour, and does not produce a well-risen loaf on its own; and **cracked wheat** or **bran flours**, all purpose flours to which cracked wheat or bran has been added. While unbleached and bleached flours are processed differently, the two can be used interchangeably, although many professional bakers insist that foods made with unbleached flour rise higher and have a better texture than those made with bleached flour.

Banana-nut bread

CALLED A QUICK BREAD BECAUSE IT DOESN'T USE YEAST, AND THEREFORE REQUIRES NEITHER RISING NOR KNEADING, THIS BREAD IS EASY TO MAKE. IT'S ALSO A GREAT USE OF OVERRIPE BANANAS. SIMPLY PEEL THEM AND FREEZE IN A RESEALABLE PLASTIC BAG UNTIL YOU'RE READY TO MAKE THIS BREAD.

1¾ cups all purpose flour

2 teaspoons baking powder

¾ teaspoon salt

¼ teaspoon baking soda

1 cup mashed ripe bananas

½ cup whole milk

1 teaspoon vanilla extract

½ cup solid vegetable shortening

1 cup sugar

2 large eggs

1 cup pecans, toasted, chopped

MAKES 1 LOAF

Preheat oven to 350°F. Butter and flour 9¼x5x2½-inch loaf pan. Whisk together flour, baking powder, salt and baking soda in medium bowl. In small bowl, mix mashed bananas, milk and vanilla. Using electric mixer, beat shortening in large bowl until creamy. Gradually beat in sugar. Add eggs 1 at a time, beating well after each addition. Beat banana mixture and flour mixture alternately into shortening mixture in 2 additions each. Stir in pecans. Transfer to prepared pan.

Bake bread until tester inserted into center comes out clean, about 1 hour 10 minutes. Cool 5 minutes. Turn out onto rack and cool completely. *(Can be prepared 2 days ahead. Wrap tightly in aluminum foil and let stand at room temperature.)*

Chocolate chip scones

SCONES ARE A KIND OF QUICK BREAD. THESE CONTAIN CHOCOLATE CHIPS INSTEAD OF THE MORE EXPECTED RAISINS. BAKE THEM ON THE TOP RACK OF THE OVEN TO AVOID BURNING THE BOTTOMS.

2 cups unbleached all purpose flour

⅓ cup plus 2 tablespoons sugar

1 teaspoon baking powder

½ teaspoon baking soda

½ teaspoon salt

6 tablespoons (¾ stick) chilled unsalted butter, diced

1 teaspoon (packed) grated lemon peel

¾ cup miniature semisweet chocolate chips

¾ cup chilled buttermilk

1 large egg yolk

1 teaspoon vanilla extract

Milk (for glaze)

MAKES 6

Butter and flour baking sheet. Sift flour, ⅓ cup sugar, baking powder, baking soda and salt into large bowl. Add butter and lemon peel; rub in with fingertips until butter is reduced to size of rice grains. Mix in chocolate chips. Whisk buttermilk, egg yolk and vanilla in small bowl to blend. Add buttermilk mixture to flour-butter mixture; mix until dough comes together in moist clumps. Gather dough into ball. Press dough out on lightly floured surface to 8-inch round; cut round into 6 wedges. Transfer wedges to prepared baking sheet, spacing 1 inch apart. *(Can be prepared 1 day ahead. Cover and refrigerate.)*

Preheat oven to 400°F. Brush scones lightly with milk; sprinkle with 2 tablespoons sugar. Bake until scones are crusty and tester inserted into center comes out clean, about 20 minutes. Serve warm.

11

Where there is celebration, there is cake. And whether it's a birthday, a baby shower or a "just-because" party, every celebration deserves a cake made from scratch. Trust us, it's easier and quicker to whip up a cake than you think.

Not convinced? Just take it one step at a time, starting with the simple techniques outlined here. We begin with accurate measuring and foolproof mixing, before moving on to tips for making the lightest whipped cream and the prettiest chocolate curls. We'll progress one layer at a time through flourless chocolate cakes, layer cakes and angel food, all the way to cheesecakes.

And before long, you'll be baking from scratch as confidently as you used to mix from a box.

Cakes

Vanilla Angel Food Cake with Mango-Ginger Sauce (page 152)

Powdered sugar pound cake

POUND CAKE WAS ORIGINALLY MADE WITH ONE POUND EACH OF FLOUR, BUTTER, SUGAR AND EGGS. THIS VARIATION HAS BEEN UPDATED WITH DIFFERENT PROPORTIONS. IT ALSO USES POWDERED SUGAR INSTEAD OF GRANULATED. THE TRICK TO THE CAKE'S TEXTURE IS TO BEAT THE BUTTER UNTIL IT'S SOFT AND FLUFFY.

1½ **cups (3 sticks) unsalted butter, room temperature**

1 **1-pound box powdered sugar**

1½ **teaspoons grated lemon peel**

1 **teaspoon vanilla extract**

½ **teaspoon salt**

6 **large eggs**

2⅓ **cups all purpose flour**

12 TO 16 SERVINGS

Preheat oven to 325°F. Butter and flour 12-cup angel food cake pan with removable bottom. Using electric mixer, beat butter in large bowl until fluffy. Gradually beat in sugar, then lemon peel, vanilla extract and salt. Beat in eggs 1 at a time. Add flour in 3 additions, beating just until blended each time. Transfer batter to prepared pan.

Bake cake until tester inserted near center comes out clean, about 1 hour 10 minutes. Cut around center tube and pan sides to loosen cake. Remove pan sides. Cool cake completely.

Equipment

Baking a cake is one of the great kitchen pleasures—and one that requires surprisingly little equipment. Start with the appropriate measuring cups: metal or plastic for dry ingredients (so that flour, for example, can be leveled off), clear glass for liquid (so that the fluid level is visible). And pans: Many cake recipes call for pans with an eight- or nine-inch diameter and sides that are 1½ to 2 inches high. The pans can be made of aluminum or aluminized steel, but if you are using nonstick, turn your oven down 25 degrees and check for doneness about five minutes earlier than the recipe recommends. For cheesecakes, you may need a springform pan; select one with a leakproof base, or buy the inexpensive version, wrap it in foil and set it on a baking sheet. Even decorating can be done simply—beginners may start with an inexpensive decorating kit, which has a small pastry bag, a few decorating tips and a coupler.

Also useful: a handheld mixer, a heavy-duty standing mixer, large bowls, a flour sifter, offset spatulas for frosting and rubber spatulas in various sizes. Some equipment never goes out of style.

Flourless chocolate cake with raspberry sauce

INSTEAD OF FLOUR, EGGS PROVIDE THE VOLUME HERE. ESPRESSO ADDED TO THE BATTER OF THIS DENSE, FUDGY CAKE GIVES IT EXTRA DEPTH OF FLAVOR. FOR EASIER SLICING, CHILL OVERNIGHT BEFORE SERVING.

SAUCE

3 10-ounce packages frozen raspberries in syrup, thawed

CAKE

12 ounces semisweet chocolate, coarsely chopped

4 ounces unsweetened chocolate, chopped

1 pound (4 sticks) unsalted butter, diced

1 cup freshly brewed espresso or 1 tablespoon instant espresso powder dissolved in 1 cup water

1 cup (packed) golden brown sugar

8 large eggs, beaten to blend

Fresh raspberries

20 SERVINGS

FOR SAUCE: Working in batches, puree raspberries and syrup in processor. Strain puree into medium bowl. Cover and chill. *(Sauce can be prepared 2 days ahead.)*

FOR CAKE: Preheat oven to 350°F. Line bottom of 9-inch-diameter cake pan with 2-inch-high sides (not a springform pan) with parchment. Place all chocolate in large bowl. Bring butter, espresso and brown sugar to boil in medium saucepan, stirring to dissolve sugar. Add to chocolate; whisk until smooth. Cool slightly. Whisk in beaten eggs.

Pour batter into prepared pan. Place cake pan in roasting pan. Pour enough hot water into roasting pan to come halfway up sides of cake pan. Bake until center of cake is set and tester inserted into center comes out with a few moist crumbs attached, about 1 hour. Remove pan from water. Chill cake overnight.

Cut around pan sides to loosen cake. Using oven mitts as aid, hold pan bottom over low heat 15 seconds, warming slightly. Place platter over pan. Hold pan and platter together tightly and invert. Lift off cake pan; peel off parchment. Serve with sauce and fresh berries.

Espresso whipped cream

AS AN ALTERNATIVE TO THE RASPBERRY SAUCE INCLUDED IN THE RECIPE ABOVE, SERVE SLICES OF THE FLOURLESS CHOCOLATE CAKE TOPPED WITH THIS ESPRESSO-FLAVORED WHIPPED CREAM.

1 cup chilled whipping cream

3 tablespoons golden brown sugar

1 teaspoon vanilla extract

1 teaspoon instant espresso powder

MAKES ABOUT 2 CUPS

Beat all ingredients in medium bowl to soft peaks. *(Can be made 4 hours ahead; cover and chill.)*

Basic white cake

HERE'S AN EASY, ALL-PURPOSE BUTTER CAKE. IT CAN BE BAKED IN A SHEET PAN OR AS A LAYER CAKE, AS IN THE FOUR-LAYER CAKE WITH LEMON CURD (OPPOSITE). A SIMPLE WHIPPED CREAM FROSTING IS ADDED.

3¼ cups cake flour

1½ teaspoons cream of tartar

¾ teaspoon baking soda

¼ teaspoon salt

2 cups plus 3 tablespoons sugar

1 cup (2 sticks) unsalted butter, room temperature

8 large egg whites, whisked until blended but not foamy

4 teaspoons vanilla extract

1 cup whole milk

1¾ cups chilled whipping cream

12 SERVINGS

Position rack in center of oven and preheat to 375°F. Butter and flour 13x9x2-inch metal baking pan. Sift first 4 ingredients into medium bowl. Using electric mixer, beat 2 cups sugar and butter in large bowl until fluffy. Add egg whites in 4 additions, beating well after each. Beat in 2 teaspoons vanilla. Beat in dry ingredients alternately with milk, beginning and ending with dry ingredients.

Pour batter into prepared pan. Bake until cake is golden and tester inserted into center comes out clean, about 30 minutes. Transfer pan to rack and cool completely. (*Cake can be prepared 1 day ahead. Wrap cake in aluminum foil and store at room temperature.*)

Beat whipping cream, remaining 3 tablespoons sugar and 2 teaspoons vanilla in large bowl to stiff peaks. (*Can be prepared 4 hours ahead. Cover and refrigerate.*) Spread frosting over cake. Refrigerate at least 2 hours and up to 8 hours.

Is it possible to cut a cake recipe in half?

The short answer is: Don't try it. Technically, you should be able to halve a cake recipe that is "balanced"—in which the weights of the components (flour, milk, fat and so forth) are in standard ratio. However, cake baking is an exact science; so many factors come into play that altering a recipe is tricky at best. For example, a large cake needs a smaller proportion of leavening and a larger amount of liquid than a small cake. Even using different sizes of cake pans with the same ratio of ingredients can produce different results.

Four-layer cake with lemon curd

THE BASIC WHITE CAKE BATTER (OPPOSITE) IS DIVIDED AMONG FOUR PANS FOR THIS LAYER CAKE.
A HOMEMADE LEMON CURD IS USED FOR THE FILLING AND GLAZE.

LEMON CURD

1½ cups sugar

½ cup plus 1 tablespoon fresh lemon juice

½ cup (1 stick) butter

8 large egg yolks

2 tablespoons (packed) grated lemon peel

¼ teaspoon salt

CAKE

3¼ cups cake flour

1½ teaspoons cream of tartar

¾ teaspoon baking soda

¼ teaspoon salt

2 cups sugar

1 cup (2 sticks) unsalted butter, room temperature

8 large egg whites, whisked until blended but not foamy

2 teaspoons vanilla extract

1 cup whole milk

Mint sprigs

12 SERVINGS

FOR LEMON CURD: Combine all ingredients in heavy medium non-aluminum saucepan. Whisk over medium heat until mixture thickens and candy thermometer registers 170°F, about 8 minutes (do not boil). Pour into medium bowl and cool.

FOR CAKE: Position rack in center of oven and preheat to 375°F. Butter and flour four 9-inch-diameter cake pans with 1½-inch-high sides. Sift first 4 ingredients into medium bowl. Using electric mixer, beat sugar and butter in large bowl until fluffy. Add egg whites in 4 additions, beating well after each. Beat in vanilla. Beat in dry ingredients alternately with milk, beginning and ending with dry ingredients.

Divide batter among prepared pans. Bake until cakes are golden and tester inserted into center comes out clean, about 20 minutes. Transfer pans to racks and cool 5 minutes. Turn cakes out onto racks; cool completely. Layers will be thin. *(Lemon curd and cakes can be prepared 1 day ahead. Cover and chill curd. Wrap cake layers separately and store at room temperature.)*

Place 1 cake layer on platter. Spread 6 tablespoons lemon curd over. Top with second cake layer. Spread 6 tablespoons curd over. Top with third layer. Spread 6 tablespoons curd over. Top with remaining layer. *(Can be prepared 6 hours ahead. Cover cake and remaining curd separately; chill. Bring cake to room temperature before continuing.)* Whisk remaining curd in saucepan over low heat until heated through and slightly thinner. Pour atop cake, spreading evenly and allowing some to run down sides. Garnish with mint.

Vanilla angel food cake

THIS CLASSIC ANGEL FOOD CAKE USES ONLY BEATEN EGG WHITES FOR VOLUME. TO ENSURE A LIGHT AND AIRY TEXTURE, SIFT THE DRY INGREDIENTS FIVE TIMES, BEAT THE EGG WHITES UNTIL VERY LIGHT AND FILLED WITH AIR, AND FOLD THE DRY INGREDIENTS EVENLY AND THOROUGHLY INTO THE EGG WHITES.

1½ cups sugar

1 cup sifted cake flour

½ teaspoon salt

1½ cups egg whites (about 11 large)

2 teaspoons warm water

1 teaspoon cream of tartar

2 teaspoons vanilla extract

Powdered sugar

8 TO 10 SERVINGS

Preheat oven to 350°F. Sift ½ cup sugar, flour and salt into medium bowl 5 times. Using electric mixer, beat egg whites in large bowl (at least 4-quart capacity) until foamy. Add 2 teaspoons warm water and cream of tartar and beat until soft peaks form. Gradually add remaining 1 cup sugar and vanilla and beat until stiff but not dry. Sift sugar-flour mixture over whites ¼ cup at a time and gently fold in.

Transfer batter to ungreased 12-cup angel food cake pan with removable bottom (do not use nonstick pan). Bake until cake is light golden, top springs back when touched lightly and cake begins to pull away from sides of pan, about 45 minutes. Remove cake from oven. Turn cake pan upside down; place center tube of pan over narrow bottle neck or funnel. Cool cake completely.

Using knife, cut around sides and center tube of pan to loosen cake. Push up cake. Cut cake from bottom of pan. Transfer to platter. *(Can be prepared 1 day ahead. Wrap tightly with plastic and store at room temperature.)* Dust cake with powdered sugar.

Vanilla angel food cake with mango-ginger sauce

THE ANGEL FOOD CAKE ABOVE IS ENHANCED BY THIS SWEET-AND-SPICY MANGO AND GINGER SAUCE (PICTURED ON PAGE 147). TRY USING THE SAUCE AS A TOPPING FOR ICE CREAM OR FROZEN YOGURT, IF YOU LIKE.

2¾ cups finely chopped peeled pitted mangoes (about 2 mangoes)

2 tablespoons sugar

¼ cup chopped crystallized ginger

2 teaspoons fresh lime juice

Vanilla Angel Food Cake (see recipe above)

Thinly sliced crystallized ginger (optional)

8 TO 10 SERVINGS

Place 1 cup chopped mangoes in medium bowl. Combine remaining 1¾ cups chopped mangoes and sugar in processor. Puree until smooth. Add to bowl with chopped mangoes. Stir in chopped crystallized ginger and lime juice. Let stand at least 30 minutes. *(Can be prepared 1 day ahead. Cover and refrigerate.)*

Garnish cake with ginger slices, if desired. Serve with sauce.

Cinnamon swirl coffee cake

COFFEE CAKES CAN BE MADE WITH OR WITHOUT YEAST. THIS VERSION, WHICH USES BAKING POWDER AS THE LEAVENING AGENT, WOULD BE GREAT FOR DESSERT OR BREAKFAST, OR AS A SNACK.

1¾ cups sugar

½ cup chopped walnuts, toasted

1 tablespoon ground cinnamon

1 tablespoon unsweetened cocoa powder

3 cups all purpose flour

1 tablespoon baking powder

¾ teaspoon salt

¾ cup (1½ sticks) unsalted butter, room temperature

4 large eggs

1 tablespoon vanilla extract

1 cup whole milk

12 SERVINGS

Preheat oven to 350°F. Butter 10-inch-diameter by 4-inch-deep angel food cake pan; dust with flour. Mix ½ cup sugar, walnuts, cinnamon and cocoa in small bowl. Sift next 3 ingredients into medium bowl.

Beat butter in large bowl until smooth. Gradually beat in remaining 1¼ cups sugar. Beat in eggs 1 at a time, then vanilla. Mix in flour mixture in 3 additions alternately with milk in 2 additions. Spoon ⅓ of batter into prepared pan. Sprinkle with half of walnut mixture. Top with half of remaining batter, then remaining walnut mixture and remaining batter. Using knife, cut through batter to swirl walnut mixture.

Bake cake until tester inserted near center comes out clean, about 55 minutes. Cool cake in pan on rack. (*Can be made 1 day ahead. Cover pan with foil; store at room temperature.*)

Cut around pan sides and center tube to loosen cake. Turn cake out; transfer cake, rounded side up, to plate.

Tips

TO MAKE fluffy whipped cream, start with very cold cream. Pour it into a chilled bowl and beat with chilled beaters or whisk, adding sugar about halfway through. Beat just until soft peaks form. Whipped cream can be stored for several hours, covered, in the refrigerator.

IF A RECIPE says to sift, do so. Besides mixing the ingredients, sifting adds air and gives the flour a lighter texture. This can substantially affect the cake's volume. When measuring, scoop unsifted flour into the measuring cup and level it off. Sifted flour, however, should be spooned into the measuring cup to maintain volume, then leveled.

TO STABILIZE a tall layer cake while frosting it, insert a bamboo skewer into the center to keep the layers aligned. (Remove the skewer before serving the cake!)

Basic cheesecake with graham cracker crust

THIS BASIC CHEESECAKE IS BAKED IN A TRADITIONAL SPRINGFORM PAN WITH A REMOVABLE BOTTOM. A SOUR CREAM TOPPING SWEETENED WITH SUGAR AND VANILLA IS ALL THAT YOU NEED—BUT IF YOU WANT TO EMBELLISH THE CAKE FURTHER, MAKE THE VARIATION OPPOSITE.

CRUST

20 whole graham crackers (10 ounces total), broken

¾ cup (1½ sticks) chilled unsalted butter, diced

½ cup (packed) golden brown sugar

FILLING

4 8-ounce packages cream cheese, room temperature

1¾ cups sugar

3 tablespoons fresh lemon juice

2½ teaspoons vanilla extract

Pinch of salt

3 tablespoons all purpose flour

5 large eggs

TOPPING

2 cups sour cream

3 tablespoons sugar

½ teaspoon vanilla extract

12 SERVINGS

FOR CRUST: Position rack in center of oven and preheat to 350°F. Wrap foil around outside of 10-inch-diameter springform pan with 3-inch-high sides. Combine crackers, butter and sugar in processor. Using on/off turns, blend until crumbs begin to stick together. Press onto bottom and 2¾ inches up sides of pan. Bake crust 10 minutes. Transfer to rack; cool while preparing filling. Maintain oven temperature.

FOR FILLING: Beat cream cheese, sugar, lemon juice, vanilla and salt in large bowl until very smooth. Beat in flour. Add eggs and beat just until blended, stopping occasionally to scrape down sides of bowl. Pour batter into prepared crust.

Bake cheesecake until outer 2-inch edge of cake is puffed and slightly cracked, center is just set and top is brown in spots, about 55 minutes. Transfer cake to rack. Cool 10 minutes. Maintain oven temperature.

FOR TOPPING: Whisk sour cream, sugar and vanilla extract in medium bowl to blend. Spoon topping over cake, spreading to edge of pan. Bake until topping is just set, about 5 minutes. Remove from oven. Run knife between crust and pan.

Cool cake in pan on rack. Chill overnight. Release pan sides.

Strawberry-topped cheesecake

ADDING A FRESH STRAWBERRY TOPPING MAKES A DELECTABLE VARIATION ON THE RECIPE OPPOSITE (PICTURED BELOW). CONVENIENTLY, YOU CAN TOP THE CHEESECAKE WITH THE BERRIES UP TO SIX HOURS AHEAD.

Basic Cheesecake with Graham Cracker Crust (see recipe opposite)

2 **16-ounce baskets strawberries, hulled**

1 **18-ounce jar raspberry jelly**

12 SERVINGS

Prepare cheesecake. Arrange whole berries, points facing up, atop cheesecake, covering completely. Stir jelly in heavy small saucepan over medium-low heat until melted. Cool to barely lukewarm, about 5 minutes. Brush enough jelly over berries to glaze generously, allowing some to drip between berries. Reserve remaining glaze in saucepan. *(Cheesecake and glaze can be prepared 6 hours ahead. Cover cheesecake and refrigerate.)*

Rewarm remaining glaze until pourable. Cut cheesecake into wedges and serve, passing remaining glaze separately.

Chocolate genoise with peppermint ganache

THIS DESSERT MAY NOT BE SIMPLE, BUT IT CERTAINLY IS IMPRESSIVE. IT FEATURES TWO CLASSIC COMPONENTS: THE BUTTERY SPONGE CAKE KNOWN AS GENOISE AND THE RICH FROSTING KNOWN AS GANACHE.

SYRUP

⅓ cup water

⅓ cup sugar

1½ tablespoons dark crème de cacao

½ teaspoon vanilla extract

GENOISE

Nonstick vegetable oil spray

¾ cup plus 2 tablespoons sifted cake flour

⅓ cup plus 1 tablespoon unsweetened cocoa powder (preferably Dutch process)

¼ teaspoon baking soda

5 large eggs

1 large egg yolk

FOR SYRUP: Stir water and sugar in small saucepan over low heat until sugar dissolves. Increase heat; bring to boil. Remove from heat. Stir in crème de cacao and vanilla. *(Can be made 1 week ahead. Cover; chill.)*

FOR GENOISE: Preheat oven to 350°F. Butter and flour 9-inch springform pan with 2¾-inch-high sides; line bottom with parchment paper. Cover cake rack with paper towel; spray towel with nonstick spray.

Sift flour, cocoa and baking soda 3 times into small bowl. Combine eggs, egg yolk, sugar and salt in large stainless steel bowl. Set bowl over saucepan of simmering water and whisk until warm to touch and instant-read thermometer registers 110°F, about 2 minutes. Remove mixture from over water. Using electric mixer, beat until egg mixture triples in volume and falls in heavy ribbon when beaters are lifted, about 5 minutes. Beat in vanilla. Sift flour mixture over in 3 additions, folding gently to incorporate each time. Drizzle butter over and fold in (do not overmix or batter will deflate). Transfer batter to prepared pan.

MAKING GENOISE AND GANACHE:

STEP 1: Set the bowl over a saucepan of simmering water. Do not let the bottom of the bowl touch the water. Whisk the egg mixture until warm to touch, about 2 minutes.

STEP 2: Using an electric mixer, beat the egg mixture until it triples in volume and falls in a heavy ribbon when the beaters are lifted.

STEP 3: Add corn syrup and extracts to the ganache; whisk until smooth. Cool to room temperature, stirring occasionally.

¾ cup plus 2 tablespoons sugar

¼ teaspoon salt

1½ teaspoons vanilla extract

4 tablespoons (½ stick) unsalted butter, melted, cooled

GANACHE

36 ounces bittersweet (not unsweetened) or semisweet chocolate, finely chopped

2½ cups whipping cream

¼ cup light corn syrup

1½ teaspoons peppermint extract

1 teaspoon vanilla extract

Chocolate curls (about 6 ounces)

10 TO 12 SERVINGS

Bake cake until tester inserted into center comes out clean, about 40 minutes. Cut around pan sides to loosen cake. Release sides. Turn cake out onto prepared cake rack; peel off parchment. Cool completely. (Can be made 1 day ahead. Wrap; store at room temperature.)

FOR GANACHE: Place chocolate in large bowl. Bring cream to boil in small saucepan. Pour cream over chocolate. Add corn syrup and both extracts; whisk until smooth. Cool to room temperature, stirring occasionally, about 2 hours.

Transfer 3 cups ganache to medium bowl. Using electric mixer, beat until very thick and light colored, about 12 minutes.

Using long serrated knife, cut genoise horizontally into 3 equal layers. Place 1 layer on cardboard round or tart pan bottom. Brush cake with 3 tablespoons syrup. Spread ⅓ of whipped ganache over. Repeat 2 more times with genoise, syrup and whipped ganache. Spread 1 cup unwhipped ganache very thinly over top and sides of assembled cake. Refrigerate until coating sets, about 10 minutes.

If necessary, warm remaining unwhipped ganache until just pourable. Place cake on rack set over sheet of foil. Pour ganache over cake as glaze, spreading to cover top and sides smoothly. Refrigerate cake until glaze begins to set, about 30 minutes. Place cake on platter. Press chocolate curls onto sides. Chill at least 2 hours before serving.

How do I make chocolate curls?

For easy chocolate shavings and curls, heat a large chocolate bar in the microwave on a paper towel at five- to ten-second intervals until it's barely warm. (If it starts to melt, put it back in the refrigerator and begin again.) Using a very sharp vegetable peeler, "peel" the chocolate into curls and shavings. Rewarm the chocolate bar as necessary to keep it pliable.

Maybe you're one of the fortunate ones: You stood at your grandmother's side, flour dusting your hands, learning the secret of perfectly light and flaky pie crust. If you're like most of the world, however, you've been settling for store-bought crusts because homemade ones just seemed too complicated to make. Guess what? They're not.

Here are the modern secrets of mixing, rolling and baking that will result in a tender and delicious crust—one that's just waiting to be filled with your favorite pie ingredients. A basic tart crust is included here, too. Use it for a traditional tart or a free-form *crostata*. No matter what, you'll wind up with a dessert that anybody's grandmother would be proud of.

12

Pies & Tarts

Pear and Dried Cranberry Crostata (page 169)

Basic pie pastry

THE KEY TO A GOOD FLAKY PIE CRUST IS USING A COMBINATION OF BUTTER FOR FLAVOR AND SHORTENING FOR FLAKINESS. FOR A FANCIFUL TOUCH, FOLLOW THE STEPS BELOW TO MAKE A DECORATIVE CRUST EDGE.

2⅔ cups all purpose flour

2 tablespoons sugar

½ teaspoon salt

½ cup chilled solid vegetable shortening, cut into small pieces

½ cup (1 stick) chilled unsalted butter, cut into small pieces

1 large egg

3 tablespoons (about) ice water

MAKES ENOUGH FOR TWO 9-INCH CRUSTS

Combine flour, sugar and salt in processor. Using on/off turns, cut in shortening and butter until mixture resembles coarse meal. Beat egg and 3 tablespoons ice water in bowl to blend. Add to flour mixture. Process until moist clumps form, adding more water by teaspoonfuls if dough is dry. Gather into ball. Divide in half. Flatten each half into disk. Wrap in plastic; chill 1 hour. *(Can be made 1 day ahead. Keep chilled. Let dough soften slightly at room temperature before rolling.)*

HOW TO DECORATE A PIE CRUST:
After rolling out the dough, transfer it to a pie dish.

BRAIDED EDGE: Trim the dough so that it's flush with the rim of the dish. Press down gently on the dough around the rim to make a flat foundation. Roll second disk to form a long ⅛-inch-thick strip (a standard 9-inch pie dish will require about a 30-inch trim). Cut three ¼-inch-wide strips from the long strip. Braid the strips. Brush the dough rim on the dish with cold water; press the braid gently onto the edge of the crust.

FLUTED EDGE: Using one crust, instead of trimming the dough to line up with the rim of the dish, leave a half-inch overhang. To form a wavy edge, place your left thumb on the edge of the crust and pull up the dough on both sides of your thumb with the thumb and forefinger of your right hand. Repeat at one-inch intervals until the entire pie crust has a fluted edge.

OVERLAPPING LEAVES: Trim so that the crust is flush with the rim of the dish. Press down gently around the rim to form a flat foundation for the leaves. Roll out extra dough to ⅛-inch thickness. With a sharp knife, cut out leaf shapes. Using the dull side of the blade, mark veins on the leaf, being careful not to cut all the way through. Brush the back of each leaf with cold water; place on the edge in a decorative pattern.

Apricot-raspberry pie with hazelnut streusel

THE BASIC PIE PASTRY RECIPE OPPOSITE IS USED HERE. TO KEEP FRAGILE RASPBERRIES AT THEIR BEST, STORE THEM IN THEIR ORIGINAL CONTAINER IN THE REFRIGERATOR FOR NO LONGER THAN TWO DAYS.

STREUSEL

½ cup all purpose flour

½ cup hazelnuts (about 2½ ounces)

¼ cup (packed) golden brown sugar

¼ cup sugar

¼ teaspoon salt

5 tablespoons chilled unsalted butter, cut into ½-inch cubes

FILLING

1½ pounds ripe apricots, peeled, halved, pitted, each half cut into 4 wedges

1 cup sugar

3 tablespoons all purpose flour

¼ teaspoon ground allspice

1 ½-pint basket raspberries

½ Basic Pie Pastry (1 dough disk; see recipe opposite)

8 SERVINGS

FOR STREUSEL: Position rack in bottom third of oven and preheat to 400°F. Combine first 5 ingredients in processor. Using on/off turns, blend until nuts are coarsely chopped. Add butter and cut in, using on/off turns, until mixture begins to clump together. Transfer streusel to bowl and refrigerate.

FOR FILLING: Combine apricots, sugar, flour and allspice in large bowl; toss to blend. Let stand until dry ingredients are moistened, about 15 minutes. Carefully fold in raspberries.

Roll out pastry on lightly floured surface to 12½-inch round. Transfer to 9-inch-diameter glass pie dish. Trim overhang to ¾ inch. Fold overhang under; crimp edges decoratively. Spoon filling into crust.

Place pie on baking sheet. Bake until filling begins to bubble at edges, about 45 minutes. Sprinkle streusel evenly over pie. Cover crust edges with foil to prevent overbrowning. Bake until crust and topping are golden and filling is bubbling thickly in center, about 50 minutes. Cool pie on rack at least 2 hours and up to 8 hours.

Equipment

Metal pie pans help bottom crusts brown quickly and evenly, so they are good for custard, cream and other pies (such as lemon meringue and pumpkin-custard) that won't spend a lot of time in the oven. Glass and ceramic pie dishes are perfect for crisps, crumbles and other desserts with fruit on the bottom, and for recipes that don't require a deeply browned bottom crust. As a bonus, glass and ceramic pie dishes are extremely easy to clean.

Also useful: a food processor for making dough in a flash; a copper bowl for beating egg whites; a pastry cutter; rolling pins (*not* water-filled, since they can leave condensation on the crust and make it sticky); a pastry board; and a nine- or ten-inch tart pan with a removable bottom.

Apple-cinnamon pie with vanilla ice cream

TWO KINDS OF APPLES ARE USED FOR THIS ALL-AMERICAN CLASSIC. IT HAS BOTH A TOP AND A BOTTOM CRUST, SO YOU'LL USE BOTH DOUGH DISKS FROM THE BASIC PIE PASTRY RECIPE (PAGE 160).

1½ pounds Red Delicious apples, peeled, cored, cut into ¼-inch-thick slices

1½ pounds Golden Delicious apples, peeled, cored, cut into ¼-inch-thick slices

¼ cup plus 1 tablespoon sugar

¼ cup all purpose flour

3½ teaspoons ground cinnamon

1 tablespoon cider vinegar

½ teaspoon salt

1 Basic Pie Pastry (2 dough disks; see recipe on page 160)

¼ cup honey

1 tablespoon milk

Vanilla ice cream

8 SERVINGS

Position rack in bottom third of oven and preheat oven to 400°F. Combine sliced apples, ¼ cup sugar, flour, 2 teaspoons ground cinnamon, vinegar and salt in large bowl; toss to blend.

Roll out 1 dough disk on lightly floured surface to 13-inch round. Transfer to 9-inch-diameter deep-dish glass pie dish. Trim overhang to ½ inch. Brush edge of crust lightly with water. Transfer apple mixture to crust, mounding in center and pressing lightly to compact. Drizzle with honey. Sprinkle with 1 teaspoon cinnamon. Roll out second dough disk to 13-inch round. Place atop apples. Trim dough overhang to 1 inch. Fold top crust edge under bottom crust edge, pressing to seal. Crimp edge decoratively. Cut several slits in crust to allow steam to escape.

Place apple pie on baking sheet. Bake 45 minutes.

Combine remaining 1 tablespoon sugar and ½ teaspoon ground cinnamon in small bowl. Brush top crust of pie with milk. Sprinkle with sugar mixture. Bake until crust is golden brown, apples are tender and juices are bubbling thickly, covering crust edges with foil if browning too quickly, about 20 minutes. Transfer pie to rack and cool.

Cut pie into wedges and serve with vanilla ice cream.

Tips

OVERPROCESSING can make pastry tough. The trick is to mix the dough just until the shortening or butter is reduced to pea-size pieces. The bits of fat separate the crust into flaky layers while it bakes.

FOR EASIER pastry rolling, chill the dough first. Sprinkle the work surface, the dough and the rolling pin lightly with flour. Begin at the center of the dough and roll quickly outward with light, even pressure.

PIE DOUGH keeps well for several months in the freezer. Wrap well in plastic wrap and place in a labeled and dated resealable plastic bag.

TO KEEP pie edges from burning, fold a long piece of foil lengthwise and wrap it around the edge of the pie halfway through baking.

USE COPPER bowls when beating egg whites—a chemical reaction between the protein and the copper creates longer-lasting air bubbles.

Pumpkin pie with toffee-walnut topping

THIS SIMPLE PUMPKIN-CUSTARD PIE ALSO USES THE BASIC PIE PASTRY RECIPE (PAGE 160). THERE ARE TWO KINDS OF CANNED PUMPKIN SOLD IN SUPERMARKETS, ONE WITH SUGAR AND SEASONINGS AND ONE CONTAINING ONLY PUMPKIN. BE SURE TO BUY THE PURE PUMPKIN PUREE.

½ Basic Pie Pastry (1 dough disk; see recipe on page 160)

1 large egg yolk, beaten to blend

1 15-ounce can pure pumpkin

⅔ cup (packed) golden brown sugar

⅔ cup whipping cream

⅓ cup whole milk

2 large eggs

¼ cup sugar

1 teaspoon vanilla extract

1¼ teaspoons ground cinnamon

¾ teaspoon ground ginger

¼ teaspoon ground nutmeg

¼ teaspoon salt

⅛ teaspoon ground allspice

½ cup walnuts, toasted, chopped

⅓ cup English toffee bits (such as Skor)

10 SERVINGS

Position rack in bottom third of oven and preheat to 375°F. Roll out dough disk on floured surface to 12-inch round. Carefully transfer dough to 9-inch-diameter pie dish. Fold overhang under, forming high-standing rim. Crimp edges decoratively. Freeze crust 15 minutes. Brush crust all over with egg yolk. Bake until crust is set but still pale, about 15 minutes. Cool slightly.

Whisk pumpkin and next 11 ingredients in large bowl. Pour into warm crust. Bake pie until filling is set, about 55 minutes. Transfer to rack. Sprinkle chopped nuts and toffee bits around edge of hot pie, forming decorative border. Cool pie completely. (Can be prepared 6 hours ahead. Let pumpkin pie stand at room temperature.)

Lemon meringue pie with pecan crust

A TENDER PECAN CRUST BECOMES THE BASE FOR THIS LUSCIOUS LEMON MERINGUE PIE (PICTURED OPPOSITE).
TO KEEP THE MERINGUE FROM SHRINKING DURING BAKING, SEAL IT COMPLETELY AGAINST THE CRUST EDGE.

CRUST

- 1   cup all purpose flour
- ⅔   cup finely chopped pecans
- ⅓   cup cake flour
- 3   tablespoons (packed) golden brown sugar
- ½   teaspoon salt
- 5   tablespoons chilled unsalted butter, cut into ½-inch cubes
- 3   tablespoons chilled vegetable shortening, cut into ½-inch cubes
- 3   tablespoons (about) ice water

FILLING AND TOPPING

- 1¾ cups plus ⅓ cup sugar
- ⅓   cup cornstarch
- 1½ cups water
- ½   cup fresh lemon juice
- 5   large eggs, separated
- 2   tablespoons grated lemon peel
- ½   teaspoon cream of tartar

8 SERVINGS

FOR CRUST: Mix first 5 ingredients in large bowl; add butter and shortening. Using electric mixer, beat at low speed until mixture resembles coarse meal. Add 2 tablespoons ice water. Beat until dough holds together, adding more water by ½ tablespoonfuls if dough is dry. Gather dough into ball; flatten into disk. Wrap disk in waxed paper and chill until firm enough to roll, at least 1 hour and up to 1 day.

Roll out dough between sheets of waxed paper to 12-inch round. Peel off top sheet of paper. Invert dough into 9-inch-diameter glass pie dish; peel off paper. Press dough gently into dish. Trim overhang to ¾ inch; turn under. Crimp edge decoratively. Freeze crust 30 minutes.

Position rack in center of oven and preheat to 375°F. Line crust with foil; fill with dried beans or pie weights. Bake crust until edges are golden, about 15 minutes. Remove foil and beans; continue to bake until crust is pale golden, piercing with fork if crust bubbles, about 12 minutes. Cool completely on rack. Reduce oven temperature to 325°F.

FOR FILLING AND TOPPING: Whisk 1¾ cups sugar and ⅓ cup cornstarch in heavy medium saucepan to blend. Gradually add 1½ cups water and lemon juice, whisking until cornstarch dissolves and mixture is smooth. Add egg yolks and lemon peel; whisk to blend. Cook over medium-high heat until filling thickens and boils, whisking constantly, about 8 minutes. Pour hot filling into prepared crust.

Using electric mixer, beat egg whites and cream of tartar in large bowl until soft peaks form. Gradually add remaining ⅓ cup sugar, beating until stiff and shiny. Mound meringue atop warm lemon filling, spreading to seal to crust at edges.

Bake pie until meringue is golden, about 20 minutes. Cool pie 1 hour. Refrigerate up to 6 hours; serve cold.

Coconut cream pie

ANOTHER KIND OF PIE CRUST ALTOGETHER, THIS VERSION STARTS WITH SHORTBREAD COOKIE CRUMBS; COCONUT ADDS CRUNCH AND FLAVOR. SERVE THE PIE ON ITS OWN OR GIVE IT A FLOURISH WITH THE MANGO-CREAM TOPPING INCLUDED IN THIS RECIPE.

CRUST

1⅓ cups shortbread cookie crumbs

⅔ cup sweetened flaked coconut, toasted

6 tablespoons (¾ stick) unsalted butter, melted

FILLING

½ cup plus 1 tablespoon sugar

2 large eggs

1 large egg yolk

3 tablespoons all purpose flour

1½ cups whole milk

1½ cups sweetened flaked coconut

1½ teaspoons vanilla extract

1½ cups chilled whipping cream

TOPPING

1 ripe mango, peeled, pitted, diced

1 tablespoon sugar

1 teaspoon lime juice

Mango slices

Lime slices

8 SERVINGS

FOR CRUST: Preheat oven to 325°F. Butter 9-inch-diameter glass pie dish. Combine all ingredients in medium bowl and stir until crumbs are moistened. Press crumbs evenly onto bottom and up sides of prepared dish. Bake until crust begins to color, about 10 minutes. Cool crust completely on rack. *(Can be prepared 1 day ahead. Cover and let stand at room temperature.)*

FOR FILLING: Whisk ½ cup sugar, eggs, egg yolk and flour in medium bowl to blend. Bring milk and coconut to simmer in heavy medium saucepan over medium heat. Gradually add hot milk mixture to egg mixture, whisking constantly. Return mixture to same saucepan and cook until filling thickens and boils, stirring constantly, about 4 minutes. Remove from heat. Mix in 1 teaspoon vanilla. Transfer filling to medium bowl. Press plastic wrap directly onto surface to prevent formation of skin. Refrigerate until cold, at least 2 hours. *(Can be prepared 1 day ahead. Keep refrigerated.)*

Beat whipping cream, remaining 1 tablespoon sugar and ½ teaspoon vanilla in bowl until peaks form. Whisk filling until smooth and slightly softened. Fold in 1 cup whipped cream. Spread filling in crust. Chill remaining whipped cream for topping.

FOR TOPPING: Puree diced mango, sugar and lime juice in processor until very smooth. Strain into bowl. Fold into reserved whipped cream. Spoon mango cream around edge of pie. Garnish with mango slices and lime slices. Chill. *(Can be prepared 2 hours ahead. Keep chilled.)*

What can be done to keep pie crusts from becoming soggy?

One solution is to bake an empty pie crust partially before adding the filling. Prebaking gives the pie crust a chance to set and will protect it from the liquids in the filling. You might also try putting double-crust fruit pies, which can't be prebaked, in the bottom third of the oven. That way the pies will be exposed to more bottom heat, ensuring that the crust sets and cooks completely.

Basic tart crust

THIS RECIPE CAN BE USED AS THE CRUST FOR ANY NUMBER OF FILLINGS. TO RELEASE A FINISHED TART FROM ITS PAN, PLACE THE PAN ON TOP OF A COFFEE CAN. THE RIM WILL DROP TO THE COUNTER. NEXT, RUN A SPATULA BETWEEN THE CRUST AND THE BOTTOM METAL DISK; TRANSFER THE TART TO A PLATTER.

1   cup all purpose flour

¼   cup powdered sugar

6   tablespoons (¾ stick) chilled unsalted butter, cut into pieces

1   tablespoon chilled whipping cream

MAKES ONE 9-INCH CRUST

Blend flour and sugar in processor. Add butter; using on/off turns, cut in until mixture resembles coarse meal. Add cream; process until moist clumps form. Turn dough out onto work surface. Gather into ball; flatten to disk. Wrap dough in plastic; chill 15 minutes.

Preheat oven to 350°F. Roll out chilled dough on lightly floured surface to 11-inch-diameter round. Transfer to 9-inch-diameter tart pan with removable bottom. Press gently into place. Fold dough edges over to form double-thick sides. *(Can be prepared 1 day ahead. Cover and refrigerate.)* Bake crust until just beginning to color, about 15 minutes. Transfer pan to rack and cool.

Peach-frangipane tart

THE TERM *FRANGIPANE* REFERS TO AN ALMOND FILLING OR TOPPING FOR PASTRIES OR CAKES. USE THE TART CRUST RECIPE ABOVE FOR THIS AMARETTO-LACED FILLING TOPPED WITH FRESH PEACHES.

¾   cup slivered blanched almonds (about 3½ ounces)

⅓   cup sugar

3   tablespoons amaretto or other almond-flavored liqueur

2   tablespoons (¼ stick) unsalted butter, room temperature

1   tablespoon all purpose flour

1   large egg

    Basic Tart Crust (see recipe above)

5   peaches

½   cup peach or apricot preserves

6 SERVINGS

Preheat oven to 400°F. Finely grind slivered almonds in processor. Add sugar, 2 tablespoons amaretto, butter and flour and puree. Add egg and process until well blended. Pour into prepared crust. Bake until filling begins to brown and is springy to touch, about 15 minutes. Cool on rack. *(Can be prepared 6 hours ahead. Let stand at room temperature.)*

Bring medium pot of water to boil. Add peaches and blanch 30 seconds. Using slotted spoon, transfer to bowl of cold water. Peel peaches. Cut into slices. Drain well. Combine preserves and remaining 1 tablespoon amaretto in heavy small saucepan. Bring to boil, stirring to melt preserves. Boil until slightly thickened, about 30 seconds. Brush some preserves over tart filling. Arrange peaches atop preserves in concentric circles, overlapping slices. Brush with preserves. *(Can be prepared 3 hours ahead. Let stand at room temperature.)*

Blackberry lattice tart

A NUT CRUST IS USED HERE. TO MAKE THE LATTICE, PLACE FROZEN DOUGH STRIPS IN A CRISSCROSS FORMATION ACROSS THE TOP OF THE TART. SERVE IT WITH WHIPPED CREAM OR ICE CREAM, IF DESIRED.

CRUST

- 2 cups all purpose flour
- 1 cup walnuts or pecans (about 4 ounces)
- ⅓ cup sugar
- ¾ cup (1½ sticks) chilled unsalted butter, cut into ½-inch pieces
- 1 large egg
- 1 teaspoon vanilla extract

FILLING

- ¼ cup apricot preserves
- 1½ pounds frozen blackberries (about 6 cups)
- ⅔ cup sugar
- 2 tablespoons cornstarch

10 SERVINGS

FOR CRUST: Blend flour, nuts and sugar in processor until nuts are finely chopped. Add butter, egg and vanilla extract; process just until dough holds together, occasionally scraping down sides of bowl. Press ⅔ of dough onto bottom and up sides of 11-inch-diameter tart pan with removable bottom. Refrigerate tart crust and remaining dough at least 1 hour. *(Can be made up to 1 day ahead. Cover tart crust and remaining dough separately and keep refrigerated.)*

Position rack in top third of oven and preheat to 400°F. Roll out remaining ⅓ of dough on lightly floured foil to 12x7-inch rectangle. Cut dough lengthwise into ½-inch-wide strips. Freeze strips on foil. Bake crust until golden, pressing down with back of fork if crust bubbles, about 25 minutes. Remove crust from oven.

FOR FILLING: Reduce oven temperature to 350°F. Spread ¼ cup apricot preserves over bottom of crust. Toss frozen blackberries with sugar and cornstarch in large bowl. Immediately spoon berry mixture in even layer atop preserves. Arrange frozen dough strips atop tart, forming lattice. Press ends of strips into crust edge to seal. Bake until filling is bubbling thickly, about 1 hour 10 minutes. Cool completely. *(Can be made 8 hours ahead. Let stand at room temperature.)*

Why do some recipes call for unsalted butter, then later in the instructions tell you to add salt?

Different brands of salted butter contain different amounts of salt. So if salted butter is used to make a pie crust or cookie dough, it's impossible to know exactly how much salt will end up in the dough. For the most accurate salt measurement, use sweet (unsalted) butter, and add the precise amount of salt specified in the recipe.

Pear and dried cranberry crostata

THIS ITALIAN-STYLE FREE-FORM TART (PICTURED ON PAGE 159) IS MOUNDED WITH PEARS AND DRIED CRAN-
BERRIES. WHEN FILLING THE DOUGH, LEAVE A TWO-INCH BORDER SO THAT IT CAN BE FOLDED OVER THE FRUIT.

CRUST

2½ cups all purpose flour

¼ cup sugar

1 teaspoon salt

¾ cup (1½ sticks) chilled
    unsalted butter, cut into
    ½-inch cubes

6 tablespoons (about) ice water

FILLING

½ cup plus 1 tablespoon sugar

3 tablespoons all purpose flour

¼ teaspoon ground cardamom

¼ teaspoon ground allspice

3 pounds firm but ripe Anjou
    pears (about 6 small), peeled,
    halved, cored, cut into
    ¼-inch-thick slices

¾ cup dried cranberries

3 tablespoons poire Williams
    (clear pear brandy) or brandy

1 large egg, beaten to blend
    (for glaze)

WHIPPED CREAM

2 cups chilled whipping cream

2 tablespoons powdered sugar

Additional dried cranberries
(optional)

8 TO 10 SERVINGS

FOR CRUST: Mix flour, sugar and salt in processor. Add butter. Using on/off turns, process until mixture resembles coarse meal. Add 5 tablespoons ice water; process until moist clumps form, adding more water by tablespoonfuls if dough is dry. Gather into ball; flatten into disk. Wrap in plastic. Chill until firm, about 1 hour. *(Can be pre-pared 1 day ahead. Keep chilled. Let soften slightly before rolling out.)*

FOR FILLING: Mix ½ cup sugar, flour, cardamom and allspice in large bowl. Add pears and cranberries; toss to coat. Mix in pear brandy.

Position rack in center of oven and preheat to 375°F. Roll out dough on floured parchment paper to 14- to 15-inch round. Transfer dough, still on parchment paper, to large baking sheet.

Spread filling into center of dough, leaving 2-inch border. Fold dough border over fruit, pleating loosely and pinching to seal any cracks. Brush border with egg glaze; sprinkle with 1 tablespoon sugar.

Bake tart until crust is golden, about 1 hour. Cover edges of crust with foil and continue baking until filling bubbles thickly, about 15 minutes longer. Transfer baking sheet to rack; run long knife under tart to loosen from parchment. Cool. Using tart pan bottom as aid, transfer tart to platter. *(Can be made 6 hours ahead. Let stand at room temperature.)*

FOR WHIPPED CREAM: Beat whipping cream and powdered sugar in large bowl until peaks form. Sprinkle dried cranberries over whipped cream, if desired. Serve with tart.

13

There are a few things that undeniably taste better when homemade, and ice cream is one of them. And while a few years ago, it just wasn't practical to make this treat at home, the advent of reasonably priced electric ice cream makers has changed all that. Not sold on the idea of buying another piece of kitchen equipment? Take heart: You can make sophisticated sorbets and granitas without any special tools at all.

Making frozen desserts successfully simply requires that you buy the best ingredients you can find, and that you learn a few easy techniques. The shopping is up to you, but we'll teach you the tricks, and help you avoid the pitfalls. The result? Some of the best frozen desserts you will ever taste.

Frozen Desserts

Peach-Pecan Ice Cream Pie with Caramel Sauce (page 174)

Vanilla bean ice cream

HERE, REAL VANILLA BEANS IMPART A SUPERB FLAVOR TO THE REAL THING—HOMEMADE ICE CREAM.

3   cups half and half

2   cups whipping cream

2   vanilla beans, split lengthwise

¾   cup plus 2 tablespoons sugar

8   egg yolks

MAKES ABOUT 2 QUARTS

Bring first 3 ingredients to simmer in heavy medium saucepan over medium-low heat. Remove from heat, cover and let steep 40 minutes.

Return half and half mixture to simmer. Beat sugar and egg yolks to blend in medium bowl. Gradually whisk in hot half and half mixture. Return mixture to same saucepan. Stir over medium heat until custard thickens slightly and leaves path on back of spoon when finger is drawn across, about 7 minutes; do not boil. Pour custard into large bowl and refrigerate until well chilled.

Scrape any seeds remaining inside vanilla beans into custard; discard beans. Transfer custard to ice cream maker and process according to manufacturer's instructions. Transfer ice cream to container; cover and freeze. (Can be prepared 1 week ahead. Keep frozen.)

Peanut brittle ice cream sundaes with chocolate sauce

THE VANILLA BEAN ICE CREAM RECIPE ABOVE IS USED FOR THIS ICE CREAM PARLOR SPECIAL. IF YOU'RE SHORT ON TIME, USE PURCHASED VANILLA ICE CREAM INSTEAD.

PEANUT BRITTLE

¾   cup sugar

⅔   cup light corn syrup

2   tablespoons water

½   teaspoon baking soda

1½   cups salted cocktail peanuts

2   quarts Vanilla Bean Ice Cream (see recipe above), softened

CHOCOLATE SAUCE

⅔   cup water

2   tablespoons light corn syrup

8   ounces semisweet chocolate, chopped

2   ounces bittersweet (not unsweetened) chocolate, chopped

Whipped cream

8 SERVINGS

FOR PEANUT BRITTLE: Lightly butter large baking sheet. Combine sugar, corn syrup and water in heavy medium saucepan. Stir over medium-low heat until sugar dissolves. Attach clip-on candy thermometer to side of pan. Increase heat to medium. Using wooden spoon, stir constantly but slowly until temperature reaches 300°F, occasionally brushing down sides of pan with wet pastry brush, about 20 minutes. Remove from heat; immediately add baking soda and stir until very foamy. Immediately stir in peanuts. Working quickly, pour out onto prepared baking sheet. Cool completely. Coarsely chop peanut brittle. (Can be made 3 days ahead. Store in airtight container.)

Place softened ice cream in large bowl. Mix in 2 cups chopped peanut brittle. Cover; freeze until ice cream is firm, at least 4 hours.

FOR CHOCOLATE SAUCE: Bring ⅔ cup water and corn syrup to simmer in heavy medium saucepan. Reduce heat to low. Add both chocolates and stir until smooth. Serve warm.

Top ice cream with chocolate sauce, whipped cream and brittle.

Peach ice cream

FRESH PEACHES FLAVOR A CLASSIC ICE CREAM. BE SURE TO START A DAY AHEAD.

1 cup half and half

1 cup whipping cream

1 vanilla bean, split lengthwise

½ cup plus 3 tablespoons (firmly packed) brown sugar

4 large egg yolks

2¼ pounds peaches, peeled, pitted

1½ cups sour cream

MAKES ABOUT 2 QUARTS

Bring first 3 ingredients to simmer in heavy medium saucepan over medium-low heat. Remove from heat, cover and let steep 40 minutes.

Return half and half mixture to simmer. Beat brown sugar and egg yolks to blend in large bowl. Gradually whisk in hot half and half mixture. Return mixture to same saucepan. Stir over medium heat until custard thickens slightly and leaves path on back of spoon when finger is drawn across, about 7 minutes; do not boil. Pour custard into large bowl and refrigerate until well chilled.

Coarsely puree 1½ pounds peaches in processor. Fold into custard. Mix in sour cream. Refrigerate overnight.

Discard vanilla bean. Process custard in ice cream maker according to manufacturer's instructions until almost set. Coarsely chop ¾ pound peaches; add to ice cream and process until set. Transfer ice cream to container; cover and freeze. *(Can be made 1 week ahead. Keep frozen.)*

Is there a way to keep vanilla beans from drying out?

Storing vanilla beans in a tightly sealed plastic bag in the refrigerator should keep them moist for six months. If they do become dry, add one apple wedge for every two beans. That should restore some moisture in about four days. If the beans are being used to flavor a custard or cream sauce, they can be steeped in the hot liquid until softened.

Peach-pecan ice cream pie with caramel sauce

THIS DECADENT DESSERT (PICTURED ON PAGE 171) CAN BE PREPARED UP TO A WEEK IN ADVANCE. MAKE THE PEACH ICE CREAM (PAGE 173) OR, IF SHORT ON TIME, SUBSTITUTE PURCHASED PEACH ICE CREAM.

CRUST

2½ cups finely ground or crushed pecan shortbread cookies (such as Pecan Sandies; about 11 ounces)

¼ cup (½ stick) unsalted butter, melted

CARAMEL SAUCE AND FILLING

2 cups sugar

½ cup water

1¼ cups whipping cream

¾ teaspoon vanilla extract

2 quarts (or 4 pints) Peach Ice Cream (see recipe on page 173) or purchased peach ice cream, slightly softened

1 cup pecans, toasted, coarsely chopped (about 4 ounces)

1 cup (about) pecan halves, toasted

12 SERVINGS

FOR CRUST: Preheat oven to 325°F. Butter 9-inch-diameter springform pan with 2¾-inch-high sides. Mix cookie crumbs and melted butter in medium bowl until crumbs are evenly moistened. Press crumb mixture firmly onto bottom and 1 inch up sides of prepared pan. Bake until crust is set and pale golden, about 15 minutes. Cool completely.

FOR CARAMEL SAUCE AND FILLING: Combine sugar and ½ cup water in medium saucepan. Stir over medium-low heat until sugar dissolves. Increase heat to medium-high; boil without stirring until syrup is deep amber color, occasionally brushing down sides of pan with wet pastry brush and swirling pan, about 8 minutes. Remove from heat. Gradually add cream (mixture will bubble vigorously). Stir over low heat until any caramel bits dissolve and sauce is smooth, about 1 minute. Stir in vanilla. Let stand until cool but still pourable, 1 hour.

Drizzle ¼ cup cooled caramel sauce over bottom of crust. Freeze until caramel sets, about 10 minutes. Spread 1 quart ice cream over caramel in crust. Sprinkle chopped pecans over ice cream. Drizzle ½ cup caramel sauce over. Freeze until caramel sets, about 10 minutes. Spread remaining ice cream over. Freeze until top of pie is firm, about 1 hour. Arrange pecan halves in 3 concentric circles around top of pie. Drizzle ¼ cup caramel sauce over pie. Freeze pie until frozen solid, at least 4 hours. *(Can be prepared 5 days ahead. Cover tightly with foil; keep frozen. Cover and chill remaining caramel sauce.)*

Rewarm caramel sauce over low heat, stirring often. Cut around pan sides to loosen pie. Let soften slightly at room temperature, about 10 minutes. Remove pan sides. Serve pie with warm caramel sauce.

MAKING CARAMEL:

STEP 1: Stir sugar and water in heavy saucepan over medium-low heat until sugar dissolves.

STEP 2: For best results, boil the syrup without stirring; swirl the pan occasionally for even browning, until the syrup is deep amber.

STEP 3: To keep the syrup from becoming grainy, use a pastry brush dipped into water to brush down any sugar crystals sticking to the sides of the pan.

Equipment

For making ice cream you'll need an ice cream machine. There are basically three types: the old-fashioned manual crank machine, the expensive (read hundreds here) all-electric machine that can go from off to freezing in just a few minutes, and the not-too-pricey electric ice cream makers that churn the ice cream ingredients in buckets that are pre-frozen. All three produce terrific ice cream, so the choice can be based on finances, storage capacity (the electric ice cream maker with the pre-freeze bucket is the smallest) and patience. Type A ice cream eaters should at least consider the expensive but fastest type.

Also useful: ice cream scoops, a blender or food processor for pureeing ingredients for desserts and sauces, a handheld mixer, a whisk, a nonstick pot for cooking up the ice cream base, and a sieve for straining it, along with a metal baking pan for granitas. Some frozen desserts, like the delicious ice cream pie here, call for a springform pan.

Watermelon-berry granita

AN ITALIAN GRANITA IS FLAVORED LIQUID THAT HAS BEEN FROZEN, THEN SCRAPED WITH A FORK TO MAKE A FLAKY, ICY TREAT (KIND OF LIKE A SNOW CONE FOR GROWN-UPS).

7 cups ¾-inch cubes seeded watermelon (from 4¼ pounds)

½ cup sugar

2 tablespoons fresh lemon juice

1 large ripe strawberry, hulled
Pinch of salt

6 TO 8 SERVINGS

Working in batches, puree watermelon in blender until smooth. Return 4 cups puree to blender. Add all remaining ingredients. Blend until smooth. Pour mixture into 13x9x2-inch metal baking pan. Freeze until icy at edges of pan, about 45 minutes. Whisk to distribute frozen portions evenly. Freeze again until icy at edges of pan and overall texture is slushy, about 45 minutes.

Whisk granita to distribute frozen portions evenly. Freeze until solid, about 3 hours. Using fork, scrape granita down length of pan, forming icy flakes. Freeze granita at least 1 hour. (*Can be prepared 1 day ahead. Cover and keep frozen.*)

Watermelon-berry granita with melon and berries

TRY THE WATERMELON GRANITA ABOVE WITH THIS FRESH BERRY AND MELON TOPPING (PICTURED OPPOSITE) OR THE COFFEE GRANITA (PAGE 178; PICTURED OPPOSITE) THE NEXT TIME YOU WANT A COOLING DESSERT.

3 cups ½-inch cubes seeded watermelon

1 cup diced hulled strawberries

1 cup fresh raspberries

1 cup fresh blueberries

3 tablespoons sugar

1 tablespoon thinly sliced fresh mint

Watermelon-Berry Granita (see recipe above)

6 TO 8 SERVINGS

Mix first 6 ingredients in large bowl. Let topping stand at least 30 minutes and up to 2 hours.

Working quickly, scoop granita into bowls. Spoon topping alongside granita and serve immediately.

Coffee granita with white chocolate-sambuca cream

IN ITALY, COFFEE GRANITA IS SERVED IN TALL GLASSES FILLED HALFWAY WITH GRANITA AND THEN TOPPED WITH WHIPPED CREAM. HERE, THAT WHIPPED CREAM IS FLAVORED WITH MELTED WHITE CHOCOLATE AND SAMBUCA, AN ANISE-FLAVORED LIQUEUR, FOR A DECADENT TREAT (PICTURED ON PAGE 177).

COFFEE GRANITA

- 4 cups freshly brewed strong coffee (made from 6 cups water and 2½ cups ground French roast coffee)
- 1 cup sugar
- 1 tablespoon grated orange peel
- 1 teaspoon vanilla extract
- 1 tablespoon sambuca or other anise-flavored liqueur

WHITE CHOCOLATE CREAM

- 2 cups chilled whipping cream
- 4 ounces good-quality white chocolate (such as Lindt or Baker's), chopped
- 2 tablespoons sambuca
- 1 teaspoon vanilla extract

  Orange peel strips or chocolate-covered coffee beans

  8 SERVINGS

FOR COFFEE GRANITA: Stir first 4 ingredients in bowl until sugar dissolves. Pour into 13x9x2-inch metal pan. Chill 2 hours; mix in sambuca.

Freeze coffee mixture until icy at edges of pan, about 45 minutes. Whisk to distribute frozen portions evenly. Freeze again until icy at edges of pan and overall texture is slushy, about 45 minutes. Whisk to distribute frozen portions evenly. Freeze until solid, 3 hours. Using fork, scrape granita down length of pan, forming icy flakes. Freeze at least 1 hour. *(Can be prepared 1 day ahead. Cover; keep frozen.)*

FOR WHITE CHOCOLATE CREAM: Combine ⅓ cup whipping cream and chocolate in medium metal bowl. Set over saucepan of barely simmering water (do not let bottom of bowl touch water). Stir until mixture is smooth. Remove from over water. Cool 15 minutes. Beat remaining 1⅔ cups whipping cream, sambuca and vanilla in large bowl until soft peaks form. Fold ¼ of whipped cream into white chocolate mixture to lighten. Fold in remaining whipped cream in 2 additions. Refrigerate topping up to 8 hours.

Working quickly, scoop granita into glasses, filling halfway. Fill to top with cream. Garnish with peel or coffee beans; serve immediately.

Quick coconut sorbet

A SORBET IS SIMILAR TO A SHERBET, EXCEPT THAT IT CONTAINS NO DAIRY INGREDIENTS. (CREAM OF COCONUT IS A THICK MIXTURE OF COCONUT PASTE, WATER AND SUGAR; IT DOES NOT ACTUALLY CONTAIN CREAM.)

- 1 15-ounce can cream of coconut (such as Coco López)*
- 1 cup ice-cold water
- ¼ teaspoon rum extract

  MAKES ABOUT 2 CUPS

Whisk all ingredients in medium bowl. Transfer to 11x7x2-inch glass baking dish. Freeze until frozen, stirring every 30 minutes, about 3 hours. *(Can be made 2 days ahead. Cover and keep frozen.)*

*Available in the liquor department of most supermarkets nationwide.

Quick coconut sorbet with rhubarb compote

COMPOTES ARE CHILLED FRUIT MIXTURES THAT HAVE BEEN COOKED IN A SUGAR SYRUP OVER MODERATELY LOW HEAT. FRESH RHUBARB (AVAILABLE FROM LATE WINTER TO EARLY SUMMER) AND MINCED CRYSTALLIZED GINGER ARE USED IN THIS VERSION. SERVE IT WITH THE COCONUT SORBET OPPOSITE.

2   pounds fresh rhubarb, trimmed, cut into 1-inch pieces (about 7 cups)

½   cup currant jelly

½   cup sugar

¼   cup minced crystallized ginger

2   tablespoons fresh lemon juice

1   teaspoon grated lemon peel

Quick Coconut Sorbet (see recipe opposite) or 1 pint purchased coconut sorbet

6 SERVINGS

Combine first 6 ingredients in heavy pot. Bring to boil, stirring occasionally. Reduce heat to medium-low, cover and simmer until mixture thickens slightly, about 10 minutes. Transfer to medium bowl. Refrigerate compote until cold. (Can be made 1 day ahead. Cover and chill.) Spoon into bowls. Top with sorbet and serve.

Tips

ICE CREAM recipes that include eggs should *always* call for cooking the eggs in a custard first (as do the vanilla and peach ice cream recipes here). Although the chance is small, raw eggs could contain the salmonella bacterium; cooking the eggs kills any bacteria.

MELTING chocolate for an ice cream sundae sauce? Go slow: When overcooked, chocolate can become grainy. Always melt chocolate over very low heat and stir frequently.

FRUIT-FLAVORED frozen desserts require the ripest, most flavorful fruits: Cold foods tend to dull our taste buds and reduce the impact of flavors.

FOR SMOOTH slicing of frozen dessert pies and cakes, dip the serving knife into hot water between slices.

14

Custards and puddings are the ultimate comfort food. Rich, creamy, sweet and satisfying, they provide an instant antidote for the worst of bad days. As for soufflés, well, these elegant finales offer the best of all worlds—dramatic presentation and heavenly flavor.

In this chapter, we'll guide you through all the essential techniques, so that your soufflés stand tall and your custards and puddings are lump-free. And in the end you'll take comfort in knowing that these soothing foods can be prepared perfectly again and again.

Custards & Soufflés

Honey Crème Brûlée (page 183)

Basic baked custards

CUSTARDS SHOULD BE COOKED SLOWLY OVER LOW HEAT; IF ALLOWED TO BOIL, THEY WILL SEPARATE AND CURDLE. THE BEST WAY TO PREVENT THIS IS TO BAKE THEM IN A WATER BATH, CALLED A *BAIN-MARIE*.

½ cup sugar

2 large eggs

2 large egg yolks

2 teaspoons vanilla extract

   Pinch of salt

2 cups half and half

   6 SERVINGS

Preheat oven to 350°F. Whisk sugar, eggs, egg yolks, vanilla and salt in medium bowl. Heat half and half in small saucepan over medium heat until tiny bubbles form around edge of pan.

Gradually whisk half and half into egg mixture. Divide custard mixture evenly among six ¾-cup custard cups or ramekins. Set cups in 13x9x2-inch baking pan. Pour enough hot water into baking pan to reach halfway up sides of cups.

Place pan with custards in oven; bake until custards are just set in center, about 35 minutes. Remove custards from water and cool 10 minutes. Refrigerate at least 2 hours. *(Can be prepared 1 day ahead. Cover and keep refrigerated.)*

Blueberry custards

USING THE TECHNIQUE OUTLINED FOR THE PLAIN BAKED CUSTARDS ABOVE, YOU CAN MAKE A FLAVORED VERSION BY ADDING FRUIT PRESERVES AND FRESH FRUIT TO THE CUSTARD CUPS BEFORE BAKING. YOU COULD MAKE THIS RECIPE WITH RASPBERRIES, BOYSENBERRIES OR PEACHES INSTEAD OF BLUEBERRIES.

6 tablespoons blueberry preserves

1 ½-pint basket fresh blueberries or 1 cup frozen unsweetened blueberries, thawed

½ cup sugar

2 large eggs

2 large egg yolks

2 teaspoons vanilla extract

   Pinch of salt

2 cups half and half

   6 SERVINGS

Preheat oven to 350°F. Place 1 tablespoon preserves in each of six ¾-cup custard cups or ramekins. Top with blueberries, dividing equally. Whisk sugar, eggs, egg yolks, vanilla and salt to blend in medium bowl. Heat half and half in small saucepan over medium heat until tiny bubbles form around edge of pan. Gradually whisk half and half into egg mixture. Evenly divide custard mixture among cups with berries. Set cups in 13x9x2-inch baking pan. Pour enough hot water into baking pan to reach halfway up sides of cups.

Place pan with custards in oven; bake until custards are just set in center, about 35 minutes. Remove custards from water and cool 10 minutes. Refrigerate at least 2 hours. *(Can be prepared 1 day ahead. Cover and keep refrigerated.)*

Honey crème brûlée

WITH THIS RECIPE (PICTURED ON PAGE 181), PREPARING THE CLASSIC RESTAURANT DESSERT IS ALMOST AS EASY AS ORDERING IT. HERE, TWO DIFFERENT METHODS ARE GIVEN FOR CARAMELIZING THE TOP OF THE CREAMY CUSTARD: USE A MINIATURE BLOWTORCH, CALLED A KITCHEN TORCH IN COOKWARE STORES, OR THE BROILER.

8 large egg yolks

¼ cup plus 8 teaspoons sugar

⅓ cup honey

3 cups whipping cream

Chopped unsalted pistachios (optional)

Assorted fresh berries (optional)

8 SERVINGS

Preheat oven to 350°F. Place eight ¾-cup ramekins or custard cups in roasting pan. Whisk egg yolks, ¼ cup sugar and honey in large bowl to blend. Bring cream to simmer in medium saucepan. Gradually whisk cream into yolk mixture. Pour custard into ramekins, dividing equally.

Pour enough hot water into roasting pan to come halfway up sides of ramekins. Bake until custards are set in center, about 45 minutes. Remove from water; cool. Cover; chill overnight.

Sprinkle 1 teaspoon sugar over each custard. *To brown under broiler:* Preheat broiler. Arrange ramekins on baking sheet. Broil until sugar browns, rotating baking sheet for even browning and watching closely, about 2 minutes. *To brown with blowtorch:* Working with 1 custard at a time, hold blowtorch so that flame is 2 inches above surface. Direct flame so that sugar melts and browns, about 2 minutes.

Refrigerate until custards are firm again but topping is still brittle, at least 2 hours but no longer than 4 hours or topping will soften. Garnish crèmes brûlées with pistachios and berries, if desired.

MAKING CRÈME BRÛLÉE:

STEP 1: While gradually pouring the hot cream into the yolk mixture, whisk constantly but gently to form a smooth custard base.

STEP 2: Before baking the custards, pour hot water into the pan. Using this method, called a *bain-marie* or water bath, keeps the custards from curdling by cooking them gently.

STEP 3: Hold the blowtorch two inches from the layer of sugar on top of the chilled custards. The heat melts and burns the sugar, which forms a crisp layer as it cools.

Milk chocolate parfaits with raspberries

GROWN-UPS ARE SURE TO ENJOY THIS CHILDHOOD FAVORITE—CHOCOLATE PUDDING—ESPECIALLY WHEN IT'S
LAYERED IN CHAMPAGNE GLASSES WITH FRESH RASPBERRIES AND WHIPPED CREAM.

½ cup plus 2 tablespoons sugar

¼ cup unsweetened cocoa powder

2 tablespoons cornstarch

3¼ cups whole milk

4 large egg yolks

2 large eggs

8 ounces milk chocolate, finely chopped

2 tablespoons unsalted butter

1 teaspoon vanilla extract

2 ½-pint baskets fresh raspberries

1½ cups chilled whipping cream

6 SERVINGS

Whisk ½ cup sugar, cocoa and cornstarch in heavy large saucepan. Gradually whisk in milk. Whisk over medium heat until mixture boils and thickens slightly, about 4 minutes. Remove from heat.

Whisk egg yolks and 2 eggs in large bowl. Gradually whisk in hot milk mixture. Return mixture to saucepan. Whisk over medium heat until mixture thickens, about 5 minutes; do not boil. Remove from heat. Add chocolate, butter and vanilla; whisk until pudding mixture is smooth. Cool 10 minutes, whisking occasionally.

Spoon ¼ cup pudding into each of 6 Champagne glasses. Top each with 4 berries. Repeat layering ¼ cup pudding and 4 berries in each glass. Divide remaining pudding among glasses. Cool completely.

Beat whipping cream and remaining 2 tablespoons sugar in large bowl to peaks. Top parfaits with cream. Chill at least 2 hours and up to 8 hours. Top cream with remaining berries.

Because most recipes call for only small amounts of extracts, spices and other ingredients, I end up storing them for long periods of time. How long will they stay fresh?

Most baking products (including flour, sugar, baking powder and baking soda) will last more than a year if they are stored properly. They should be kept in a cool, dark place in airtight containers. The exceptions: VANILLA EXTRACT has a shelf life of four years, and it actually improves with age. It should not be kept in the refrigerator. WHOLE CLOVES, cinnamon sticks and whole nutmeg are good for about four years. Ground spices, such as cinnamon, cloves and nutmeg, keep for about three years. Don't store the spices near the stove, as heat can diminish their flavors.

CHOCOLATE CHIPS are good for about two years. Keep them in a cool, dark place, or wrap tightly and store in the refrigerator. SHREDDED COCONUT, in an unopened package, lasts for 18 months. After it has been opened, seal it in a resealable plastic bag, and use it within two months. Or the coconut can be wrapped in foil, sealed in a plastic bag and frozen for up to six months. WALNUTS and almonds last about 18 months if stored in the freezer. DRIED FRUITS should be stored in sealed plastic bags in the freezer. They stay fresh for about a year.

Rice pudding with almonds and cherry sauce

MEDIUM- OR SHORT-GRAIN RICE GIVES THE PUDDING A WONDERFUL CREAMINESS AND DOES NOT HARDEN
WHEN CHILLED, AS LONG-GRAIN RICE SOMETIMES WILL.

4¾ cups whole milk

7 tablespoons plus ¾ cup sugar

¾ cup short-grain or
    medium-grain rice

1 vanilla bean, split lengthwise

½ cup sliced almonds, toasted

1 cup chilled whipping cream

1 16-ounce package frozen
   pitted cherries, thawed

1 lemon, quartered

1 tablespoon cornstarch mixed
   with 1 tablespoon water

6 TO 8 SERVINGS

Combine milk, 5 tablespoons sugar and rice in heavy medium sauce-pan. Scrape in seeds from vanilla bean; add bean. Bring to boil. Reduce heat to medium; simmer until rice is tender and mixture is thick, stirring frequently, about 35 minutes. Discard bean. Mix in almonds. Pour rice pudding into 13x9x2-inch metal baking dish; cool completely.

Using electric mixer, beat cream and 2 tablespoons sugar in medium bowl until medium peaks form. Fold cream into rice pudding mixture in pan. Cover and refrigerate until cold, about 4 hours. *(Can be pre-pared 1 day ahead. Keep refrigerated.)*

Cook cherries, lemon and remaining ¾ cup sugar in heavy medium saucepan over medium heat until cherries are tender, stirring occa-sionally, about 5 minutes. Add cornstarch mixture and bring to boil, stirring constantly. Discard lemon. Spoon pudding into bowls. Spoon hot cherry sauce over and serve.

Equipment

One whisk is not enough. When you're beating egg whites into stiff peaks or whipping cream into soft mounds—basically, when you're pumping any ingredient full of air—what you need is a big balloon whisk. A medium whisk works well for creams and custards, as well as for soups and sauces. And a small whisk, ten inches long or so, is the all-purpose utensil that handles everything from folding flour into batter to making salad dressings. In any size, look for a whisk with as many wires as possible, since each wire multiplies the whisk's action.

Also useful: a small nylon pastry bag, a handheld mixer, a strainer, a double boiler, ramekins and soufflé dishes, a copper bowl for coaxing optimum volume out of each egg white, mousse molds, a large flat roasting pan for hot-water baths, and a small propane blowtorch (or your oven broiler) for crème brûlée.

Basic vanilla soufflé

THE SIMPLE SOUFFLÉ IS CONVENIENT BECAUSE YOU CAN MAKE THE BASE A DAY AHEAD. ADD A DUSTING OF POWDERED SUGAR FOR THE CROWNING TOUCH.

1   **cup whole milk**

½   **large or 1 medium vanilla bean, split lengthwise**

3   **large egg yolks, room temperature**

5   **tablespoons sugar**

¼   **cup all purpose flour**

5   **large egg whites, room temperature**

    Pinch of cream of tartar

    Powdered sugar

4 TO 6 SERVINGS

Combine milk and vanilla bean in heavy small saucepan. Bring just to simmer. Remove from heat, cover and let steep 30 minutes.

Remove vanilla bean from milk; reserve for another use. Return milk to simmer. Remove from heat. Whisk egg yolks and 3 tablespoons sugar in medium bowl until creamy, about 1 minute. Add flour to yolks and whisk until just blended. Gradually whisk in hot milk. Return mixture to saucepan. Whisk over medium-low heat until custard boils and is very thick, about 3 minutes. Remove custard from heat. Scrape from sides of pan. Cool until just warm to touch. *(Can be prepared 1 day ahead. Press plastic wrap onto surface of custard. Chill. Before continuing, whisk custard over low heat until barely warm. Do not let custard boil.)*

Position rack in center of oven and preheat to 400°F. Generously butter 6- to 7-cup soufflé dish and coat with sugar. Using electric mixer, beat egg whites with cream of tartar to soft peaks. Gradually add remaining 2 tablespoons sugar and beat until stiff but not dry. Whisk custard until smooth. Fold ¼ of whites into custard to lighten; gently spoon remaining whites over custard and fold in. Pour into prepared dish, spreading evenly. Bake soufflé until puffed and almost firm to touch, 20 to 25 minutes. Dust with powdered sugar. Serve immediately.

Tips

THE SECRET to light soufflés? Egg whites that are beaten until stiff but not dry, and ingredients that are properly folded together. First, fold a quarter of the whites into the batter to lighten the mixture. Spoon the remaining whites on top of the batter, then gently bring a rubber spatula down through whites, across the bottom of the bowl and up the side. Turning the bowl after each fold, continue folding only until a few streaks of white remain.

TO ENSURE that the coating of sugar on a crème brûlée caramelizes evenly, start with a thick, even layer of granulated or brown sugar across the surface. (If using brown sugar, force the sugar through a fine sieve.)

Individual cappuccino soufflés

WE'VE TAKEN THE BASIC VANILLA SOUFFLÉ (OPPOSITE) AND INCORPORATED IT INTO THIS RECIPE FOR INDIVIDUAL COFFEE- AND CHOCOLATE-FLAVORED SOUFFLÉS. ANOTHER VARIATION TO TRY—ORANGE: MIX 1 TABLESPOON GRATED ORANGE PEEL AND 2 TABLESPOONS ORANGE JUICE INTO THE COOKED CUSTARD; ADD 1 TABLESPOON GRAND MARNIER TO THE CUSTARD BEFORE ADDING THE EGG WHITES.

1 cup whole milk

½ large or 1 medium vanilla bean, split lengthwise

2 tablespoons plus 1 teaspoon instant espresso powder

2 tablespoons plus 1 teaspoon very hot water

3 large egg yolks, room temperature

5 tablespoons sugar

¼ cup all purpose flour

1 ounce semisweet chocolate, finely chopped

5 large egg whites, room temperature

Pinch of cream of tartar

1 teaspoon unsweetened cocoa powder

1 teaspoon powdered sugar

½ teaspoon cinnamon

Sweetened whipped cream

6 SERVINGS

Combine milk and vanilla bean in heavy small saucepan. Bring to simmer. Remove from heat, cover and let steep 30 minutes.

Meanwhile, dissolve espresso in 2 tablespoons plus 1 teaspoon very hot water. Cool to room temperature.

Remove vanilla bean from milk; reserve for another use. Return milk to simmer. Remove from heat. Whisk egg yolks and 3 tablespoons sugar in medium bowl until creamy, about 1 minute. Add flour to yolks and whisk until just blended. Gradually whisk in hot milk. Return mixture to saucepan. Whisk over medium-low heat until custard boils and is very thick, about 3 minutes. Remove custard from heat. Add chocolate and whisk until melted. Gradually whisk in espresso. Scrape sides of pan. Cool until just warm to touch. (Can be prepared 1 day ahead. Press plastic wrap onto surface of custard. Chill. Before continuing with recipe, whisk custard over low heat until barely warm.)

Position rack in center of oven and preheat to 400°F. Generously butter six 1-cup soufflé dishes. Coat with sugar. Using electric mixer, beat egg whites with cream of tartar to soft peaks. Gradually add remaining 2 tablespoons sugar and beat until stiff but not dry. Whisk custard until smooth. Fold ¼ of whites into custard to lighten; spoon remaining whites over custard and fold in. Spoon into prepared dishes, spreading evenly. Bake until puffed and brown and almost firm to touch, about 15 minutes.

Mix cocoa, powdered sugar and cinnamon in small bowl. Sift over tops of soufflés. Serve immediately with whipped cream.

Panna cotta with strawberry-Vin Santo sauce

ITALIAN FOR "COOKED CREAM," *PANNA COTTA* IS AN EGGLESS (USUALLY) CUSTARD, OFTEN TOPPED WITH PINE NUTS AND HONEY. THIS RECIPE (PICTURED OPPOSITE) INCORPORATES THOSE INGREDIENTS INTO THE CUSTARD, THEN TOPS IT OFF WITH A DELICIOUS STRAWBERRY SAUCE LACED WITH VIN SANTO, A TUSCAN DESSERT WINE.

1   **pound fresh strawberries, hulled, quartered (about 4 cups)**

1⅓   **cups sugar**

3   **tablespoons Vin Santo,* Muscat wine or cream Sherry**

½   **teaspoon vanilla extract**

¼   **teaspoon (packed) grated lemon peel**

¼   **cup cold water**

4   **teaspoons unflavored gelatin**

4   **cups whipping cream**

1   **tablespoon orange blossom honey**

2   **cups pine nuts (about 9 ounces)**

    Additional pine nuts

10 SERVINGS

Puree strawberries in processor. Transfer puree to heavy large saucepan. Mix in ⅓ cup sugar, 2 tablespoons Vin Santo, ¼ teaspoon vanilla and lemon peel. Simmer over medium-low heat until sauce is reduced to 2 cups, stirring often, about 15 minutes. Cool. *(Can be prepared 2 days ahead. Cover and refrigerate.)*

Pour ¼ cup cold water into metal bowl; sprinkle gelatin over. Let stand until gelatin softens, about 10 minutes. Set bowl in saucepan of simmering water. Stir just until gelatin dissolves, about 1 minute.

Combine cream, remaining 1 cup sugar, honey and remaining ¼ teaspoon vanilla in heavy large saucepan. Bring to boil, stirring until sugar dissolves. Remove cream mixture from heat. Add gelatin mixture and remaining 1 tablespoon Vin Santo; whisk until well blended.

Divide 2 cups pine nuts among ten ¾-cup custard cups. Divide cream mixture among cups. Chill overnight.

Set cups in small bowl of warm water to loosen panna cotta, about 20 seconds each. Run small knife between panna cotta and custard cups. Invert panna cotta onto plates. Spoon sauce over. Sprinkle with additional pine nuts; serve.

*An Italian dessert wine available at some liquor stores and specialty foods stores.

What's the difference between whipping cream and heavy cream?

Two words: *fat content.* Whipping cream (also called light whipping cream) has 30 to 36 percent milk fat. Heavy cream (or heavy whipping cream) has at least 36 percent—and often up to 40 percent. Substituting one for the other is generally acceptable. But the higher the fat content, the faster and more firmly the cream will whip up.

15

Other desserts may be more sophisticated, and many are more complex, but nothing gets the kids (and the grown-ups) lined up outside your kitchen like the aroma of freshly baked cookies. Of course, we have a killer recipe for America's favorite cookie—chocolate chip—along with many other familiar (and some not-so-familiar) treats. None is difficult to make, but each benefits from a few handy tricks.

This chapter will cover the basics of good cookie making, and answer a few questions, too. How can you soften butter quickly? What's the best baking sheet? And most important: When the craving strikes, how fast can you get a batch of brownies in the oven?

Cookies

Sour Lemon Bars (page 199)

Cookie-jar chocolate chip cookies

FOR CHEWY COOKIES, BAKE UNTIL GOLDEN BROWN BUT STILL SLIGHTLY UNDERDONE IN THE CENTER. THE COOKIES WILL CONTINUE TO COOK A BIT ON THE HOT BAKING SHEETS ONCE REMOVED FROM THE OVEN.

Nonstick vegetable oil spray

3 cups all purpose flour

1 teaspoon baking soda

1 teaspoon salt

1 cup (2 sticks) unsalted butter, room temperature

1 cup sugar

1 cup (packed) golden brown sugar

2 large eggs

2 teaspoons vanilla extract

1 12-ounce package semisweet chocolate chips

MAKES ABOUT 30

Preheat oven to 325°F. Spray large baking sheet with nonstick spray. Whisk flour, baking soda and salt in medium bowl to blend. Using electric mixer, beat butter in large bowl until light and fluffy. Add sugar and brown sugar; beat until well blended. Add eggs and vanilla; beat until mixture is creamy and well blended. Gradually add flour mixture, beating just until blended. Stir in chocolate chips.

Working in batches, drop dough by generously mounded table-spoonfuls onto prepared baking sheet, spacing 3 inches apart. Bake cookies until pale brown, about 15 minutes. Cool slightly on sheet. Transfer cookies to racks; cool completely. *(Can be prepared 2 days ahead. Store airtight at room temperature.)*

Equipment

In cookie baking, almost nothing is as crucial as the quality of your baking sheets. Heavy-duty aluminum baking sheets are the best choice because they heat quickly and evenly. Buy the largest baking sheets that will fit into your oven while still allowing two inches of air space all around. Avoid black metal sheets, which can burn cookies quickly, or insulated baking sheets, which may keep cookie bottoms from browning. Parchment paper, either silicone-coated or regular, can transform well-worn baking sheets into even browners to which nothing sticks.

Also useful: a standing mixer; a rolling pin, either French style or with handles; and cookie cutters in whatever shapes suit the occasion—and your mood.

Brown sugar-oatmeal cookies

ANOTHER POPULAR "DROP" COOKIE, SO CALLED BECAUSE SPOONFULS OF DOUGH ARE DROPPED ONTO THE BAKING SHEET. USING VEGETABLE SHORTENING INSTEAD OF BUTTER WILL PRODUCE A CRISPER COOKIE.

3 cups old-fashioned oats

1 cup all purpose flour

1 teaspoon baking soda

1 teaspoon salt

1 teaspoon ground cinnamon

1 cup vegetable shortening

1 cup (packed) dark brown sugar

1 cup sugar

2 large eggs

1 teaspoon vanilla extract

MAKES ABOUT 36

Preheat oven to 350°F. Butter 2 baking sheets. Combine first 5 ingredients in medium bowl; whisk to blend. Set aside. Using electric mixer, beat shortening, brown sugar and sugar in large bowl until blended. Beat in eggs 1 at a time, then vanilla. Reduce mixer speed to low; beat in dry ingredients.

Drop dough by rounded tablespoonfuls onto prepared baking sheets, spacing 1½ inches apart. Bake cookies until golden brown and crisp to touch, about 15 minutes. Let cool 5 minutes on baking sheets. Transfer cookies to racks; cool completely. *(Can be prepared up to 3 days ahead. Store in airtight container at room temperature.)*

Old-fashioned peanut butter cookies

DIFFERENT RECIPES MAY CALL FOR DIFFERENT TYPES OF PEANUT BUTTER: CREAMY VARIETIES FOR SMOOTHNESS, CRUNCHY FOR ADDED TEXTURE, NATURAL FOR ITS LACK OF SEASONINGS. FOR BEST RESULTS, USE THE TYPE SPECIFIED IN THE RECIPE. THESE CAN BE MADE WITH EITHER THE CREAMY OR THE CHUNKY KIND.

3 cups all purpose flour

1 teaspoon baking powder

1 teaspoon salt

1 cup (2 sticks) unsalted butter, room temperature

1 cup creamy or chunky peanut butter (do not use old-fashioned style or freshly ground)

2 teaspoons vanilla extract

1 cup (packed) golden brown sugar

1 cup sugar

2 large eggs

MAKES ABOUT 48

Preheat oven to 350°F. Line 2 large baking sheets with parchment paper. Mix flour, baking powder and salt in medium bowl. Using electric mixer, beat butter, peanut butter and vanilla in large bowl until well blended. Beat in both sugars. Scrape down sides of bowl. Stir half of dry ingredients into mixture. Add eggs 1 at a time, stirring well after each addition. Mix in remaining dry ingredients.

For each cookie, roll 1 heaping tablespoonful dough into 1¾-inch-diameter ball. Arrange dough balls 2½ inches apart on prepared baking sheets. Using back of fork, flatten dough balls and form crosshatch design on top. Bake cookies until dry on top and golden brown on bottom, about 14 minutes. Cool cookies on baking sheets 5 minutes. Transfer cookies to racks and cool completely. *(Can be prepared up to 3 days ahead. Store in airtight container at room temperature.)*

Frosted sugar cookies

USE THIS "REFRIGERATOR" DOUGH RECIPE TO MAKE ROLLED CUTOUT COOKIES NOT JUST AROUND THE HOLIDAYS BUT ALL YEAR LONG. BE SURE TO ROLL OUT THE DOUGH EVENLY SO THAT THE COOKIES ARE ALL THE SAME THICKNESS. THIS, AND ROTATING THE BAKING SHEETS OCCASIONALLY IN THE OVEN, WILL HELP THE COOKIES COOK EVENLY.

COOKIES

- 1 cup (2 sticks) unsalted butter, room temperature
- 1 cup (packed) golden brown sugar
- 1 large egg
- 1 teaspoon vanilla extract
- 2⅔ cups all purpose flour
- 1 teaspoon baking powder
- ½ teaspoon salt
- ½ teaspoon ground nutmeg

FROSTING

- 9 cups (or more) powdered sugar (about 2¼ pounds)
- 4½ tablespoons Just Whites (pasteurized powdered egg whites)*
- 12 tablespoons (or more) water
  Assorted liquid food colorings

- 4 (or more) small disposable pastry bags**

MAKES ABOUT 36

FOR COOKIES: Using electric mixer, beat butter and brown sugar in large bowl until fluffy. Beat in egg and vanilla. Sift flour, baking powder, salt and nutmeg over; stir to blend well. Turn dough out onto lightly floured surface and knead gently 1 minute. Shape dough into ½-inch-thick rectangle. Cut into 4 equal pieces; wrap in plastic and refrigerate at least 3 hours and up to 1 day. Let dough soften slightly at room temperature before rolling out.

Position rack in center of oven and preheat to 350°F. Butter large baking sheet. Working with 1 dough piece at a time, roll out dough on lightly floured surface to ⅛-inch thickness, lifting and turning dough often and dusting surface very lightly with flour to prevent sticking. Using floured 3- to 4-inch cutters, cut out cookies. Pull away excess dough from around cookies. Transfer cookies to prepared baking sheet, spacing 1 inch apart (cookies will not spread). Gently reroll dough scraps; cut out more cookies. Transfer cookies to same baking sheet.

Bake cookies until light brown, about 11 minutes. Let cool 5 minutes on baking sheet. Transfer cookies to rack; cool completely.

Repeat with remaining dough pieces, baking 1 sheet of cookies at a time. Cool sheet completely and butter sheet lightly between batches.

FOR FROSTING: Whisk 9 cups sugar and powdered egg whites in large bowl to blend. Whisk in 12 tablespoons water. If necessary, whisk in more water by teaspoonfuls or more sugar by tablespoonfuls until frosting is medium-thick and very smooth. Place ½ cup frosting in each of 4 small bowls; mix in colors of your choice. Thin frosting in each bowl as needed by mixing in ¼ teaspoon water at a time.

Using pastry brush or small metal offset spatula, spread frosting on cookies; set cookies aside and let frosting dry, about 30 minutes. Fold down top 2 inches of 1 disposable pastry bag, forming collar. Holding bag under collar and using small rubber spatula, fill bag with 1 color of frosting. Cut off small tip from end. Repeat with remaining pastry bags, filling each with 1 color of frosting. Pipe decorations onto frosted cookies in desired patterns and colors. Let cookies stand until decorations are firm and dry, at least 4 hours. *(Can be prepared 3 days ahead. Place cookies in single layer between sheets of waxed paper in airtight container; store at room temperature.)*

*Just Whites can be found in the baking-products section of most supermarkets.

**Disposable pastry bags are available at cake and candy supply stores.

MAKING FROSTED SUGAR COOKIES:

STEP 1: To make the chilled sugar cookie dough easier to roll, begin by firmly pressing a generously floured rolling pin into the dough several times to flatten slightly.

STEP 2: Whisk powdered sugar, powdered egg whites and water to make the icing. Add more sugar or water as needed to achieve a medium-thick, pourable consistency.

STEP 3: An alternative to the standard pastry bag is a disposable plastic bag. After filling the plastic bag with icing, use scissors to cut off the very bottom of the tip, allowing the icing to come out.

Pecan crescent cookies

TO MAKE THE "REFRIGERATOR" DOUGH FOR THESE COOKIES EASIER TO WORK WITH, START A DAY IN ADVANCE SO THAT THE DOUGH HAS A CHANCE TO CHILL OVERNIGHT.

2 cups all purpose flour, sifted

1 cup pecans, toasted

½ teaspoon salt

1 cup (2 sticks) unsalted butter, room temperature

¾ cup powdered sugar

2 teaspoons vanilla extract

Additional powdered sugar

MAKES ABOUT 36

Preheat oven to 325°F. Combine 1 cup flour, pecans and salt in processor. Using on/off turns, finely chop pecans. Using electric mixer, beat butter, ¾ cup powdered sugar and vanilla in large bowl until blended. Add pecan mixture and remaining 1 cup flour; mix thoroughly. Divide dough in half. Wrap each half in plastic; chill overnight.

Working with 1 tablespoon dough at a time, shape dough into 3-inch-long logs. Pinch ends of logs to taper and turn in slightly, forming crescents. Place cookies on ungreased baking sheets, spacing 1 inch apart (cookies will not spread).

Bake cookies until light brown around edges and firm to touch, about 18 minutes. Cool cookies 10 minutes on baking sheets. Roll cookies in additional powdered sugar. Cool completely on racks. (*Cookies can be prepared 2 weeks ahead. Store in airtight container.*)

Simple shortbread

NOT A BREAD AT ALL, THIS CRISP, BUTTERY COOKIE IS A SCOTTISH CLASSIC. TRADITIONALLY, THE DOUGH IS PRESSED INTO A SHALLOW EARTHENWARE MOLD. HERE, YOU CAN USE EITHER A CAKE PAN OR A PIE DISH. BE SURE TO CUT THE SHORTBREAD WHILE IT'S STILL HOT; IT WILL CRACK AND CRUMBLE IF CUT AFTER IT COOLS.

½ cup sugar

½ teaspoon salt

1 cup (2 sticks) chilled unsalted butter, cut into ½-inch cubes

¼ teaspoon vanilla extract

2 cups all purpose flour

MAKES 24

Blend sugar and salt in processor. Mix in butter until blended and smooth. Blend in vanilla. Add flour; using on/off turns, process until just blended but still slightly crumbly, occasionally scraping down sides of bowl. Gather dough into ball; flatten into disk. Wrap dough in plastic wrap and refrigerate 30 minutes.

Position rack in top third of oven and preheat to 250°F. Divide dough in half. Press each half onto bottom of 8-inch-diameter cake pan or 9-inch-diameter pie dish. Bake shortbread 30 minutes. Rotate pans and continue baking until cooked through and very pale golden, about 30 minutes longer. Cool in pans on racks 10 minutes. Cut each warm shortbread while still in pan into 12 wedges. Cool completely. Using thin spatula, carefully transfer wedges to platter. (*Can be prepared up to 4 days ahead. Store airtight at room temperature.*)

Honey and almond biscotti

THE TWICE-BAKED ITALIAN COOKIES KNOWN AS BISCOTTI ARE MADE BY FIRST BAKING THE COOKIE DOUGH IN A LOAF, THEN SLICING THE LOAF WHILE IT IS STILL WARM AND BAKING THE SLICES UNTIL CRISP. THE RESULT IS A CRUNCHY COOKIE THAT IS IDEAL FOR DIPPING IN HOT COFFEE.

2½   cups all purpose flour
1½   cups plus 1 tablespoon sugar
2   teaspoons baking powder
¾   teaspoon salt
5   large eggs
1   tablespoon honey
1   tablespoon grated lemon peel
1½   teaspoons vanilla extract
1   cup whole almonds, toasted
     MAKES ABOUT 36

Preheat oven to 375°F. Butter and flour large baking sheet. Whisk flour, 1½ cups sugar, baking powder and salt in large bowl to blend. Make well in center of dry ingredients. Add 4 eggs, honey, lemon peel and vanilla to well. Stir egg mixture until blended; gradually mix with dry ingredients. Mix in almonds.

Drop dough by tablespoonfuls onto prepared sheet, forming two 12-inch-long by 2-inch-wide logs. Space logs 3 inches apart. Using moistened fingertips, shape logs neatly. Beat remaining egg in small bowl. Brush logs with egg glaze; sprinkle with 1 tablespoon sugar. Bake logs until golden and firm to touch, about 15 minutes. Cool on baking sheet 10 minutes. Reduce oven temperature to 325°F.

Transfer warm logs to work surface. Cut on slight diagonal into ½-inch-thick slices. Arrange slices, cut side down, on 2 clean baking sheets. Bake until pale golden, about 8 minutes. Cool completely. *(Store in airtight container up to 1 week at room temperature.)*

Tips

THE IMPORTANCE of a properly calibrated oven cannot be overstated. Once a year, use an oven thermometer to check that your oven is baking at the temperature indicated on the dial.

USE a self-releasing ice-cream scoop to form cookie dough into balls; a three-tablespoon scoop makes a perfect three-inch cookie. (Hint: Freeze some dough balls, and you can bake them straight from the freezer whenever the urge for a cookie strikes.)

MAKE SURE cookies have cooled completely before freezing them; otherwise, they will end up soggy. Pack them in a double layer, separated with waxed paper, in an airtight container. Freeze frosted cookies for no longer than three months, and unfrosted cookies for up to six months.

BEFORE creaming butter and sugar, the butter should be slightly softened. If necessary, cut it in cubes and microwave it for ten seconds.

Pistachio meringues

MERINGUES ARE CLASSIC COOKIES MADE WITH BEATEN EGG WHITES AND SUGAR AND BAKED IN THE OVEN AT A VERY LOW TEMPERATURE. HERE, CREAM OF TARTAR IS BEATEN WITH THE EGG WHITES TO HELP MAKE THE MERINGUE MORE STABLE. CHOPPED PISTACHIOS ADD INTEREST.

1¼ cups shelled natural pistachios, chopped

½ cup powdered sugar

3 large egg whites

¼ teaspoon cream of tartar

⅔ cup sugar

MAKES ABOUT 24

Preheat oven to 225°F. Line 2 large baking sheets with aluminum foil; butter and flour foil. Mix pistachios and ½ cup powdered sugar in small bowl to blend. Beat egg whites and cream of tartar in medium bowl until soft peaks form. Gradually add ⅔ cup sugar, beating until whites are stiff and shiny. Fold nut mixture into egg whites. Drop meringue onto prepared sheets by rounded tablespoonfuls, spacing 1 inch apart and spreading to form 2½-inch rounds.

Bake meringues until dry and almost crisp but not yet colored, about 45 minutes. Cool meringues on baking sheets. *(Can be prepared 1 week ahead. Wrap airtight in foil and freeze.)*

Chocolate chip fudge brownies

BAKING BROWNIES (A KIND OF BAR COOKIE) FROM SCRATCH IS SIMPLER THAN MIGHT BE IMAGINED. ONE TRICK: BE SURE YOU DON'T OVERBAKE THEM. TO VARY THE RECIPE, ADD CHOPPED NUTS, CHOPPED DRIED CHERRIES OR DIFFERENT FLAVORED CHIPS, SUCH AS WHITE CHOCOLATE OR BUTTERSCOTCH.

¾ cup (1½ sticks) unsalted butter

4 ounces unsweetened chocolate, chopped

4 large eggs

1¾ cups sugar

1½ teaspoons vanilla extract

¾ cup all purpose flour

1 cup semisweet chocolate chips

Powdered sugar

MAKES 24

Preheat oven to 350°F. Butter 13x9x2-inch metal baking pan. Stir butter and unsweetened chocolate in heavy medium saucepan over medium-low heat until melted and smooth. Remove from heat. Whisk eggs and 1¾ cups sugar in large bowl until pale yellow and light, about 3 minutes. Gradually whisk in warm chocolate mixture. Whisk in vanilla, then flour. Mix in chocolate chips. Pour batter into prepared pan.

Bake brownies until tester inserted into center comes out with moist crumbs attached, about 25 minutes. Cool brownies completely in pan on rack. Cut into squares. *(Can be prepared 1 day ahead. Store in airtight container at room temperature.)* Sift powdered sugar over.

Sour lemon bars

THESE LEMON BARS (PICTURED ON PAGE 191) ARE ANOTHER TYPE OF BAR COOKIE—AND A DELICIOUS TAKE ON AN OLD FAVORITE. THE LEMON TOPPING SHOULD BE POURED OVER THE CRUST AS SOON AS IT COMES OUT OF THE OVEN. THE HOT PAN WILL SET THE EDGES SO THAT THE TOPPING DOESN'T RUN UNDER THE CRUST.

CRUST

1½   **cups all purpose flour**

¼   **cup powdered sugar**

  Pinch of salt

½   **cup (1 stick) chilled unsalted butter, cut into pieces**

½   **teaspoon vanilla extract**

TOPPING

5   **large eggs, room temperature**

2   **cups sugar**

1   **cup strained fresh lemon juice**

3   **tablespoons all purpose flour**

2½   **tablespoons grated lemon peel**

  Powdered sugar

MAKES 32

FOR CRUST: Position rack in center of oven and preheat to 350°F. Line 9-inch square baking pan with 2-inch-high sides with foil, extending 1 inch above sides of pan. Combine flour, powdered sugar and salt in processor. Add butter; using on/off turns, cut in until mixture appears sandy. Add vanilla and process until dough begins to come together. Press dough evenly into prepared baking pan. Bake until golden brown, about 28 minutes.

MEANWHILE, PREPARE TOPPING: Whisk eggs and 2 cups sugar in medium bowl to blend. Whisk in lemon juice, then flour. Strain into another bowl. Mix in lemon peel.

Reduce oven temperature to 325°F. Pour topping over hot crust. Bake until sides are set and filling no longer moves in center when pan is shaken gently, about 22 minutes. Cool on rack. Cover and refrigerate at least 4 hours or overnight.

Using foil sides as aid, lift dessert from pan. Fold down foil sides. Cut into 16 squares. Cut each square diagonally in half, forming 2 triangles. Sift powdered sugar over lemon bars. *(Can be prepared 1 day ahead. Store in airtight container in refrigerator.)*

I know the white inner pith of a lemon is bitter, so I am careful to grate only the outermost skin. Yet some cookies and other baked goods still turn out bitter. Any advice?

Avoid using the tiniest grater holes for this task. No matter how careful you are, they always tend to remove some pith along with the peel. Also, they usually compact the finest shreds, so that you might actually end up with more peel than the recipe requires. Instead, try the smaller of the two cheese-grating holes, and use very fresh, firm lemons. Or use a zester: When it is drawn across the skin of a lemon, the zester cuts thin threads of peel that can be easily chopped with a knife.

Chocolate-almond macaroons

UNLIKE COCONUT MACAROONS, WHICH ARE MADE WITH FLAKED OR SHREDDED COCONUT, TRADITIONAL LIGHT AND SLIGHTLY CHEWY FRENCH MACAROONS LIKE THESE ARE MADE WITH ALMOND PASTE OR GROUND ALMONDS. PIPING THE COOKIE BATTER FROM A PASTRY BAG WILL HELP YOU MAKE PERFECTLY FORMED ROUNDS.

1 **1-pound box powdered sugar**

2 **cups whole blanched almonds**

6 **tablespoons unsweetened cocoa powder**

¾ **cup egg whites (about 6 large)**

MAKES 48

Preheat oven to 400°F. Line 2 large baking sheets with parchment paper. Blend powdered sugar and almonds in processor until nuts are ground to powder, scraping sides of bowl often, about 8 minutes. Add cocoa and blend 1 minute more. Using electric mixer, beat egg whites in large bowl until stiff but not dry. Fold nut mixture into whites in 4 additions, making thick batter.

Spoon half of batter into pastry bag fitted with ½-inch plain round tip. Pipe batter onto each prepared sheet in 12 walnut-size mounds, spacing mounds apart (cookies will spread slightly). Bake cookies, 1 sheet at a time, until firm to touch in center and dry and cracked on top, about 11 minutes. Slide parchment with cookies onto work surface; cool cookies. Repeat with remaining batter, cooling sheets completely and lining with clean parchment for each batch. *(Can be prepared 1 day ahead. Store airtight between sheets of waxed paper.)*

Macaroons with chocolate or caramel filling

THE MACAROON RECIPE ABOVE IS USED TO CREATE THESE INDULGENT SANDWICH COOKIES (PICTURED OPPOSITE). EACH FILLING MAKES ENOUGH FOR ONE BATCH OF COOKIES. WHICHEVER FILLING YOU CHOOSE, BE SURE TO PREPARE IT ONE DAY AHEAD.

CHOCOLATE FILLING

¾ **cup whole milk**

5 **tablespoons unsalted butter**

8 **ounces bittersweet (not unsweetened) or semisweet chocolate, finely chopped**

CARAMEL FILLING

2 **large egg yolks**

6 **tablespoons (¾ stick) unsalted butter, room temperature**

¼ **cup whipping cream**

FOR CHOCOLATE FILLING: Bring milk and butter to simmer in heavy medium saucepan. Remove from heat. Add bittersweet chocolate; whisk until melted and smooth. Transfer to small bowl. Cool. Cover and refrigerate until thick and cold, at least 1 day and up to 3 days.

FOR CARAMEL FILLING: Place yolks in medium bowl. Bring 4 tablespoons butter and cream to simmer in heavy small saucepan. Gradually whisk hot cream mixture into yolks. Anchor bowl with yolk mixture by placing bowl on wet kitchen towel; set aside.

2 cups (packed) powdered sugar

6 tablespoons water

Chocolate-Almond Macaroons (see recipe opposite)

MAKES 24 SANDWICH COOKIES

Stir sugar and 6 tablespoons water in heavy medium saucepan over low heat until sugar is dissolved. Increase heat and boil without stirring until syrup is deep amber color, occasionally brushing down sides of pan with wet pastry brush and swirling pan so caramel will color evenly, about 10 minutes. Slowly whisk hot caramel into yolk mixture, then whisk until smooth. Transfer caramel mixture to small bowl; let stand until no longer warm to touch (caramel will become too thick if it cools too long), about 1 hour. Whisk in 2 tablespoons butter. Cover and chill until thick and cold, at least 1 day and up to 3 days.

Arrange 1 macaroon, flat side up, on work surface. Drop 1 scant tablespoon filling onto cookie. Top with second macaroon, flat side down. Press lightly to adhere, making sandwich. Repeat with remaining macaroons and filling. Arrange macaroons on platter. Cover; chill at least 2 hours and up to 1 day. Serve cold.

Index

Page numbers in *italics* indicate color photographs.

Acknowledgments

THE FOLLOWING PEOPLE CONTRIBUTED THE RECIPES INCLUDED IN THIS BOOK:

Bruce Aidells
Rick Anderson
Brad Avooske
Mary Barber
Melanie Barnard
Nancy Verde Barr
Caroline Belk
Anne Bianchi
Lena Cederham Birnbaum
Bistro 921, Hilton Hotel, Portland, OR
Emily and Dick Boenning
Marilynn Bonecki
Georgeanne Brennan
David Burke, Le Pont de la Tour, London, England
Emma and Simon Burns
Taryn and Gene Cafiero
Floyd Cardoz, Tabla, New York, NY
Kathy Cary
Circle Line Restaurant, Prague, Czechoslovakia
C Lazy U Ranch, Granby, CO
Shirley Corriher
Lane Crowther
Sanford D'Amato, Coquette Cafe, Milwaukee, WI
Gary Danko, San Francisco, CA
Molly Shannon Daum
Robin Davis
Lorenza de' Medici
Brooke Dojny
Kathy Donahue
Mark Dorian, Un Grand Café, Chicago, IL
John Dudek
Suzanne Dunaway
Judy and Wash Falk
Tarla Fallgatter
Fat Cats, Cleveland, OH
Lynae Fearing
Barbara Pool Fenzl
Fidel Murphy's Irish Pub, Grand Cayman
Bobby Flay
Janet Fletcher
Jim Fobel
Fregatten Sct. Georg III, Copenhagen, Denmark
Fringale, San Francisco, CA
Monique Gaspais
Michael Gebel
Rozanne Gold

Victoria Granof
Lauren Groveman
Anita Hacker
Ken Haedrich
Beth Hensperger
Pierre Hermé
Cameron and Gerald Hirigoyen
Inn of the Anasazi, Santa Fe, NM
Blanche Johnson
Michele Anna Jordan
Karen Kaplan
Marlin Kaplan, Marlin, Cleveland, OH
Mollie Katzen
Karen Keisir
Sarah and Paul Keith
Thomas Keller
Jeanne Thiel Kelley
Kristine Kidd
Elinor Klivans
Mary Klonowski
Michael Kornick, MK Restaurant, Chicago, IL
Emeril Lagasse, Emeril's, New Orleans, LA
Virginia and David Larkin
Susan Lasken
Las Ventanas, Cabo San Lucas, Mexico
Faye Levy
Emily Luchetti
Lucia Luhan
Ronni Lundy
Marcuccio's, Boston, MA
Peggy Markel
Michael McLaughlin
Susie and Bruce Meyer
Flora Mikula, Les Olivades, Paris, France
Katie Morford
Jinx and Jefferson Morgan
Selma Brown Morrow
Gina and Rich Mortillaro
Nancy Oakes
Ada Olcese, Trattoria Bar Ligagin, Pannesi di Lumarzo (Genoa), Italy
Paprika Bistro, Victoria, British Columbia, Canada
Scott Peacock
Luciano Pellegrini, Valentino, Las Vegas, NV
Sherrie and Fred Petermann
Provisions, Nantucket, MA
Mary Risley
Rick Rodgers
Betty Rosbottom

Vilma Rozansky
Susan C. Samuel
Cathy Sandrich
Richard Sax
Amy Scherber
Chris Schlesinger
Laurence Senelick
Martha Rose Shulman
Stephanie Silva
Marie Simmons
Sarah and Andy Spongberg
Daniela and Gionata Tedeschi
Frances Teasley
Sandy Soto Teich
Sarah Tenaglia
Mary Jo Thoresen
Mary Tripoli
Priscilla Unger
Marcela Valladolid Rodriguez
Joanne Weir
Sara Whiteford
Dede Wilson
Wyldewood, Boynton Beach, FL
Zin Restaurant & Wine Bar, Healdsburg, CA

THE FOLLOWING PEOPLE CONTRIBUTED THE PHOTOGRAPHS INCLUDED IN THIS BOOK:

Jack Andersen
Noel Barnhurst
Beatriz da Costa
Dāsha Wright Ewing
Delbert Garcia
Brian Leatart
Scott Peterson
Rick Szczechowski
Mark Thomas
Elizabeth Watt
James Worrell

ORIGINAL PHOTOGRAPHY, JACKET AND PAGES 2, 5 (right), 6, 7 (right), 8, 9, 11, 21, 31, 33, 47, 51, 59, 69, 75, 91, 113, 135, 143, 147, 159, 164, 171, 175, 179, 181, 189 and 191 by Mark Thomas Studio.
Mark Thomas, PHOTOGRAPHER
William Smith, FOOD STYLIST
Nancy Micklin, PROP STYLIST